BLOOD
MONEY

BLOOD MONEY

BIKIES, TERRORISTS AND MIDDLE EASTERN GANGS

CLIVE SMALL & TOM GILLING

ALLEN&UNWIN

This edition published in 2011
First published in 2010

Allen & Unwin
Sydney, Melbourne, Auckland, London

83 Alexander Street
Crows Nest NSW 2065
Australia
Phone: (61 2) 8425 0100
Fax: (61 2) 9906 2218
Email: info@allenandunwin.com
Web: www.allenandunwin.com

Cataloguing-in-Publication details are available
from the National Library of Australia
www.trove.nla.gov.au

ISBN 978 1 74237 606 6

Index by Garry Cousins
Internal design by Lisa White
Set by Midland Typesetters, Australia
Printed in Australia by McPherson's Printing Group

10 9 8 7 6 5 4 3 2 1

'*I am fed-up with no investigations; dead-end investigations; incompetence; the long arm of coincidence which allows key principals to escape; the lack of will; the lack of expertise; and the indolence or deliberate cover-up.*'

John Hatton MP, speaking in the New South Wales Legislative Assembly on 17 May 1990, on the mafia and organised crime

Contents

Preface

This book is a natural sequel to *Smack Express: How organised crime got hooked on drugs,* picking up the themes we explored in that book and following them in different directions. We will meet new criminals, often more violent and more reckless than their predecessors, and show how they have taken organised crime into new areas. Furthermore, we will show how the structure of organised crime has changed through the formation of alliances—such as those between Middle Eastern crime gangs, outlaw motorcycle gangs and the Calabrian Mafia—that would once have been unthinkable.

We will look at the emergence of terrorism and its impact on Australia and Australians, how it increasingly relies on crime to fund its activities, and how the boundaries between organised crime and terrorism have become porous. These developments represent both a grave new threat and, we argue, new opportunities for law enforcement to seize the initiative after decades of political complacency.

Organised crime is now permanently hooked on drugs. It is also becoming hooked on weapons—not just handguns but assault rifles, explosives and rocket launchers. Its suppliers are often the same as those used by terrorists.

In Australia, as in many other countries, jail has become a place where criminals don't just acquire new skills but, increasingly, a new religion and a new ideology—the ideology of jihad. Men imprisoned as car thieves and drug dealers emerge as holy warriors. This book attempts to show how these changes happened, what they mean and where they might lead.

One of the difficulties of writing an up-to-the-minute account of organised crime and terrorism is that some matters are still before the courts. The trials are rarely straightforward and defence lawyers are increasingly likely to ask for—and be granted—suppression orders. In editing this book we have had to delete some names altogether. Sometimes we have used pseudonyms. We hope that real names can be restored in future editions.

Acknowledgements

Our sincere thanks to those on both sides of the law—many of whom must remain nameless—who helped directly or indirectly in the writing of this book. Thanks also to the journalists who over the decades have reported fearlessly on the growth and influence of organised crime.

Special gratitude to Yoni Bashan, Bob Bottom, Angela Handley, John Hatton, Rebecca Kaiser, Mark Loves, Kate McClymont, Michael McGann, Neil Mercer, Natalie O'Brien, David Penberthy, Bruce Provost, Gerard Ryle, Jennifer Sexton, Peter Smith, Brian Toohey, Dylan Welch and Marian Wilkinson for their support and advice.

About the authors

In 2009 Clive Small and Tom Gilling published the bestselling book *Smack Express: How organised crime got hooked on drugs*, which exposed the growth and transformation of organised crime in Australia since the late 1960s.

CLIVE SMALL is a 38-year New South Wales police veteran. Much of his time was spent in criminal investigation. He was awarded several commendations. From 1977–80 he worked as an investigator with the Woodward Royal Commission into Drug Trafficking. During 1987–88 he was an investigator on Strike Force Omega which reinvestigated the 1984 shooting of Detective Michael Drury. In the early 1990s Small led the backpacker murder investigation, which resulted in the conviction of Ivan Robert Milat for the murder of seven backpackers in the Belangalo State Forest, south of Sydney, between 1989 and 1992. In 2001, as head of the Greater Hume Police Region, he helped dismantle the Vietnamese street gangs that had made Cabramatta Australia's heroin capital. After retiring from the police he joined the New South Wales Independent Commission Against Corruption as the Executive Director of Operations. Since March 2007 he has been writing full-time.

TOM GILLING's first two novels, *The Sooterkin* (1999) and *Miles McGinty* (2001), were both shortlisted for major awards and chosen as notable books of the year by the *New York Times*. They have been translated into several languages. His third novel, *Dreamland*, has been published in Australia, Britain and the United States. As a journalist he has worked for numerous publications including the *Sydney Morning Herald*, *Rolling Stone*, the *Guardian* (UK) and the *New York Times*. Before *Smack Express* he co-wrote two non-fiction books, *Trial and Error* (1991), about the Israeli nuclear whistleblower Mordechai Vanunu; and *Bagman: The final confessions of Jack Herbert* (2005), about the events that led to the Fitzgerald Inquiry into Queensland police corruption.

Cast of major characters and gangs

George David Freeman (born 23 January 1934) was in jail when he met Lennie McPherson. The pair became lifelong friends and partners in crime. In the 1960s Freeman's SP bookmaking empire was protected by police and corrupt politicians. Freeman died in 1990 of an asthma attack.

Leonard Arthur McPherson (born in May 1921) established himself alongside Freeman as one of the 'bosses' of organised crime. Their main businesses were illegal gambling, SP bookmaking, protection and skimming money from licensed clubs. McPherson died in jail in 1996.

Fayez 'Frank' Hakim (born 1930) was around 20 when he arrived in Australia. By the mid 1960s Hakim was in partnership with McPherson and Freeman in their gambling, protection and corruption rackets. Known as the 'Lebanese godfather', Hakim introduced Louis Bayeh to organised crime. Hakim was the subject of at least 26 state and federal police corruption investigations during the 1980s. He survived Sydney's gang war of the mid 1980s and died in January 2005.

Louis Bayeh (born 5 April 1953) came to Australia from Lebanon in the late 1960s. While working as a bouncer at Kings Cross nightclubs owned by Abe Saffron and at illegal casinos and ethnic gambling clubs, Bayeh met Hakim. Through Hakim, McPherson hired him to provide protection and collect debts. After starting his own gambling club, Bayeh became an integral part of crime and corruption at Kings Cross and played a key role in resolving the gang war. After serving time for perverting the course of justice and for drug and extortion offences, he was released from jail in 2002. He lives in western Sydney.

Bill Bayeh (born 4 August 1955), Louis's brother, joined his family in Sydney at the age of 13. He followed Louis into the world of crime and illegal gambling but did not become part of Hakim's circle. From at least the late 1970s, Bill's focus was the Kings Cross drug trade. He formed a volatile relationship with Danny Karam and later teamed up with corrupt detective Trevor Haken. In 1999 Bayeh was convicted of supplying drugs and perverting the course of justice and sentenced to 18 years' jail.

Thomas Christopher 'Tom' Domican (born 1 February 1941) first hit the headlines in 1980 over allegations of vote rigging in the Enmore branch of the Australian Labor Party. During the 1980s his interests were illegal gambling and protection. In Sydney's gang war he sided with Barry McCann against Lennie McPherson and George Freeman. Domican has been charged and acquitted of one murder, one attempted murder and five counts of conspiring to murder. He now spends much of his time in Western Australia.

Trevor Haken (born 1950) joined the NSW Police in 1969. After transferring to Kings Cross in 1989 he formed a corrupt relationship with Bill Bayeh to control the local drug trade.

Haken admitted his corruption at the Wood Royal Commission and entered the federal witness protection program.

William 'Bill' El Azzi (born 25 December 1958) joined the police in 1981, using Frank Hakim as a referee. He was a close associate of Tom Domican. El Azzi left the police and became an amphetamine cook for a major Sydney drug syndicate. In 2003 he was convicted of conspiring to manufacture amphetamines and sentenced to seven years' jail. El Azzi now lives in Sydney's western suburbs.

Hassan 'Sam' Ibrahim (born 9 September 1965) migrated from Lebanon with his family in the 1970s. The Ibrahims became friends with the Bayeh family. For a time Sam was Louis Bayeh's driver, bodyguard and debt collector. He also provided protection to drug dealers. In the mid 1990s Ibrahim's alliance with the Nomads outlaw motorcycle gang helped make them one of Sydney's most influential crime groups. Despite being arrested around 30 times, Ibrahim has spent relatively little time in jail.

Michael Ibrahim (born 30 April 1978) was charged in 2006 with the stabbing murder of Robin Nassaur and the wounding of his brother, George, at Chiswick in Sydney's inner west. The cause of the stabbings was an argument on New Year's Eve between the Nassaurs and Michael Ibrahim at the UN Nightclub in Paddington, which was run by his brother John and where Michael worked as a bouncer. Michael is serving a nine-year jail sentence for manslaughter.

Fadi Ibrahim (born 23 May 1974) survived an attempted assassination in June 2009 when he was shot five times while sitting in his Lamborghini outside his Castle Cove home on

Sydney's north shore. Six weeks before the shooting, police had raided the house and seized $300,000 and a further $3 million in cash hidden in the ceiling of his sister's home.

John Ibrahim (born 25 August 1970) had bought his first nightclub, the Tunnel, by the time he was twenty. John has been charged with murder and threatening witnesses but has beaten all charges. He is in business with the sons of the late crime boss George Freeman. He has extensive business interests at Kings Cross and elsewhere and owns multimillion-dollar homes in Sydney's east.

Roger Caleb Rogerson (born 3 January 1941) joined the NSW Police and became one of its most decorated detectives. He formed corrupt relationships with various criminals, including Louis Bayeh, and was accused (but acquitted) of having been involved in the attempted assassination of Detective Michael Drury in 1984. Dismissed from the police in 1986, he was later jailed for perverting the course of justice.

Christopher Dale Flannery (born 15 March 1949) was a relatively unsuccessful Melbourne criminal before moving to Sydney, where he became known as 'Rent-a-Kill'. He provided protection to George Freeman and formed a corrupt relationship with Detective Sergeant Roger Rogerson. In 1984 he shot and wounded Detective Michael Drury in his Chatswood home. Flannery killed several people during the gang war of the mid 1980s. In 1985 he was murdered on the orders of Lennie McPherson and George Freeman.

Arthur Joseph Loveday (born 3 June 1953) has a long and violent criminal record that includes kidnapping, rape, armed robbery and drugs. His history with bikie gangs goes back at least to the early 1970s. In jail Loveday met former detective Roger Rogerson. Released in 1996, six months after Rogerson, he continued the friendship outside jail. After becoming president of the Bandidos' north coast chapter, Loveday married Catherine Vella, a cousin of Alex Vella, national president of the Rebels. The pair made the `ndrangheta's Francesco 'Fat Frank' Barbaro godfather of their twins. Several Italian crime figures have since been admitted to the Rebels. In 2002 Loveday and Barbaro were arrested for trafficking in ecstasy. Barbaro was eventually jailed but Loveday beat the charge.

Danny Georges Karam (born 19 March 1962) migrated from Lebanon in 1979 and set up his own drug operation before joining Bill Bayeh. As well as dealing in drugs, they ripped off dealers. Karam also provided protection to illegal gambling clubs. He was a heavy heroin user and served several jail terms. After the Wood Royal Commission closed in 1997, Karam formed his own gang known as Danny's Boys or DK's Boys. Its main members were:

- **Alexi 'Little Al' Taouil** (born 30 January 1976). Taouil came from the same Lebanese village as Karam and was his key lieutenant.
- **Michael 'Doc' Kanaan** (born 23 May 1975). Kanaan came to Australia from Lebanon with his family as a child. He was prone to extreme and unpredictable outbursts of violence and was to become one of the state's most dangerous criminals.
- **Alan Rossini** (a court-ordered pseudonym), also known as 'Big Al' and 'Chavez'. Rossini was by far the most intelligent and streetwise of the recruits.
- **Wassim El Assaad** (born 10 January 1977), also known

as 'Was' and 'Wassi'. Australian-born El Assaad was a cocaine user and dealer with a history of credit card fraud, car rebirthing and violence. His brother, Khaled, was a member of the Darwiche crew.

- **Charbel Geagea** (born 5 January 1977), known as 'Charlie' and 'Johnny'. Geagea, known for his involvement in drugs and his willingness to use violence, became an enforcer for the gang.
- **Rabeeh 'Rabs' Mawas** (born 1 March 1977). A follower rather than a leader, Mawas has a criminal record that includes drugs and car rebirthing.

In addition, Danny's Boys had up to ten 'associate' members. From mid 1997 the gang was involved in shootings, kneecappings, drugs and protection in Kings Cross and Sydney's south. On 13 December 1998 the gang murdered its boss. Karam died in a hail of bullets as he sat in his car in Surry Hills.

Michael 'Doc' Kanaan took over Danny's Boys after Karam's murder, but his reign lasted just over six months. After being shot and wounded in a shootout, Kanaan was given three life sentences for murder and 25 years for wounding. Other members of the gang were also given long jail sentences. Two fled overseas: one was Saleh Jamal (see **Terrorists**).

Gehad Razzak (born 1 April 1979) formed a gang around himself in the mid 1990s. He was able to maintain control of the gang during the significant periods he spent in jail. The gang included:

- **Ziad,** or 'Ziggy' (born 18 July 1977), Gehad's brother.
- **Bilal, known as 'Bill'** (born 11 July 1981), **Mohamed** (born 13 November 1982) and **Samear** (born 11 March 1976)—all cousins of Gehad.

- **Ahmed Fahda** (born 10 May 1978), self-proclaimed 'king of Punchbowl'. In 2003 he was shot dead by two hooded men as he filled his car with petrol. Six years later Abdul Darwiche was shot and killed. Ahmed's brother Mohammed, or 'Blackie', has been charged with the killing of Darwiche.
- **Haissam Hannouf** (born 23 November 1974) and his brothers **Ahmad** (born 2 November 1978), **Rabbi** (born 11 May 1977) and **Wahib** (born 30 June 1981).
- **'Moukhtar'** (not his real name) (born 20 May 1976). 'Moukhtar' always carried $10,000 to $20,000 cash, spending it on lavish dinners and visits to brothels and massage parlours with his 'workers'.
- **Ali Hamka** (born 23 June 1980).
- **Robert Hanna** (born 6 November 1982).

The gang moved from the theft and rebirthing of stolen motor vehicles to large-scale insurance frauds, extortion and protection rackets. By the late 1990s they were dealing drugs in and around Bankstown. Their murderous feud with the rival Darwiche crew caused mayhem across west and south-west Sydney. By 2004 the core members of Razzak's crew were either dead or in jail.

Adnan 'Eddie' Darwiche (born 4 March 1976) formed the Darwiche crew in opposition to the Razzaks. Like the Razzaks, the Darwiche gang evolved from an earlier teenage gang. Its members included:

- Eddie's brothers **Abdul** (born 26 February 1972), **Mohammed Ali** (born 3 August 1982) and **Michael** (born 1 July 1968). On 14 March 2009 Abdul was shot and killed outside a fast food restaurant at Bass Hill in

Sydney's south-west. An arrest warrant has been issued for Mohammed 'Blackie' Fahda whose brother, Ahmed, was murdered six years earlier. Abdul was a suspect for Ahmed's murder.

- **Ali 'Biggie' Osman** (born 4 April 1983), Eddie Darwiche's right-hand man, and his brother **Abass** (born 2 December 1977).

- **Ramzi 'Fidel' Aouad** (born 26 March 1981).

- **Naseam 'Sam' El Zeyat** (born 29 July 1980), also known as 'Erdt' (Arabic for 'the monkey'). El Zeyat was previously a member of Danny's Boys and Kanaan's gang.

- **Khaled 'Crazy' Taleb** (born 26 September 1977). Taleb rolled in return for immunity when arrested. Abdul Darwiche later claimed that Taleb had received 'two million dollars, a boat, a new identity and a pension for life ... and had been indemnified on 17 attempted murders and four murders'.

- **Khaled El Assaad** (born 10 May 1979), also known as Kaled Elassaad. His brother Wassim was a member of Danny's Boys and Kanaan's gang. El Assaad took over the Darwiche gang's drug runs with Ali and Abass Osman when Darwiche went to Lebanon. In 2004, after a brawl involving El Assaad's younger brother, he was charged with the attempted murder of a bouncer at Rogues Nightclub. Two years later he beat the charge.

- **Mohammed 'MT' Touma** (born 15 April 1979). Touma was a close confidant of Eddie Darwiche and accompanied him on a pilgrimage to Mecca in Saudi Arabia. He was later arrested and charged with weapons offences. Granted bail, he fled Australia and is believed to be living in the Middle East. He is wanted for the 2003 murder of Ahmed Fahda at Punchbowl. Touma's cousin, **Mazen Touma** (born 16 April 1980), was arrested in raids on a terrorist cell in Sydney during 2005–06. In 2008 Mazen pleaded guilty to a terrorism-related charge and was jailed.

- **Ahmad 'Gary' Awad** (born 25 May 1975). Awad is alleged to have been involved in several shootings. He fled Australia when the Darwiche crew broke apart and is believed to be living in Tripoli. He is said to have demanded, and been paid, money from Darwiche for his silence.

- **Ghassam 'Easy' Said** (born 15 August 1982). A longtime criminal partner of Saleh Jamal, Said was involved in several of the Karam and Kanaan gangs' most violent crimes. He fled Australia while on bail and is believed to be living in Saudi Arabia.

- **Tony Haddad** (born 1 May 1976). A professional car thief and expert at vehicle rebirthing, Haddad joined Danny's Boys on several shooting sprees. In return for rolling, he won indemnity against a decades-long career of serious crime that included murder and attempted murder. He was sentenced to 20 months' jail for perjury.

Several members of the Darwiche crew had links with Danny's Boys and Kanaan's gang. Like the Razzak crew, the Darwiches progressed from motor vehicle theft and rebirthing to protection, standover rackets and drugs. By beating the Razzaks to the drug trade, they established a bigger and more profitable network of drug runs across Sydney's south-west. By 2004 the core members of the Darwiche crew were either dead or in jail. Eddie Darwiche, Naseam El Zeyat and Ramzi Aouad were convicted and given life sentences for various murders. Other gang members were also jailed for shootings, drugs and related crimes.

Shadi Derbas (born 12 April 1973) supplied stolen and rebirthed cars to Danny's Boys and Kanaan's gang. During the late 1990s and early 2000s his Telopea Street Boys also operated a 'drive-through' drug market in Telopea Street, Punchbowl. Swoops on the Telopea Street gang during the early 2000s saw more than 60 people arrested and convicted of murder, possession of firearms including a machine pistol, drug possession and supply, car theft, car rebirthing and fraud. Derbas was sentenced to five years' jail for his part in murders carried out by the Kanaan gang. Around $3 million in assets was seized.

Outlaw motorcycle gangs first emerged in Australia during the 1960s. Since the mid 1980s there have been more than a hundred bikie murders around Australia, together with hundreds of non-fatal shootings and violent attacks on gang clubhouses. In 2006 police estimated that there were 35 outlaw motorcycle gangs across Australia. These gangs were broken up into 212 chapters, with a total membership of up to 3500 full-patch members and as many as ten times that number of prospective members, nominees and associates. According to the Australian Crime Commission, membership is growing and the gangs' criminal activities constitute a significant threat to Australia. Bikie gangs are involved in murders, drug manufacturing and trafficking, firearms trafficking, extortion, prostitution, robbery, theft, fraud, money laundering and rebirthing of stolen motor vehicles. The main gangs include:

- the **Comancheros**, formed in the western suburbs of Sydney in 1966;
- the **Hells Angels**, formed in Sydney in 1967;

- the **Rebels, Nomads, Gypsy Jokers** and **Finks,** all formed in Sydney in 1970;
- the **Coffin Cheaters,** formed in Western Australia in 1970;
- the **Black Uhlans,** formed in Queensland in the early 1970s;
- the **Bandidos,** formed in Sydney in 1982 after a split within the Comancheros;
- **Notorious,** formed in Sydney in 2007 after a split within the Nomads. Notorious is a small 'pseudo' bikie gang with some members not even owning bikes. Since its formation it has been in constant conflict with several of the established bikie gangs.

Terrorists have been responsible for at least 200 acts or relevant events in or directed at Australia between 1966 and 2009. In 2005 it was estimated that Australia had about a dozen terrorist cells comprising up to 60 individuals in Sydney and Melbourne. Two years later the Australian Federal Police reported that in one year it had investigated 40 new terrorist cases, finalised 35 cases, and still had 76 cases on hand. As in other countries, jails have become prime recruiting and training grounds for jihadist criminals. Those who have committed terrorist acts against Australia include:

- **Jack Roche** (born 31 October 1953). Roche migrated from the UK to Australia in 1978 and converted to Islam around 1992. After meeting the head of Jemaah Islamiyah in Sydney, Roche travelled to Indonesia, where he studied Islam. In 2000 he travelled to Pakistan and Afghanistan for military training. In 2003 Roche was jailed for nine years for conspiring to destroy the Israeli embassy in Canberra and the Israeli consulate in Sydney.

- **Willie Brigitte** (born 10 October 1968), also known as Mohammed Abderrahman, Mohammed Ibrahim Abderrahman, Abou Maimouna, Salahouddin, Jamal and 'Abderrahman the West Indian'. He was known to French anti-terrorist investigators since at least the late 1990s. In 1999 he studied at a religious school in Pakistan and later underwent military training. Brigitte arrived in Sydney in 2003 and married Australian Melanie Brown, a Muslim convert. They had been introduced by Mohamed Ndaw who, in 2004, was deported to his native Senegal on security grounds. Ndaw was the brother-in-law of Australian-born 'Abdul' (real name withheld for legal reasons), who trained at terrorist camps in New South Wales and was convicted in 2008 of a terrorism-related offence and jailed. Brigitte was deported to France. In 2007 he was jailed for nine years for planning terrorist attacks in Australia.

- **Saleh Jamal** (born 26 October 1972). Jamal came under the influence of radical Islamic teachers while in jail, having been convicted of supplying cannabis, and having had his bail refused on a range of charges including the drive-by shooting of the Lakemba Police Station. After completing his jail sentence on the drug charge, Jamal was bailed. In March 2004 he fled Australia on a false passport. Two months later he was arrested in Lebanon for terrorism offences and sentenced to five years' jail. After the Lebanese Court of Appeal overturned Jamal's conviction, he was extradited to Sydney. In 2007 he was sentenced to nine years' jail on nine counts of shooting with intent to cause grievous bodily harm. Two years later he was convicted of the drive-by shooting of the Lakemba Police Station.

- **'Hussein'** (real name witheld for legal reasons). 'Hussein' has been involved in terrorist training and planning since at least 2000. In 2003 he bought five rocket launchers through Eddie Darwiche, head of the Darwiche crime gang. The launchers, which have not been recovered, were stolen from an Australian Defence Force establishment in Sydney's west. In 2004 'Hussein', Mazen Touma and Bangladeshi 'Azooz' (not his real name) were apprehended by police within the 1.6-kilometre exclusion zone around Sydney's Lucas Heights nuclear reactor. None was charged. In 2005 'Hussein' and Touma were arrested and convicted of a terrorism-related crime.

- **'Rajab'** (real name withheld for legal reasons) is an Algerian who arrived in Australia in 1989 on a visitor's visa. He became a prohibited person and for more than six years fought attempts to deport him. In 1992 he married a Lebanese woman who was an Australian citizen. In 1996 'Rajab' was granted Australian residence. Two years later he became an Australian citizen, though he retained his Algerian citizenship. In 2008 he was convicted of a terrorism-related crime.

CHAPTER ONE

Frank Hakim and Louis Bayeh

The Lebanese involvement in organised crime in New South Wales began almost 50 years ago and reached a peak during the late 1990s and early 2000s. Sydney's Lebanese underworld could have been the inspiration for the popular US television show *The Sopranos*, with embattled crime bosses suffering a range of medical conditions from anxiety and mental instability to memory loss, heart problems and breathing difficulties, gambling addiction and drug abuse.

The original Lebanese godfather, Fayez 'Frank' Hakim, was born in Lebanon in 1930 and was about 20 when he arrived in Australia. During the late 1950s and early 1960s he built an extensive network among Lebanese migrants, helping many, and became a prominent member of the Lebanese community. He bought and ran a delicatessen in the inner Sydney suburb of Redfern, across the road from the Redfern courthouse and conveniently close to the New South Wales Police training centre, home of the Gaming Squad, which was responsible for the policing of gambling laws across the state. Hakim befriended many in the local court system and was soon on good terms with members of the squad.

By the mid 1960s Hakim had cemented a corrupt partnership with the Gaming Squad which was to endure for two decades. As a Justice of the Peace he was frequently called upon to sign warrants. In 'Report on Investigation into the Relationship Between Police and Criminals: First Report' in 1994, the New South Wales Independent Commission Against Corruption (ICAC) observed that between 1971 and 1979 'Hakim signed almost every warrant taken out by the Gaming Squad' even though the Police 'Bureau of Criminal Intelligence had quite extensive holdings concerning Hakim, one of which connected him with ... illegal gaming premises in ... Redfern or East Sydney'. Hakim had been involved in illegal gaming from at least 1974. He admitted to signing warrants from as early as 1966 but denied doing anything wrong.

The corrupt activities of the Gaming Squad were part of a broader enterprise controlled by Leonard Arthur 'Lennie' McPherson and George David Freeman—two 'Mr Bigs' of organised crime—that provided protection to ethnic-based illegal gambling clubs, casinos, illegal starting price bookmakers and vice operations. Hakim became a senior figure in this operation and reported directly to McPherson.

Louis Bayeh was born in Kafardlakos, a small village in north Lebanon, in 1954 and came to Australia in the late 1960s. Over the next few years his mother and brothers also migrated to Australia. Bayeh had no formal education and can neither read nor write English. Rather than go to school, he worked as a bouncer at various Kings Cross nightclubs owned by Abe Saffron and at illegal casinos and ethnic gambling clubs. While working at these places Bayeh met Hakim—he was about 17 at the time—and they quickly struck up a friendship and business relationship. It was only a short time before Hakim took Bayeh to meet McPherson, who hired him to provide protection, collect debts and supply muscle to resolve disputes. During the 1970s Bayeh was convicted and fined for a number of relatively minor offences. Most related to his work for McPherson.

About two years after meeting Hakim, Bayeh opened his own illegal gambling club at West Ryde. According to evidence Bayeh gave to the Wood Royal Commission into the New South Wales Police Service, he obtained approval for the illegal club from McPherson through Hakim and paid Hakim for protection from both the police and crime gangs. The club operated for about a decade until the early 1980s when it was closed as a result of a police crackdown brought about by revelations of gambling-related corruption involving both police and politicians. Bayeh's connections had shielded him from the crackdown for nearly two years. He also told the commission that for decades he had paid bribes to around a hundred police, many of whom he used to invite to barbecues at his western Sydney home. He claimed to have showered the notorious and corrupt former detective Roger Rogerson with gifts, including $1000 cash towards his daughter's wedding.

In 1977 one of Bayeh's brothers, Fred, was bashed. He had entered the Palace nightclub—one of his Kings Cross haunts—without paying the two-dollar entrance fee, just as he had done many times before. But on this occasion Fred was ordered to pay. He refused. He was taken away and bashed by three bouncers. Louis Bayeh described Roger Brealey, one of the assailants, as a man who, in addition to looking after several clubs, was 'Abe Saffron's bouncer'. Bayeh and his brothers had known Abe Saffron, Peter Farr (Farrugia) and Jim Anderson, the owners of the nightclub, for years and had 'done business' with them. All three were well-known local criminals.

In evidence to the commission, Louis Bayeh said he confronted Brealey, who told him he had bashed Fred 'because he refused to pay [the] cover charge'. Not happy with the explanation, Bayeh replied, 'We know each other for a long time. If you rang me up I give you two bucks. There was no need to break his nose.' Later he picked up a rifle, and with an accomplice went looking for Brealey. Around four o'clock in the morning they found him: 'I know Roger Brealey will have a gun ... and I was concerned if I come by myself empty handed he will shoot me or will do something, so that's the reason I brought a rifle ... I tell Brealey, "Don't move or I'll shoot you." Then I belt him up with the rifle.' It was a savage beating. Bayeh broke the wooden butt of the rifle over Brealey's back and head.

Bayeh knew that his actions would not be forgotten. He had just publicly bashed one of Saffron's bodyguards. It would be seen as a personal affront to Saffron. Louis Bayeh needed help and protection—fast. He went straight to Hakim who rang Darlinghurst Police. The news was bad: the investigation had been taken over by the Armed Robbery Squad and Bayeh had to be charged.

What had started out as a failure to pay a two-dollar cover charge was now dragging in people at the highest levels of both the police and organised crime. Hakim arranged to meet Louis Bayeh at Wilson's Restaurant in Cleveland Street, Redfern, the godfather's preferred meeting place for business as well as pleasure. According to Bayeh, Hakim told him, 'I [Hakim] go and see Merv Wood [the then New South Wales police commissioner] and explain the situation to him, that [Louis] should be charged with assault, but not with robbery. I [Hakim] go and see Merv Wood and explain everything to him, and he will go and see Abe.'

Hakim later claimed that he had spoken with Merv Wood and that Wood had spoken with Saffron. Hakim told Bayeh, 'Abe Saffron, he don't want to get involved. He [Merv Wood] spoke to Abe. He brush him off ... He [Abe] don't want to be involved.' A few months later Bayeh spoke directly with Saffron and was told the same: Saffron would not get involved because his partners, Peter Farr and Jim Anderson, wanted Bayeh charged.

If Bayeh had to be charged, perhaps the charge could be watered down as he and Hakim had originally discussed. Again Hakim and Bayeh met at Wilson's Restaurant. According to Bayeh, Detective Rogerson and his partner came in and they went straight to the back of the restaurant with Hakim. They spoke with Hakim for about half an hour before leaving, exchanging pleasantries with Bayeh on their way out. Hakim sat down and said, 'We can't do anything, because they have been told to charge you. You have to be charged with assault and robbery.' The next day Bayeh was charged. Three years later on 10 March 1980 Bayeh pleaded guilty to a lesser charge of malicious wounding. He was placed on a four-year bond and ordered to pay $2500 compensation to Brealey.

Bayeh later told the commission that just before the District Court hearing of the charge he spoke to Rogerson who told him he would receive a fine if he pleaded guilty to the lesser offence. It was not exactly what he had been promised but Bayeh said he was happy with the court result. Most importantly for Bayeh, he had not gone to jail. According to Bayeh, a few weeks after the conviction he met Rogerson and paid him $6000—the price for his lenient treatment at court. The payment had been agreed at their earlier meeting. From this time, said Bayeh, he and Rogerson became good friends and socialised regularly. Like Arthur 'Neddy' Smith, Bayeh always paid Rogerson's entertainment bills. In return, Rogerson sorted out problems and gave him access to other police.

Despite some of Hakim's protection networks having been severely damaged as a result of the police crackdown on illegal betting and gambling clubs in the late 1970s and early 1980s, Hakim was a known fixer and was still profiting from those parts of the network that remained intact. Between January and August 1983 the Australian Federal Police's Operation Spendthrift intercepted more than 7000 calls on Hakim's home and office telephones. As a result the New South Wales Police Internal Security Unit conducted 26 separate corruption investigations. Six resulted in criminal prosecutions involving police while other investigations resulted in the dismissal or resignation of several police. Meanwhile, Hakim's troubles continued.

The Labor Government's corrective services minister, Rex Jackson, was addicted to gambling. Like most gamblers he was not very successful. Money became an obsession and Jackson found a way of making good his losses at the racetrack: he started accepting bribes for the early release of prisoners. The racket didn't last. In 1984 Hakim and three other men were charged over the early release scheme. Three years later Hakim and his co-conspirators were convicted at the District Court and jailed. Hakim got six and a half years. Jackson was also charged with conspiracy and in 1987 he was convicted and sentenced to ten years' jail for taking bribes. He was released after three.

It wasn't only the police who were causing problems for Hakim. In the mid 1980s there was growing discontent among a number of criminal gangs over the lucrative protection and amusement machine rackets in Sydney's small illegal ethnic gambling clubs. On 15 January 1985 these tensions became the trigger for a gang war.

In his role of approving and organising protection for these clubs on behalf of McPherson and Freeman, Hakim had given permission to Tom Domican and Bill El Azzi, a former police officer and longtime associate of Hakim, to put their machines into a gambling club in Enmore. El Azzi would become a drug trafficker and amphetamine cook and serve jail time. It appears Hakim had 'forgotten' that McPherson already had a profitable arrangement with the club and had also 'forgotten' to tell McPherson that he had allowed Domican and El Azzi to move in. McPherson wouldn't tolerate their involvement in the club and sent a group of his musclemen to trash the club, throwing Domican's amusement machines onto the street.

Christopher 'Rent-a-Kill' Flannery, a notorious criminal who moved to Sydney in the early 1980s to escape the violence in Melbourne, declared that he was supporting Freeman and McPherson, although he was not at the trashing of the club. Behind the scenes Flannery was planning to be the last man standing at the end of the gang war. Only a couple of weeks earlier Flannery and Neddy Smith had called on Michael Sayers, another Melbourne criminal who had moved to Sydney, and told him that Flannery was setting up a 'new' protection racket. Sayers was an illegal starting price book-maker and heroin dealer. He was already paying Freeman for protection and when Flannery demanded payment for the same service, Sayers refused. Flannery backed off: he knew he was not yet in a position to take on Freeman.

Flannery's ambitions and his belief in his own invincibil-ity had grown as a result of his attempted hit on Detective Michael Drury in the kitchen of his Chatswood home. There had not been any retribution from the police: Flannery appeared to have got away with it despite widespread suspi-cion that he was the shooter. Indeed Flannery still had the support of some police.

Following the trashing of the club and several unsuccess-ful attempts to negotiate a truce, the gang war exploded. But as in many wars, this one soon became a series of wars within a war. Eventually McPherson and Freeman ordered the murder of Flannery in a bid to restore peace. Flannery disappeared on 9 May 1985, soon after having answered a phone call from Freeman, but the war dragged on and there were several more murders and attempted murders before peace was finally restored.

On 21 February 1985, just over a week after the trashing of the Enmore gambling club, the then Detective Inspector Tony Lauer—later to become police commissioner—led a raid on Hakim's Redfern office. Hakim was charged with possession of just over a gram of heroin, failure to secure a licensed firearm, having goods in custody of $5000 cash, together with another $1600 cash and a New Zealand passport in the name Strathdee, an unidentified woman. The charges relating to his possession of $1600 cash and the passport were later dismissed, but Hakim was convicted over possession of the $5000 cash and fined $400. In January 1987 Hakim was convicted of possessing heroin and fined $1000, but he beat the charge of failing to secure a firearm.

In 1989, after Hakim complained that police had planted the heroin, the then Police Board referred allegations of corruption by police in Hakim's arrest to ICAC. The ICAC hearings began soon after Hakim had completed his jail sentence over the early release of prisoners racket. The ICAC Commissioner, Mr Ian Temby QC, found that the heroin had not been planted on Hakim. The explanation for it being in his possession, the commissioner concluded, 'lies in Mr Hakim's doubtful memory. I believe that although he expected the police to call upon him at some time, he had simply forgotten that the heroin was there. There was evidence that his serious medical condition, which is of many years standing, has a detrimental effect upon memory.' It was the same 'forgetfulness' that had caused all the trouble at the Enmore Club.

Two years later Lauer became the New South Wales police commissioner. After five years in the job, as the Wood Royal Commission was about to release its first damning report on police corruption, Lauer resigned.

While Hakim's empire foundered, the career of his criminal protégé Louis Bayeh was on the rise. By the early 1980s Bayeh was well on his way to becoming a major player in the Kings Cross underworld. Around 1983 he went into partnership with McPherson and Kostas 'Con' Kontorinakis, buying a share in the Love Machine nightclub. In evidence to the Wood Royal Commission the Lebanese drug trafficker and murderer Danny Karam (see Chapter 3) described Kontorinakis as 'one of the big figures up the Cross, in the strip—you know, owning nightclubs and that'. It was also alleged that he regularly paid corrupt police.

As a business associate of McPherson and Kontorinakis and a provider of protection to clubs at Kings Cross, Bayeh socialised regularly with local police.

Early in 1983 Detective Roger Rogerson, Bayeh, McPherson and Chris Flannery met at the 73 York Street Seafood Restaurant in Sydney's central business district. The restaurant, which was owned by one of Rogerson's close friends, was a popular dining spot for members of Sydney's underworld. Rogerson and his workmate Detective Bill Duff ate there with Flannery. Rogerson and Neddy Smith both socialised and did business there and, according to Alan Williams (the Melbourne criminal who organised the hit on Detective Michael Drury), it was there that he (Williams), Flannery and Rogerson planned Drury's murder. Freeman and Flannery also dined and did business there.

According to Bayeh, McPherson suggested the meeting, while McPherson said it was Rogerson's idea. The purpose of the lunch was for Bayeh and McPherson to meet Flannery. Rogerson outlined Flannery's background and reputation while Flannery told the others that he was on Freeman's payroll.

Around the same time as the lunch with McPherson and Flannery, Rogerson introduced Bayeh to Duff. According to Bayeh, he started making corrupt payments to Duff about five months later.

In the mid 1980s Kontorinakis left Kings Cross and moved into Sydney's business district. He sold his interest in the Love Machine and bought the Eros Cinema in Goulburn Street, which ran private peep shows and had a thriving sex shop. He also invested in several other clubs. But Kontorinakis did not leave crime behind. In 1991 he was one of five men, including McPherson, who bashed an accountant (identified as 'B' in the subsequent criminal proceedings) after a commercial dispute between McPherson's nephew and B. In 1994 Kontorinakis pleaded guilty to maliciously inflicting grievous bodily harm (including a fractured right arm and multiple facial injuries) and was eventually sentenced to three years' jail.

Between 1997 and 1999 the New South Wales Police Integrity Commission (PIC) investigated the involvement of current and former members of the New South Wales Police Service in improper and/or illegal conduct with Kostas Kontorinakis or his associates. In its report of the investigation, 'Oslo', the PIC found that between 1996 and 1998 Kontorinakis paid Rogerson, through an associate, $500 a week for an unknown purpose. Rogerson described the money as repayment of a loan, although the figures did not add up and he could not produce any documentation for the loan. Kontorinakis would neither confirm nor deny that he had paid Rogerson any money.

Kontorinakis told the PIC that one of his many jobs was a 'consultancy' at the Lady Jane men's club (later renamed Little Jenny's) owned by Tony Vincent, an important underworld figure with a history in Kings Cross going back to the 1970s. Like Kontorinakis, Vincent also had a close relationship with Rogerson. In October 2004 police raided Vincent's club and Vincent and others were arrested and charged with drug trafficking (see Chapter 9).

During 1991 Kontorinakis had been picked up on National Crime Authority telephone intercepts. The calls were played to him during the PIC hearing. The person on the other end of the line was Branko Balic, a well-known criminal and Kings Cross identity and a close associate of McPherson. The intercepts record the two discussing payments to 'coppers' in relation to a business in Cabramatta. The payments included $5000 in the first month. Kontorinakis claimed that he was lying and bragging and the apparent bribes were not pursued by the PIC. The claimed payments coincided with a wave of police corruption in the Cabramatta–Fairfield area involving a small group of detectives known as the Rat Pack. The corruption included the protection of illegal gambling, drug and other rip-offs, armed robberies and the falsification of evidence, and is discussed in detail in our earlier book *Smack Express*.

During the 1980s Bayeh stuck largely with the traditional protection rackets, but was not averse to drug dealing on the side. The mid 1980s saw Bayeh heavily involved in the gang war on the side of McPherson and Freeman. He was a key figure in meetings between police and criminals who both had an interest in restoring peace so that they could get on with the business of making money.

In January 1990 Bayeh was arrested for discharging a firearm outside his home in Hughes Avenue, Ermington, in Sydney's north-west. The gun had been fired in the direction of a neighbour. In late 1992, while under remand, Bayeh approached longtime colleague Tom Domican and told him that he had been warned by a detective that police had put out a contract on his (Bayeh's) life. Domican arranged a lunchtime meeting with senior police, but Bayeh came out of the meeting considerably poorer (he had to pick up the bill) and little the wiser. In 'Report on Investigation into the Relationship Between Police and Criminals' ICAC was critical of police for attending the lunch and found that 'Domican's main purpose in organising the lunch was to bolster his reputation and standing within the criminal fraternity'. The lunch 'became known amongst the criminal fraternity, in such a manner as to increase Domican's apparent influence. Domican could boast that he had "in his pocket" the Assistant Commissioner responsible for integrity within the Police Service.'

Early on the morning of 12 July 1993, six months after his lunch with police and three months after his claims about a police contract on his life were made public at the ICAC hearings, Bayeh's Ermington home was the target of a drive-by shooting. No-one was injured but bullets peppered the rooms where his children, then aged between four and eleven, were sleeping. Bayeh claimed the attack was the result of his having told ICAC about the contract but few believed him: Bayeh's list of enemies was endless.

At the time of the shooting Bayeh was playing snooker in Kings Cross with his brother Bill and Robert Daher. The game was intended to patch up a quarrel between the Bayehs and Daher over the local drug trade during which Daher had threatened to kill Bill. The quarrel was eventually resolved, but not that night.

Asif Dibb and Norm Korbage, two of Daher's crew, were charged with the drive-by shooting of Bayeh's home by then Detective Sergeant Trevor Haken, who would later become the Wood Royal Commission's number 1 rollover (see Chapter 2). The case went to court but Dibb and Korbage beat the charges. Bayeh later claimed that 'Robert Daher told them [Dibb and Korbage] to do the shooting', and said they had admitted bribing the police to help them beat the charges. Daher denied any involvement in the shooting at Louis Bayeh's house to the royal commission.

It was Kings Cross identity John Ibrahim who put the shooting in context, telling the Wood Royal Commission, 'Even though they [Daher's crew] had shot up his brother's house, he [Bill] was still … friends with them.' The various criminal groups at the Cross, Ibrahim explained, had 'a falling out every two weeks, they sort it out and everything goes back to normal'.

On 30 September 1993 Bayeh pleaded guilty to the three-year-old charge of discharging a firearm and was ordered to perform 350 hours' community service, but not before he had attempted to avoid conviction by having a criminal associate, who was in Lebanon at the time, make a statement claiming that he, not Bayeh, had fired the gun. The plan failed and four years later Bayeh was convicted of attempting to pervert the course of justice and sentenced to four years' jail.

Five months after his January 1990 arrest Bayeh was arrested again. This time the charges included the possession and supply of heroin. He approached state Labor MP Paul Gibson and complained of widespread police corruption and the fabrication of evidence against him. Gibson supported Bayeh's cause over several years and in July 1993 the drug and other charges against Bayeh were dismissed.

Gibson and Bayeh fell out the following year. Their relationship continued to deteriorate and in July 1997 Bayeh complained to ICAC that he had provided Gibson with various benefits including payments of cash, a mobile telephone, a Fijian holiday and several thousand dollars spending money for Gibson and a friend, jewellery and clothing. In 1998 Gibson was cleared of corruption allegations. However, in 'Report on Investigation into Allegations Made by Louis Bayeh Against the Member for Londonderry, Paul Gibson MP', ICAC said, 'In respect of the particular allegations against him, the Commission has in general not accepted Gibson's evidence.'

Bayeh served two years' jail for attempting to pervert the course of justice before being released on parole on

17 November 1999. Eight months later he was involved in a gunfight as he left the El-Bardowny Lebanese restaurant in the outer Sydney suburb of Narwee. As he returned fire, Bayeh shot buildings, fences, one rival and an innocent 17-year-old bystander. Bayeh himself was shot three times, but survived.

None of those involved was eager to help police investigating the shootout. Someone claimed that it had been the result of an argument over the sale of a man's leather jacket. More likely it was the result of a dispute over protection rackets and drugs: after his enforced lay-off in prison, Bayeh had been attempting to force his way back in. Whatever the truth of the matter, Bayeh was the big loser. His parole was revoked and he went back to jail.

A year later on 27 July 2001 Bayeh pleaded guilty to supplying cocaine and heroin and demanding money with menaces (he had forced two brothel owners to pay $180,000 protection money which he split with police) and was sentenced to another three years' jail.

Back in prison Bayeh sought special treatment due to the dozen or so medications he was taking for his heart, hypertension, claustrophobia, stomach problems, hernia, sleep apnoea, memory loss, and the stress he claimed to be suffering from the number of contracts said to be out on his life. One contract alone was reputedly for $200,000; others were for lesser amounts and some were said to be matters of 'honour'. To Bayeh all the contracts were the result of misunderstandings that could be traced to his mother's death in the mid 1980s. This happened to be the period of the Sydney gang war in which Bayeh had played a prominent part. The war and its aftermath of double-crosses and triple-crosses were more probable explanations for the contracts—if they existed at all.

Bayeh was released from the Junee Correctional Centre on 14 December 2002. Two and a half years later he stood trial over the El-Bardowny shootout. This time he won. For the first time in many years Bayeh left the court free of all charges. He remains free to this day.

Bayeh is resentful at the way he has been treated by both police and criminals and believes he has not been given credit for helping keep the peace—most of the time—in Sydney's underworld. He has few friends. He is not liked by his former friends in the police who survived the Wood Royal Commission, by those who once paid him for protection or by his old colleagues in the rackets and drug trade in Kings Cross. Bayeh's chances of getting back into the game are slight: he has nothing to offer but problems and his habit of rolling over makes it unlikely anyone would trust him.

Hakim was 75 years old and a broken man when he died in January 2005. His networks had long collapsed and he had lost his influence with the criminal milieu. Freeman had died in his bed in 1990 of an asthma attack and McPherson had been jailed in 1994 and died there two years later of a heart attack. But more than 400 mourners attended Hakim's funeral at Redfern. Police controlled the crowd of mourners and provided an escort to the Botany cemetery where he was laid to rest. After the funeral the *Sydney Morning Herald*'s Malcolm Brown noted that it was the first time in two decades that Hakim had received any assistance from the police.

By the late 1980s the Kings Cross underworld was changing dramatically. Louis Bayeh and his cronies were a spent force, but Louis's brother Bill was a criminal on the rise.

CHAPTER TWO

The Bayehs and
the Ibrahims

Bill Bayeh, who changed his name to Bill Michael, is nearly two years younger than his brother Louis. In the late 1960s, a year after his father and brothers had migrated, 13-year-old Bill accompanied his mother to Australia. He had little time for school and once in Sydney followed Louis into the world of crime and illegal gambling. Like Louis, Bill can neither read nor write. Unlike him, Bill shunned the opportunity to fall in with the Lebanese godfather Frank Hakim and his partner Lennie McPherson and went his own way—though he was happy enough to accept protection and the odd job via his older brother.

The drug trade was Bill's focus from at least the late 1970s, but he was still a small-time operator when he and Danny Georges Karam began their volatile criminal relationship in the mid 1980s. Karam was born in Lebanon in 1962.

He left home at the age of 11, joined the Lebanese Christian Army and fought against the Muslim militia. He remained in the infantry for several years before joining the commandos and later 'another elite group within the army', according to the Wood Royal Commission into the New South Wales Police Service (1994–1997). Karam moved to Australia in 1979 but remained only a short time before returning to Lebanon where he rejoined the army. Four years later he moved to Australia permanently for reasons 'associated with his safety' (they concerned his political associations) and entered the local drug trade.

Introduced to heroin by friends, Karam quickly became addicted and developed a $1000-a-day habit. He claimed that he and Bill Bayeh made a living 'rolling dealers, grabbing them, keeping them in their room till their drugs had been used, then letting them go, getting another one when I needed another one'. Karam also provided muscle and protection to illegal gambling clubs in the Sydney suburbs of Marrickville, Campsie and Belmore. He had an arrangement, he said, with Bill's brother Louis, who was also providing protection: 'If I looked after something, he kept away from it and I kept away from something he looked after.' The arrangement continued until November 1985 when Karam went to jail for six months over a stolen car, using heroin and possession of a replica pistol.

Karam was out of jail for only a few weeks when he was arrested for robbery and assault occasioning actual bodily harm. Convicted, he was sentenced to 12 years' jail. On his release three and a half years later, Karam found the Cross had changed. The protection of clubs 'had become a tight organisation [and] Louis [Bayeh] had quite a grip on it'. Within months Karam was back in jail; his parole had been revoked. It was early 1991 before Karam was again released on parole.

*

By the early 1980s two longtime friends and fellow country-men of the Bayeh family, Sam and John Ibrahim, had begun to work at Kings Cross. Sam and John were born in Lebanon and during the 1970s migrated to Australia with their family and settled in south-western Sydney, where they became friends with the Bayeh family.

As with Louis and Bill, Sam's schooling was limited. His first job as a doorman and bouncer was at an illegal gambling club at Fairfield: he was 13 years old and had been kicked out of school. Within two years he was working as a doorman in Kings Cross and providing muscle at several clubs. He became Louis's driver and minder for several years during the early to mid 1980s and also collected protection and debt money for Louis from illegal gambling clubs and massage parlours in Kings Cross, Parramatta and other places. At the Wood Royal Commission Sam Ibrahim boasted of his skills in fighting and martial arts and explained how he used these skills to make a living.

By his early teens Sam's younger brother John was also providing muscle at nightclubs around Kings Cross. At the age of 16 he incurred his only criminal conviction. Arrested for assault, John overstated his age and was convicted as an adult in the Parramatta Local Court. By the late 1980s, aged 19, John became the licensee of the Tunnel nightclub at Kings Cross. Appearing at the Wood Royal Commission, John claimed that he never worked for the Bayehs but had done 'favours' for Louis that included taking his side in disputes and fights with other factions in Kings Cross and elsewhere, and had 'given him money' from time to time. None of this was business, John said—it was just 'family friendship'.

During the late 1980s Bill was still doing drug rip-offs

and street-level dealing as he tried to change the drug of choice at Kings Cross from heroin to cocaine. He explained to Thierry Botel, one of his distributors and a long-term heroin and cocaine user, that 'heroin junkies only had one shot every day or if they got a bad habit, a couple of shots or three shots a day, but with cocaine apparently the junkies had to shoot up every twenty minutes, so you got much bigger turnover [and profits].'

About 1990 Sam Ibrahim went to work for John at the Tunnel nightclub. He also provided protection to drug dealers working out of other nightclubs and on the streets. According to Sam, '[I] wasn't actually employed [by drug dealers] like there was a set wage. It was, like, if someone was getting hassled by somebody else, I'd tell them to lay off and then look after them, but there wasn't a set wage where I worked for someone.' Sam explained that at times he 'got paid in drugs. I had a habit before, a coke habit, and that's the reason why I used to protect them. I used to look after them in the street and they used to give me my drugs free.' Sam claimed that he had never been involved with Bill Bayeh in drugs, but that he had looked after Lasers nightclub for Bayeh and protected the drug dealers who worked out of there. Despite what the Ibrahims said, everyone else thought they worked for Louis and Bill.

In May 1989 Detective Sergeant Trevor Haken arrived at the Kings Cross Local Area Command. Well experienced in corruption and, in particular, corruption in the drug trade, Haken set about identifying opportunities. He and Bill Bayeh quickly formed an alliance. It was the start of a relationship that was to see them both prosper for several years.

Another police officer, Charlie Staunton, based at Darlinghurst Police Station, had befriended Bill in the mid

1980s and was soon receiving corrupt payments from him. After leaving the police in 1988 Staunton continued to help Bill in his bid to take control of the local drug trade and protection rackets. Staunton used and dealt in cocaine, paid bribes to Haken on behalf of Bill and others, and was present when Bill paid Haken thousands of dollars in bribes. He also helped Bill rig evidence in court cases. Staunton was also increasingly involved with an international cannabis trafficking network that imported shipments of tens of tonnes into Ireland, Canada, the United States and Australia.

On 7 November 1990 the police raided a room used by Bill at the Bondi Beach Inn and found cocaine with a street value of around $12,000, plastic bags, a set of electric scales and cash. Bill was charged with possessing and supplying cocaine and goods in custody and bailed. His and Haken's operation was now so big that the police raid was little more than an annoying distraction.

According to Karam: 'From about 1991 things started changing for [Bill], I guess, and he went on to bigger and better things.' Bill Bayeh and Sam Ibrahim 'wanted to make a move on the street dealers and take them under their wings and sort of turn it into an operation, a proper drug operation' and they could do this with the help of Haken. One of their first moves was to take over Lasers and several other nightclubs and turn them into 'twenty-four by seven' drug-dealing operations.

Arguably, the biggest problem for Bill was his reputation. As Karam explained: 'Bill didn't have a great name. He'd robbed every dealer in this country and he was trying to get ... people to start trusting him again and doing things.' He also 'employed' dealers rather than taking a commission from them, keeping the lion's share of the profits for himself. It was an arrangement that the dealers disliked, Karam told the commission. 'They'd been put on wages and when people take chances like that, I guess, they're risking their lives on the street, they don't want to be put on a wage. They're entitled to the profits. The person giving the protection should only be entitled to a wage themselves, but it was done the other way around, I guess.'

Karam claimed to have taken his own advice when setting up a protection racket in opposition to Bill. He put himself on a 'wage' of $100 a week from each dealer in return for protection. It was worth $100 a week to be left alone and not hassled by other organisers, such as Bill. It was also a cost that was more than covered by increased sales. If anyone did attempt to stand over protected dealers, Karam would sort out the matter—using violence if he had to.

Others, such as Sam Ibrahim, gave the commission a very different picture of Karam: 'Danny wanted to belt everybody in the street and everybody was feared from [sic] him so everybody ran back to me, "Please get him off my back," so that's what I done.'

Ongoing competition and disputes between Karam and Bill Bayeh were seen as just the way business was done in the drug trade in Kings Cross. Disputes usually started with an outbreak of violence followed quickly by a negotiated if uneasy and, for the most part, short truce. These truces, however unstable, were critical to the functioning of the Kings Cross underworld. They allowed the players to get back to the main business of selling drugs.

Around mid 1993 Karam spoke to Bill about 'doing shifts' to sell drugs at his nightclub, but Bill rejected the proposal and 'a bit of pushing' followed. Once again he called on his older brother, Louis, who had a meeting with

Karam. An altercation followed, and in the ensuing brawl Louis was beaten up. Later that night Karam was stopped by police while driving his car. Taken to Kogarah Police Station and charged with possession of heroin, Karam later pleaded guilty and was given a bond. Despite the guilty plea, Karam told the commission that the police had loaded him and that he believed it had been done at the request of Louis. The facts did not support this claim.

A few nights after his arrest, an intermediary arranged a meeting between Karam and Bill. Bill proposed that they work together and offered Karam $5000 a week 'to clean the streets [and] to make sure every drug dealer who worked the streets worked for him'. Karam accepted the offer. He hired his own muscle and 'anybody who wasn't working for Billy were [sic] moved along'. At this time, Bill had up to eight street dealers a shift working for him and a number of nightclubs and other places where off-street dealing was conducted.

Bill now controlled the streets. He was known as 'the boss' and demanded to be called the boss—'otherwise you got sacked'. His team included such colourful names as Kiwi Michael, Shifty Sam, Shifty Tony (also known as the Inspector because he liked to pretend that he was a police officer), the Frenchman (also known as French Thierry), Tongan George, Chinese Kim, Lebanese Danny, Italian Danny (also known as the Little Fella), JC (also known as Fat John and Greek John, he was Bill's driver in the early 1990s), Roly Poly Roland, Skinny Steve, Fat Steve (also known as Fatso), American Mark (who wasn't an American but put on an American accent and, like Shifty Tony, pretended to be a police officer).

In return for regular cash payments to Detective Haken

and some of his colleagues the police got rid of Bayeh's competition and picked up easy arrests. Karam described it as a good deal for everyone. 'The police's main concern through all this was that people wouldn't be hurt in the street and they were happy to go along with whatever happened.' By and large Karam was right: as long as things were peaceful the police didn't intervene.

At this time Robert Daher ran the only other major drug operation in the Cross. Although there were ongoing disputes between the two groups, they mostly left each other alone. For a while everyone—those supplying drugs and protection, street dealers, users and police—was happy. Each was getting what they wanted, or most of it. But the peace did not last long. By mid July 1993 Louis and Bill Bayeh were again at loggerheads with Robert Daher. Daher threatened to kill Bill. Sam Ibrahim tried and failed to negotiate a truce. Louis's Ermington home was shot up after he slapped Daher around for making insulting remarks about his and Bill's mother. With honour seemingly satisfied, business demanded—as always—that the antagonists pull back. A fragile peace returned.

The drug business was thriving and Karam was now a recognised and well-paid player in Bill's network, but violent challenges from rivals in the drug trade remained a constant threat. In 1993 a hit was ordered on Karam. Describing the contract to the commission, Karam casually pointed out that there had been several attempts on his life. 'I'd had priors before that,' he said. Explaining the February 1993 shooting, Karam said: 'Somebody had attempted a shooting, I believe, on my life and ended up getting a neighbour of mine ... [I] lived at 50 Moons Avenue, Lugarno, and the two people came to 15 Moons Avenue, Lugarno, and shot the person that lived there ... [H]e was an older person, a retired person; he lived across the road from me.'

Sixty-one-year-old Leszic Betcher died from a single shot to the chest when he answered his front door. Betcher was not involved in crime and had no involvement with Karam. The Supreme Court described Betcher as 'a recently retired gentleman of unquestioned respectability ... who ... lived with his wife.'

Karam claimed he did not know who ordered the hit or what it was for, other than it was something to do with the Cross. However, on 24 March, a month after the shooting, an ambulance was called to a drug overdose in a Potts Point flat. The patient was 36-year-old Jon Leslie Baartman, a career criminal and well-known freelance standover man. In the course of treating him, an ambulance officer came upon a .32 calibre Beretta pistol. The officer contacted the police, who confiscated the pistol. Ballistic testing found it to be the weapon used to kill Betcher.

Three months later Baartman and 29-year-old Paul Thomas Crofts—who had a long criminal record that included jail sentences for assault and rob, robbery in company, possessing a shortened firearm, and breaking and entering—were charged with Betcher's murder. Both were convicted and sentenced to 20 years' jail. In court they claimed they had been contracted by 'Chris' to carry out the shooting, which they said was intended to be a wounding. Chris was never identified.

As the trial approached for Bill Bayeh's 1990 drug arrest, one of his sellers, Thierry Botel, swore an affidavit that the cocaine, plastic bags and scales were his, and that he had been using the Bondi hotel room with Bayeh's permission. In March 1994 Bayeh pleaded guilty in the District Court to a lesser charge of knowingly taking part in the supply of the cocaine and was sentenced to 300 hours of community service.

Around the same time, Bill told Karam that he could no longer afford to pay him $5000 a week to keep the streets clean and suggested dropping the payments to $1500. Karam was not happy. At this time Bill was, according to Karam, the biggest heroin dealer in the Cross with about 40 dealers operating out of clubs and drug houses. There was little competition and business was good. However, Bill insisted and Karam was told that he could take the offer or leave it. Karam left it and set up his own drug protection business.

Unknown to Karam, Bill had a problem that was nothing to do with drugs. For nearly a decade Bill had been a serious gambler. His losses had begun to outstrip the profits from his drug operations. By the mid 1990s he owed about $2 million to various people, including $80,000 to his bookmaker. In less than 12 months Bill lost $1 million more than he won. In addition, he was spending about $400,000 a year, not including payments to police. His declared income to the Taxation Office was around $36,000 a year.

Karam approached the street dealers and offered them protection in return for $10 for every cap they sold. He also lured back to the Cross a number of dealers who had left because they did not want to work for Bill. Before long, Karam had eight to ten dealers and was getting between $10,000 and $12,000 a week, but he had overheads. He 'hired a few people to be up at the Cross 24 hours, just as muscle, because at that time there was a lot of tension'.

Bill quickly lost control of street dealing. But Karam wasn't the only one trying to grab a share of the Kings Cross drug trade. Local muscle working for rival drug groups and police were also harassing Karam's dealers. His solution, like Bill's, was to pay the police. Three thousand dollars a week was enough to stop the police harassment.

Karam also went into business with Russell Townsend, one of Bill's main competitors and a man with a reputation in the Cross. A former two-time Mr Australia and world record power lifter, Townsend weighed in at 130 kilograms. In intercepted telephone calls played to the commission, Bill was heard complaining to Haken that Townsend, Sam and John Ibrahim were making over $100,000 a week and were becoming too big.

Early in 1994 Karam's parole was once again revoked. With Karam in jail Townsend took over the business, but a few days later he was shot in a Kings Cross street. It was Friday 25 February 1994 and the shooting was payback for the assault of George 'Tongan George' Akula, a muscleman for Bill Bayeh. The assault had been triggered by an earlier rip-off. 'He [Akula] ripped off somebody in the street,' said Sam Ibrahim 'and he got bothered for it and that was the argument.' Karam, Townsend and two others were charged over the assault of Tongan George.

A few months later the charges were dismissed. Tongan George decided that his original statement to police, in which he identified the attackers, was wrong. The men he had named were not his attackers but his friends, he told police. The thought of living under a police protection program did not suit Tongan George's lifestyle (How would he earn a living? Would the police sell him out?) and, once again, the gangs agreed to settle their differences.

In the underworld survival was what mattered and you could not survive if you were known as a police 'dog'— even though, behind the scenes, many were. To have given evidence against Karam and Townsend would have been severely detrimental to Tongan George's health. Despite his acquittal, Karam freely admitted to the commission that he had bashed Tongan George, but denied stabbing him or knowing who did stab him. He casually explained that after one of his dealers had been assaulted and ripped off by Tongan George he had to do something—after all, he was being paid to provide protection. If he couldn't protect a dealer, the least he could do was dish out retribution.

Released from jail in May 1994, Karam returned to the Cross and resumed his drug operations and his payments to police, but declined the offer of further police protection in return for increased payments. Karam's return to the streets did not last. Four months later his parole was again revoked and he was returned to jail. Six months later he was convicted of assault and sentenced to a further 18 months' jail with a six-month non-parole period.

If Karam was having a bad run, life for Bill Bayeh was even worse. By 1995 his drug operation was starting to fall apart: profits were shrinking and he was deeply in debt to both his drug suppliers and his gambling associates. Both were known for their willingness to use violence against those who failed to pay up. To add to his problems, there was a change in the police leadership at Kings Cross. Superintendent Mal Brammer, an experienced drug investigator, had taken command and was cracking down on drugs. The Wood Royal Commission was also underway. Unknown to Bayeh, his partner in crime, Detective Sergeant Trevor Haken, had already rolled and was reporting Bayeh's every move to the commission. In addition, telephone intercepts and listening devices were recording both Bayeh's desperation and his corrupt dealings with Haken. The intercepts revealed Bayeh giving up both his opposition and his partners, asking Haken to get rid of them and to install him at the top of the drug heap—to make him not only the 'boss' but the 'godfather'.

In a series of telephone conversations Bayeh told Haken that there was too much violence at the Cross and that it was in everyone's interest for it to be controlled. 'It used to be controlled but now it isn't,' he complained. At one point Bayeh even offered to guarantee the quality of heroin sold in order to prevent drug overdoses. It was his competitors, said Bayeh, not him, who were responsible for the the rise in drug overdoses and violence in the Cross. 'What happens, everybody laughing and say to me, your old boys are not good any more. They're all saying your boys are nothing, they're finished ... Fuck the younger generation ... They've got to wait for their turn.'

Haken responded to Bayeh's lament by goading him: 'Now you tell me which ones have got to go.'

Believing he had a deal, Bill eagerly rolled off a list of competitors who had to be dealt with: Karam, Townsend, John and Sam Ibrahim and Robert Daher. Townsend was 'looking after' Lennie McPherson and Tony Vincent. He's 'looking after the whole world', Bayeh complained. He urged Haken to speak to Superintendent Mal Brammer and tell him they should go back to the days when 'nobody got murdered and there was no violence'. Brammer would be 'well rewarded' if this happened.

The 'old days' Bayeh referred to were all in his imagination. Murder and violence had been part of Kings Cross culture since at least the 1920s, when it was called Darlinghurst and the razor gangs controlled the streets. In conspiring with Haken to eliminate his rivals, Bayeh was honouring timeworn Kings Cross traditions of treachery and double-cross. At one time or another Bayeh had been in business with all those he named and had used them whenever it suited him. Now he had no qualms about sacrificing them to ensure his own survival. It was Kings Cross at its most brutal.

Bayeh told Haken that Sam Ibrahim was making big money, 'doing heaps down there, eckies, speed, everything'. Yet only months earlier he had employed Sam as muscle and taken advantage of Sam's reputation to intimidate competitors. John Ibrahim had also stood up for both Bill and Louis. Before hearing the tapes, John had described how he and Sam had regarded Bill as a family friend for '11 to 12 years'. He then told the commission, 'After hearing that taped conversation [our relationship is] not very good.' In spite of this, John Ibrahim maintained that he was not involved: 'I have no idea what Bill was talking about. I'm not sure that Bill has any idea what he's talking about half the time.'

Trying hard to enlist Haken's support, Bayeh explained that Tom Domican was in his corner and would be willing to deal with any repercussions: 'If I had any trouble, Tom will help me, yes ... Yes, he's my friend. He'll help me if I'm in a fight.' It was not the first time Bayeh had traded on Domican's name and reputation. He had a habit of telling business partners and competitors alike that he was paying Domican $1000 a week to stay on side and keep out of the Cross. Bayeh denied these claims to the commission, insisting it was all talk designed to boost his influence with partners and intimidate his enemies. But Bayeh did have a business relationship with Domican and feared him.

Despite the commission's daily exposure of police corruption and drug networks, and despite his own appearances before it, Bayeh continued his drug operations. Commission or no commission, the Cross had a voracious appetite for drugs and its needs had to be met. Throughout the first half of 1996 he sold cocaine and heroin through a network of runners operating out of the Cosmopolitan coffee shop—known as the Cosmo. One former dealer involved in the operation estimated that 80 to 120 caps, mostly cocaine, were sold each shift, while another estimated that at the peak of Bayeh's operation some dealers were selling 'more than 120 caps every shift'. The runners sold each cap of cocaine for $70 to $80. Of that Bayeh received $50—totalling between $4000 and $6000 a shift from each runner—while the runners and the supervisor split what was left.

Estimates varied of the number of runners Bayeh had on the streets at this time but four runners—the lower end of the estimates—gave Bayeh a weekly income well in excess of $100,000 while 15 runners—the higher end of the estimates—gave him a weekly income in excess of half a million dollars. Despite his income, Bill still had financial problems. He was gambling on the horses and at the Sydney casino and, as usual, was losing heavily. His debts to his drug suppliers were increasing and he was having trouble getting supplies.

One of Bill's suppliers, a violent criminal living in Balmain who had been heavily involved in the gang war a decade earlier, had to be paid: he had a reputation for murder. Bayeh collected cocaine from him in person. The cocaine was then taken to Michael 'Kiwi Mick' Wills's flat in Potts Point—one of Bayeh's cutting and packaging points. Kiwi Mick and Bayeh had known each other since the late 1980s and were bound by their common interests in gambling and drugs. Kiwi Mick became one of Bill's most trusted distributors but his own drug habit would cause problems for both.

As Bayeh struggled to keep his drug business going, the commission began Operation Caesar, which targeted Bayeh's operations out of the Cosmo café in Kings Cross. Four weeks later Bayeh and several of his distributors met at a Gladesville hotel, where they cut and packaged another supply of drugs for delivery to the streets of Kings Cross. The next day, 18 July 1996, Bill Bayeh, Kiwi Mick and others of the group appeared before the commission. Later that day they were arrested for heroin and cocaine trafficking. Kiwi Mick's Potts Point apartment had been under surveillance for about a month. Around 1500 capsules of cocaine and heroin were estimated to have been packaged at the apartment and sold during this time.

Bayeh was also charged with perverting the course of justice in relation to his 1990 Bondi drugs arrest and conviction. The affidavit made by Thierry Botel, which caused the charge and sentence against Bayeh to be reduced, had been false. Bayeh had offered him $50,000 to say the cocaine was his. The former police officer Charlie Staunton had helped Bayeh fabricate his defence.

In 1999, after several trials, Bayeh was convicted of supplying drugs, perverting the course of justice and other offences and sentenced to 18 years' jail. His 1994 conviction and 300 hours' community service sentence were quashed and replaced with jail sentences. He is not due to be released until 2014. In jail Bayeh quickly attracted a following among Lebanese inmates and became a gang leader, but his time as a powerbroker in the jail didn't last long. Regarded as a high-risk prisoner, he was moved to Lithgow Correctional Centre to serve his sentence. Bayeh's time as a major Kings Cross player and crime figure was over.

Writing in the *Sydney Morning Herald*, Candace Sutton

quoted a small-time crook and former associate of the Bayehs as saying, 'Louis is the older brother, the big, dumb brother. Bill Bayeh is smaller, smarter and better dressed, not that either of them is really smart.' Time would prove that assessment right.

The conviction and jailing of Bill Bayeh were a major success for the commission, but Operation Caesar would have tragic consequences. The operation had begun after the commission rolled one of Bayeh's main street dealers, known by the code name KX15. After giving up Bayeh and others, KX15 was allowed back on the streets to continue buying and selling heroin and cocaine. His activities were to be monitored both electronically and physically, in the hope of trapping not only other drug dealers but also corrupt cops. But it wasn't long before the operation started to go horribly wrong.

In a 2004 paper 'Who Guards the Guards', former New South Wales Police detective Mick McGann describes the heroin sold by KX15 as being 'of a higher purity than the average street junkie was used to'. New South Wales Police Task Force Bax, which was not aware of the commission's operation, was also surveilling KX15. It picked up a conversation between KX15 and another dealer. '[The heroin] is too strong,' the second dealer tells KX15. 'We have to cut it down, they're dropping [overdosing] in the streets.' In another recorded conversation, a commission investigator was heard telling KX15 to use one part heroin to three parts of whatever substance was being used for dilution of the drug, before adding: 'We [the Royal Commission] do not have the authority to sell drugs where people are OD'ing.' During the period KX15 was back on the streets the number of overdoses increased dramatically and in just three weeks 13 addicts died in Kings Cross.

In a District Court drug trial relating to the operation, *Regina v Peter and Roula Kay*, Judge Viney said of the commission's role: 'It would be at least improper for people in the position of the Royal Commission investigators and their advisers to permit and encourage that man to continue with his drug dealing. That is what they did.'

The commander of Task Force Bax, Detective Superintendent Jeff Wegg, spoke about the operation in a March 2003 *60 Minutes* report called 'Dirty Work':

> What did shock me was the fact that he [KX15] was still allowed to sell drugs without supervision, without any accountability, without any accountability for the drugs, the quantity of the drugs, the strength of the drugs, the money that was involved, [or] the profits that he was making ... from those particular sales. There was no accountability on their [the commission's] behalf ... it just went against standard procedures. It was not the right way to do it.

These exposures, made in the lead-up to a state election, led to the then police minister, Michael Costa, declaring that ICAC should investigate the allegations about KX15. However, the election came and went and nothing was done. The allegations were referred to at least ten state and federal bodies but all of them declined to investigate.

The combined effects of the Wood Royal Commission between 1994 and 1997, and the jailing of Bill Bayeh in 1996 and Louis Bayeh in 1997, created a void in the Kings Cross drug trade. Task Force Bax had been set up in early 1996 to target the drug gangs fighting for control of the Cross.

During its 18-month operational life more than 80 major drug dealers were arrested. Twenty faced charges carrying life imprisonment. All were convicted. However, Bax was disbanded after it became the subject of corruption investigations by the Special Crime and Internal Affairs Unit and the Police Integrity Commission.

In *Peter Ryan: The inside story,* written by Sue Williams, Ryan, as the police commissioner at the time of the Bax investigation, claimed personal leadership of the operation to clean up Bax: 'It was set to be one of the most daring [anti-corruption] operations ever undertaken by a Commissioner of Police in Australia ... Ryan had led a massive covert surveillance program ... within one of its [the police service's] most prized squads, Task Force Bax.' The result, Ryan declared, was a 'triumph'.

The truth was rather different. The Police Integrity Commission inquiry exposed managerial shortcomings in the conduct of the task force and found that one Bax drug investigation had been compromised. Of the task force's 30 members, one was eventually charged with various criminal offences and jailed. A second detective, not a member of Bax, was also jailed on related matters.

Twelve members of Bax launched civil action against the police and the government, claiming they had been negligently treated and falsely imprisoned as a result of the covert investigation led by Ryan. Three dropped out but nine continued with the litigation. A decade later, in December 2007, the claims of all nine were settled. The terms of settlement were not disclosed but were rumoured to have included a total payout of around $5 million. If correct, that would make it one of the biggest ever made in response to litigation by police officers against the department. Any significant settlement against nine officers was a devastating blow to the credibility of Special Crime and Internal Affairs and to the then commissioner Ryan's personally led fight against corruption.

There is no support for corrupt police, but arguably the botched investigation into Task Force Bax made life harder for police facing a new wave of criminals eager to take advantage of the openings in the drug trade created by the Wood Royal Commission.

In April 1994 Russell Townsend, John Ibrahim and Ali Sakr, an alleged muscleman for the Ibrahim family, were charged with the manslaughter of Talal Assad in a fight at Kings Cross on 21 April 1994. Assad was a street dealer who worked for Bill Bayeh.

Four years later Townsend was acquitted of Assad's killing, but convicted of assault occasioning actual bodily harm and placed on a $1000 four-year good behaviour bond. In the *Sunday Telegraph* report 'John Ibrahim gave the kiss of life', Jennifer Sexton noted that in sentencing Townsend, Justice Abadee told him:

> I accept the prisoner's statement to the jury that the victim said to him, 'Do you want to score?' I accept it because, having regard to the prisoner's enthusiasm for fitness, as further supported by character references tendered before me this morning, that he might well take umbrage at being approached for the purposes of seeing whether he would be interested in buying drugs. Next, there is nothing in the prisoner's antecedents that I have had regard to which would suggest that he is the sort of person who has in any way, shape or form in the past been involved in drug

activities, or even activities, more particularly relevant, involving personal use or abuse of drugs.

The judge can only make findings based on the material presented to him. However, at the April 1996 committal proceedings evidence was given by Robert Daher—a self-confessed drug dealer and heavy cocaine user and a significant witness at the Wood Royal Commission—that Townsend (but not Ibrahim) was 'selling drugs'. Daher was not called to give evidence at Townsend's trial. Nor was other evidence available from the commission called to rebut Townsend's claim that he had no involvement in drugs.

During the commission evidence was given of Townsend's involvement in the drug trade. In one secretly taped conversation Bill Bayeh is heard telling KX1, a Kings Cross drug dealer, 'When I come back [from court] I'll catch Russell [Townsend] and I'll tell him that he can't sell the nose thing [cocaine] any more. I want to tell him. If he says no to me he'll get a beating.' He went on to tell KX1 that Townsend was a 'chicken, don't worry about him'.

In another intercepted conversation between Bill Bayeh and Trevor Haken, recorded around the time of the Assad killing and recounted by Haken in his book *Sympathy for the Devil*, Bayeh asks Haken to help him get rid of the competition. One of the competitors was Townsend. Townsend was 'operating out of the Budget Private Hotel (aka the Budget Inn) ... Townsend was selling every type of drug out of the poolroom in William Street and was making over $100,000 a week ... Townsend was selling up to 250 half caps of rock heroin per day out of the Budget Private Hotel and his other places.'

Following the Wood Royal Commission the former associate of the bosses who ran the Kings Cross underworld during the 1980s and 1990s declared himself to be a changed man with a new and honest career: professional boxing. By 2002 Townsend was well known on the local circuit. His no-mercy approach made him a crowd pleaser and earned him the nickname the 'White Rhino'. But despite winning six fights, all by a knockout, Townsend retired without having broken into the big time.

In February 2007 Townsend was found unconscious in a locked toilet cubicle in the Qantas domestic terminal at Sydney airport. An ambulance was called and Townsend was taken to hospital. On regaining consciousness he discharged himself. It was a drug overdose and Townsend was not keen to speak with the police. His luggage was searched, but nothing was found. Townsend missed his flight to Brisbane. It was clear that he was still a heavy user of steroids—and, perhaps, other drugs.

Trevor Haken went into witness protection the day he was publicly revealed as a commission informant. Following the commission he 'disappeared'. Haken told his story to Sean Padraic (not the author's real name) who wrote the book *Sympathy for the Devil: Confessions of a corrupt police officer*. Padraic writes, 'Life since the Royal Commission has not been good for Trevor Haken.' According to Padraic, Haken feels anger towards the commission which he believes abandoned him. Haken now lives alone. 'He does not socialise with anyone. He cannot work.' He lives 'under a package of about four different names'. Perhaps it is Haken's daughter who best sums up Haken's situation: 'He would have done less time if he had killed someone.'

In 1995 Sam Ibrahim was admitted to hospital. He told the Wood Royal Commission: 'I nearly had a collapsed liver. I was in hospital for three weeks and they didn't think I was going to come out of the hospital because of the coke and I'm just trying to get off it.' Sam remained a heavy drug user.

The Ibrahims survived both the Wood Royal Commission and the split with the Bayeh family. As the commission laid bare the corruption that fed off the Kings Cross drug trade, Sam set about building an alliance with the Nomads outlaw motorcycle gang. As a result of the alliance, the Nomads emerged as one of the inner-city's most influential crime groups. Their interests included nightclubs, security contracts and protection rackets, tattoo parlours and a greatly extended drug network centred on the manufacture and distribution of amphetamines. Sam Ibrahim established a new chapter of the gang at Granville (it was known, confusingly, as the Parramatta chapter), becoming its vice president and later its president. Thanks to his close association with some of the Telopea Street Boys (see Chapter 5), several joined Ibrahim's Parramatta chapter.

The bouts of extreme violence caused by his cocaine addiction made Sam Ibrahim a danger to friend and foe alike. Cocaine was also a factor in some odd encounters with police—encounters that were hard to reconcile with his status as a senior crime figure. Sam's criminal record went back to the early 1980s when he was a teenager. Despite around 30 arrests for crimes ranging from street offences to murder, he had spent relatively little time in jail. While he beat some charges at court, others were dropped when witnesses refused to give evidence or disappeared.

In 2006 Ibrahim, Nomads national president Scott Orrock and other Nomad members were arrested and charged with a variety of crimes ranging from attempted murder to assault inflicting grievous bodily harm, assault, demanding money with intent to steal, riot, affray and firearms offences—all the result of a fight in Newcastle with the local chapter of the Nomads (see Chapter 9).

Ibrahim was refused bail. While he was on remand in jail, the Nomads' Parramatta chapter was disbanded and a new gang called Notorious was formed. Its members are predominantly from Middle Eastern and Pacific Islander backgrounds and the gang has members as young as fourteen. Though they wear full colours and claim to belong to an outlaw motorcycle gang, many members do not ride bikes. Notorious, which is in dispute with several other bikie gangs, has a record for violence and drugs and is involved in the protection rackets at Kings Cross and Oxford Street. Sam Ibrahim is believed to be the power behind the gang, although he denies it.

After almost two years in jail Ibrahim and the others beat the Newcastle charges. However, Ibrahim was not long out of jail when, in May 2009, he was arrested and returned to jail for abducting a 15-year-old boy who he accused of attempting to break into his estranged wife's home in Sydney's west. Ibrahim is alleged to have assaulted the youth, breaking a tooth and inflicting facial cuts. When he realised he had grabbed the wrong person, Ibrahim gave the youth $100 and let him go.

In court, police claimed that Tongan Sam's 21-year-old son, Nimilote 'Nim' Ngata, and 37-year-old Philip Kanda-rakis were also involved in the alleged abduction, though neither was charged. Nim had been charged on 2 March with the aggravated robbery and wounding of a man outside the Dragonfly nightclub in Kings Cross. Nim was described by

Sunday Telegraph journalist Yoni Bashan as 'an up-and-coming debt collector and emerging Kings Cross identity who works closely with the Ibrahim family'. He is a patched member of Notorious. While investigating the bashing, police searched Tongan Sam's home in the western Sydney suburb of Merrylands. They seized a bulletproof vest, ammunition, clothing and paraphernalia related to Notorious as well as around 700 tablets containing pseudoephedrine, a precursor for making amphetamines. Tongan Sam was charged over the tablets.

In June Sam Ibrahim pleaded guilty to four outstanding weapons charges and was placed on two separate good behaviour bonds and fined $1500. At the time of writing, the abduction charge against Ibrahim, the robbery and wounding charge against Nim and the drug charge against Tongan Sam were yet to go before the courts.

In April 2006 John and Sam's 27-year-old brother, Michael Ibrahim, and their cousins, 22-year-old Mouhamed Tajjour and 25-year-old Sleiman Sion Tajjour, were charged with the stabbing murder of 34-year-old Robin Nassaur and the wounding of his brother, 36-year-old George, in the basement carpark of an apartment block at Chiswick, in Sydney's inner west, three months earlier. Nassaur's body was found near a pink Harley Davidson motorbike with the word 'vendetta' painted on the mudguard. The cause of the stabbings was an argument on New Year's Eve between the Nassaurs and Michael Ibrahim at the UN nightclub (formerly known as DCM) in Paddington, which was run by John Ibrahim and where Michael worked as a bouncer.

An arrest warrant was issued for a fourth man, 22-year-old Faouxi Abou-Jibal, who had set up the Nassaurs to be attacked. Three weeks later Abou-Jibal's body was found in a park off Macdonald Street, Lakemba, in Sydney's south-west. He had been shot once in the back. A month earlier, Abou-Jibal's parents' Liverpool home had been the target of a drive-by shooting by two men.

In April 2008 Michael Ibrahim was sentenced to nine years and four months' jail for the manslaughter of Nassaur. Sleiman and Mahmoud Tajjour were each sentenced to three years and seven months' jail for manslaughter.

During the Wood Royal Commission, it was put to John Ibrahim by counsel assisting the commission, 'You are the new lifeblood of the drugs trade in Kings Cross, aren't you?'

'So it would seem, but no, I'm not,' Ibrahim replied.

Two years later John Ibrahim was charged with threatening a person on the witness protection program who was to give evidence against Sam and others facing cocaine conspiracy charges. It was alleged that John and three other men, believed to be members of the Nomads motorcycle gang, grabbed the woman and told her that if her boyfriend gave evidence she, her boyfriend and her 18-month-old child would be killed. The prosecution eventually dropped the case.

It was not the first time the Crown had lost a case against John Ibrahim. In 1994 Ibrahim had been charged over the killing of Kings Cross drug dealer Talal Assad but on that occasion too the charge against Ibrahim had been dropped.

In June 2009 *Sydney Morning Herald* journalists Kate McClymont and Dylan Welch wrote that 'The Wood Royal Commission into police corruption heard that the crooked officer Graham "Chook" Fowler asked for $10,000 to make a 1994 murder charge against John and his then colleague Russell Townsend go away.' Another officer gave evidence that 'when John [Ibrahim] was at court for a mention relating to the murder John said to him, "I know that you blokes don't mind what goes on up here as long as no-one gets hurt. I wish it was like how it was when Chook Fowler and the others were here."'

In October 2004 John Ibrahim was again charged with threatening a witness in a murder case involving his brother Michael and others. During the proceedings police described John as being 'a major organised crime figure' associated with 'outlaw motorcycle gangs'. However, 18 months later the charges were dismissed when the District Court (Criminal Jurisdiction) found that police had obtained the evidence 'improperly and in contravention of an Australian law'. While criticising the conduct of the police, Judge Finnane QC commented, 'I have no doubt that [the murdered man and some members of his family] were engaged in criminal activities and that those who attacked them [Michael Ibrahim and his crew] were engaged in similar activities.' In earlier court proceedings relating to the attacks, John Ibrahim had been described as a 'major organised crime figure' who had a 'team of henchmen at his disposal'.

The inadmissible evidence consisted of secret 2003 police recordings of conversations between John Ibrahim and Roy Malouf in which they were heard discussing the charges against John's brother Michael for shooting Malouf, Malouf's brother, Richard, and their father, Pierre. *Sunday Telegraph* journalist Jennifer Sexton described the evidence in an article headlined 'Secret recordings reveal Ibrahim world'. Ibrahim was heard telling Malouf, 'I've been on charges for murder, fucking attempted ... it doesn't mean they get me. Because they come up with all this bullshit to get you charged, and then; but [by] the time you get to court, everyone's gone, you know what I mean?' Later he told Malouf, 'I know, better than all of youse ... I've been charged 5000 times ... Unless they have someone else to say that I saw him do this, this, this, they can't do shit. DNA and all that, they can't do shit.'

Suggesting it would be unwise for Malouf's family to give evidence, Ibrahim said: 'If your brother and dad are thinking about doing that, they might as well move to the moon ... No point in moving houses ... So, that's not a threat. So, you can take that any way you want. Down the track, I'll stop it. I've got my own ways of stopping it ... And now your brother's got—oh yes, he's upset, he's got a limp, he's this and he's that, but he could get a lot worse, bro.'

In a 2009 profile *Sydney Morning Herald* journalist Dylan Welch described John Ibrahim as 'Standing in the middle of the Trademark's Piano Room as an A-list crowd—topped by the rent-a-celebrity Paris Hilton—swirls around him during New Year's Eve celebrations, Ibrahim looks like the king of the world.' Welch observed of Ibrahim, 'After 21 years of wheeling and dealing he is at the top of his game, and he knows it.' Ibrahim, he wrote, 'is a nightclub promoter who works with about 17 clubs in Kings Cross and Darlinghurst, and owns multimillion-dollar homes in Sydney's east ... He wears designer clothes, drives a Bentley and drops astounding amounts of money defending his brothers when they face court.'

John Ibrahim has not been convicted of a criminal offence for more than 20 years. He is now in business with the sons of the late organised crime boss George Freeman, 26-year-old Adam Sonny and 24-year-old David George. They jointly own the Ladylux nightclub in the centre of Kings Cross. The club's internet site describes it as a club 'where the big kids come out to play'. In a *Sunday Telegraph* article, 'Our Dad, the Underbelly hero', journalists Sharri Markson and Jennifer Sexton claim that Freeman asked Ibrahim to take care of his 'boys'. According to David Freeman, 'John worked for Dad too. He used to drive him around, he did security, ran errands. He was 18 when he started working for him.' In the article Adam Freeman describes Ibrahim as being 'like our father figure ... He's raised us and has given us everything. He's always supported us. We've lived with him at stages.' David and Adam Freeman's business empire extends from 'property development and building luxury boats in the Mediterranean to event promotions and running nightclubs'.

In February 2009 Adam and two friends were picked up by the coast guard of the Netherlands Antilles on his yacht, *I'l Dapprima*, with US$190,000 in cash hidden in a compartment on board. Money laundering charges were later dropped, but the yacht and the money were impounded. Markson and Sexton report that Adam is pursuing the return of the yacht through the courts.

John Ibrahim is eager for people to know that he is a person of influence in Kings Cross. He is also eager to assure people that he is different to the traditional people of influence at the Cross, telling the *Herald*'s Kate McClymont and Dylan Welch in June 2009, 'I didn't shoot my way to the top, I charmed my way there.'

John also wants people to know that he is different to his brothers. Jennifer Sexton's article 'Secret recordings reveal Ibrahim world' reports him saying, 'I don't have a criminal record. It's all my fucking, my brothers fuck up ... They [the police] think they are all working for me ... They [the police] think my brothers, Sam and Michael, work for me. Work that one out. And I know they're fucking lunatics. I can't control them.'

About 11.30 pm on 5 June 2009 a lone gunman shot John Ibrahim's younger brother, 35-year-old Fadi, five times in the upper part of his body as he sat in his black Lamborghini outside his multimillion-dollar Castle Cove home on Sydney's north shore. The gunman escaped. Fadi's girlfriend, 23-year-old Shayda Bastani Rad, who suffered a gunshot wound to the leg, is the former fiancée of Faouxi Abou-Jibal, the Ibrahim associate who was found murdered in a Lakemba park three weeks after Michael Ibrahim and two cousins were arrested and charged with the killing of Robin Nassaur.

Six weeks before the Fadi shooting, the New South Wales Crime Commission had raided the Castle Cove home and seized around $300,000 in cash. Nearly $3 million cash was seized in the home of Fadi's sister, 39-year-old Maha Sayour, at South Wentworthville in Sydney's west. Maha was later charged with 'recklessly dealing in the proceeds of crime'. The cash is the subject of confiscation proceedings by the New South Wales Crime Commission.

At least four operations were needed to save Fadi's life. Three weeks later, Fadi checked himself out of Sydney's Royal North Shore Hospital. He declined police protection: Fadi was safer in the care of his brothers.

Fadi and his brothers expressed full support for the police investigation and Fadi and John promised full cooperation. Unfortunately, Fadi did not see the shooter and had no idea who it could have been. He had no idea who might want him dead. Likewise, John knew nothing. There is an uneasy quiet.

Commenting on the shooting, one old timer observed: 'These Lebs are going to self destruct. Somebody in John's position has got four options. He can make peace with those that ordered the shooting, but that's not likely. He can kill them. They can kill him and his family. Or someone else will kill them both so things can get back to normal. This is bad for business.'

In September Fadi Ibrahim, his brother Michael (who was already in jail for the killing of Robin Nassaur) and 29-year-old former bikie Rodney 'Goldy' Atkinson were charged with conspiring to murder John Macris. Atkinson was also charged with drug and firearms offences. In court, police described Fadi as a 'known associate of people involved in high-level organised crime' and claimed he had a criminal history that included 'intent to influence a witness, hinder investigation and pervert the course of justice'. Fadi spent six weeks in jail before being released on $1 million bail. As Fadi left Long Bay jail his brother Sam became involved in an altercation with a waiting media cameraman. Later that day he was arrested and charged with allegedly damaging the man's television camera and with breaching his bail from an earlier offence. Thirty-seven-year-old Macris and his 27-year-old brother, Alexandros (Alex), had been friends and business partners of the Ibrahim family and of murdered standover man Todd O'Connor. In 2000 John Macris was arrested and charged with possession of amphetamines. He was convicted in 2006 and sentenced to two years and three months' jail, but released in March 2007. Alex, an alleged associate of Notorious, was arrested in early 2009 and charged with weapons and drug offences. At the time of writing, his court matters had not been finalised. Another nasty shock awaited the Ibrahims within days of Fadi's arrest when his sister Maha was arrested and charged over the cash found in her kitchen ceiling. The Ibrahims, or so it seemed, were being picked off one by one.

Several criminals expanded their business dramatically in the years following the Wood Royal Commission, but the most dangerous challenge to a traumatised and disillusioned New South Wales police force came from another quarter. Released from jail in October 1995, Bill Bayeh's old nemesis Danny Karam was content to bide his time while the after-shocks of the royal commission worked their way through the Kings Cross drug trade. By the time the commission closed its doors, Karam was ready to hit the streets with his new and most violent gang: Danny's Boys.

CHAPTER THREE

Danny Karam and
his Boys

The traditional arrangements that provided protection to the drug markets and other rackets in Kings Cross were in disarray by the time the Wood Royal Commission shut down in 1997. Street dealers and users now clamoured for the relative security of the pre-royal commission days.

After his release from jail Bill Bayeh's former lieutenant and rival Danny Karam went about re-establishing himself, quietly setting up both protection rackets and cocaine supply networks while appearing to cooperate with the commission. As the commission wound up, Karam struck. His new gang, known both as Danny's Boys and DK's Boys, moved into the drug supply vacuum that was Kings Cross and set about spreading its operations beyond the Cross into south-western Sydney. It was a new era for the Lebanese connection, based on the ruthless and indiscriminate use of violence and intimidation.

In jail and under strict supervision Karam had been violent and ill disciplined. On the streets his violence exploded, exacerbated by his heavy use of heroin and cocaine. Almost a decade earlier one of his probation officers had noted: '[Karam] has some significant psychological problems particularly in respect of appropriately dealing with frustration.' The same officer highlighted the deterioration in Karam's behaviour when he was on drugs. 'He became violent, difficult to reason with, suspicious bordering on paranoid and ... suicidal.' In fact, Karam had attempted suicide on at least four occasions during the late 1980s and early 1990s. Had he been successful, Sydney might have been spared much of the violence that was about to erupt.

Karam's first priority was muscle to protect his network and intimidate opponents. He chose a bunch of tough young thugs on the rise. Among them was 20-year-old Alexi 'Little Al' Taouil. Taouil and his family came from the same Lebanese village as Karam and called him 'uncle' out of respect. He had a special relationship with Karam and operated his own cocaine network outside the control of Karam's gang. Taouil was Karam's trusted lieutenant and together with five other new recruits made up the core of the gang.

Twenty-two-year-old Michael 'Doc' Kanaan had come to Australia with his family as a child. Relatively unknown to police at the time, Kanaan was prone to extreme and unpredictable outbreaks of violence and had little regard for human life. He was to become one of the state's most dangerous criminals.

Alan Rossini (a court-ordered pseudonym), also known as 'Big Al' and 'Chavez', was a 22-year-old of mixed Islander and Croatian parentage. He was by far the most intelligent and streetwise of the recruits. He studied police methodology and was the gang's chief planner. Rossini brought some calm to the gang when tensions broke out. He trained in self-defence and enjoyed a good fight on the streets. Unlike other members of the gang, Rossini rarely carried a gun.

The fourth member of Karam's gang was 19-year-old Wassim El Assaad, also known as 'Was' and 'Wassi', who was born in Australia of Lebanese parents. El Assaad was a cocaine user and dealer who also had a history of credit card fraud, car rebirthing and violence.

Rabeeh 'Rabs' Mawas, also 19 years old, was the fifth member. Born in Lebanon, Mawas had a criminal record that included drugs and car rebirthing, but he was very much a follower rather than a leader.

The sixth member of the gang was another 19-year-old, Lebanese-born Charbel Geagea, known as 'Charlie' and 'Johnny'. Geagea, who was known to other gang members through his involvement in drugs and his willingness to use violence, became an enforcer for the gang. In addition to this core of seven (including Karam), Danny's Boys had up to ten 'associate' members at any one time.

Mawas and El Assaad had been introduced to Rossini and Karam by 23-year-old Shadi Derbas, who had only a relatively minor criminal record at the time, but who ran a car theft and rebirthing business and a substantial cannabis distribution network from his home in Telopea Street, Punchbowl, in Sydney's south-west. Derbas had been supplying Kanaan and other members of the gang with pot for their own use long before the gang was formed. He later expanded his drug operations to the point where the community and local police lost control of Telopea Street (see Chapter 5).

While the Derbas crew and Danny's Boys had their

occasional disputes, Derbas remained the gang's cannabis supplier and worked with them throughout the late 1990s. Derbas was not in competition with Karam. He was not a threat to the gang but an ally who, as well as providing them with cannabis, helped out with stolen and rebirthed cars. Derbas would be an accomplice in some of their most violent crimes.

Around mid 1997 Kanaan was training at a Burwood gym in Sydney's inner west when an argument started with another club member. They went to the rest room 'so they could fight it out' in private, but Kanaan was never interested in a fair fight. As they walked into the room, Kanaan king hit Danny Sukkar and a mate of Kanaan's threw a 23-kilogram weight on him as he lay on the floor. Kanaan's victim was no insignificant opponent. He was a senior member of a powerful Lebanese crime family whose low profile in the broader community has allowed it largely to escape police crackdowns on Middle Eastern crime over the past decade.

According to Alan Rossini, a few nights after the fight in the gym 'four blokes turned up [at Kanaan's Belfield home] with baseball bats and one of them called out, "Don't fuck with the Sukkars"' and smashed up the place. Kanaan was not at home at the time but had arranged for armed men to provide protection.

Kanaan wanted revenge and was not prepared to wait. He grabbed a gun and went looking for the attackers. Not knowing where they lived, Kanaan went to a petrol station where he took a telephone directory and 'ripped out the page with all the Sukkars listed'. He went to several addresses in the Five Dock–Haberfield area, but after inspecting them decided they were 'occupied by Australians and not Lebanese'.

According to Rossini, Kanaan eventually found the house he was looking for and 'fired off a number of shots'. Screams of 'Ah fuck!' came from the house as the shots were fired.

Expecting reprisals, Kanaan rounded up more guns for his gang. They took up positions in the vacant house next to Kanaan's Belfield home and kept watch from the veranda. Three nights later a red car was seen driving up and down the street, slowing each time as it passed Kanaan's house. The car windows were down and on one pass a passenger called out, 'Michael Kanaan.' That was enough for Kanaan. He snapped and ran from the next-door house, firing wildly at the car as it sped off. Karam was impressed. Within weeks Kanaan and Rossini had been invited to join Karam's gang.

About six months later Karam and some of his boys were prowling Kings Cross late at night when they bumped into Danny Sukkar, who turned and ran. They chased him, firing indiscriminately. Innocent bystanders hit the ground in fear of their lives. Some not-so-innocent bystanders went for their guns, without knowing who was firing or which side they should be supporting. Sukkar fell down seriously wounded. Their job done, Karam and his gang left Sukkar lying on the road bleeding from his wounds. Earlier, Sukkar had been bashed by Louis Bayeh for insulting him. Danny Sukkar was getting a record for coming off second best in disputes.

By the end of 1997 DK's Boys were asserting their control over the drug trade in Kings Cross. Each member of the gang had a team of street dealers and runners selling cocaine. Karam demanded they pay him $1000 a week in advance for each street dealer they protected. As Rossini explained, protection—or 'rent', as it was called—was 'two thousand dollars per week for two runners and one runner who could relieve but you could only have two on the street [at one time]'. By early 1998 there were around 20 protected runners. In addition to collecting rent for their protection, Rossini was supplying cocaine to them. Kanaan and Rossini also provided muscle for Karam's illegal gambling club at Belmore.

The gang bought their cocaine from a number of sources for between $4200 and $5000 an ounce. They cut and packaged it in water bomb balloons for sale on the streets. Dealers carried the balloons in their mouth and swallowed them if confronted by police or other criminals attempting to rip them off. An ounce of cocaine made about 160 street deals that sold for between $60 and $70 each, allowing the gang to roughly double their money.

Karam had 'firm control of his runners and his close associates who worked for him selling drugs', according to Rossini. One of the runners, 'Sam Ham', wanted to sell heroin rather than cocaine, but Karam refused his request. When Sam Ham ignored Karam and sold heroin, Karam had him bashed. For Karam, heroin was not worth the headache of the extra heat it attracted from the police.

In another case, a runner who was not performing failed to make contact. When the gang found the runner he told them he had lost their contact numbers. The dealer was dragged to a trusted local tattoo parlour where the gang's mobile telephone numbers were tattooed on his wrists. There would be no more excuses and no more failed contacts.

By this time Karam was making around $28,000 a week but each gang member was on as little as $200. The gang did not know where the money was going; all Karam would tell them was that he was putting it in the 'piggy bank'.

Karam increasingly saw himself as the godfather. The gang's survival, he said, depended on loyalty. He spoke of them as Danny's Boys or DK's Boys and he gave each member a gold ring with the letter 'D' on it together with the member's first initial. When presenting them each with their ring Karam kissed them three times on the cheek but then—in an act the gang found humiliating—he made each member pay $900 towards the cost. He also urged them to get a tattoo so they would be easily identified as one of Danny's Boys if they went to jail and the ring was confiscated.

'We did whatever Danny told us to do,' Rossini told police. 'Danny's enemies became our enemies ... like it or not, you need to carry a gun.' Everyone had their favourite gun but there were rules: 'Any of the boys could use any of the guns [but] if a gun had been used, the other boys were to be told so the gun could have the barrel changed or [they could] dispose of it.'

Extreme violence was their trademark. Those who were not part of the network or who did not pay for protection were assaulted, robbed and barred from areas the gang regarded as its territory. But Karam and his boys did not have it all their own way. Rossini described how, towards the middle of 1998, 'the street runner teams were falling apart because of arrests and new dealers, mostly of Samoan and Tongan origin, who were taking over the streets and had their own suppliers'.

One local criminal, Semi 'Sam' Ngata, also known as 'Tongan Sam' and 'Sam the Taxman', was notorious for ripping off street dealers. He was now a particular problem for DK's Boys because he had the backing of a rival group led by the Ibrahims. The strength of this group was such that DK's Boys could not be certain of the result if it came to an all-out war. In fact, DK's Boys were outnumbered, outgunned and a war would have only one result: they would end up dead. Sam the Taxman had to be tolerated by DK's Boys—for the time being.

About the same time Karam ordered the killing of Russell Townsend, his former partner in the drug trade and his co-accused in the bashing and stabbing of Tongan George. The reason for the order was simple: Townsend was now a competitor and represented a threat to Karam's supremacy. The gang searched Kings Cross for days without success. Townsend had gone to ground. The hit was called off as abruptly as it had been ordered. No reason was given.

As their business expanded DK's Boys spent much of their time stoned on a combination of cocaine, amphetamines and cannabis—Karam himself was continually pumped up on steroids and heroin—while they watched videos about gang violence. Rossini recalls:

> From the time I first met Mick [Kanaan] and the boys we used to watch two movies almost on a daily basis. They were *Blood In, Blood Out* [the 1993 movie known in the US as *Bound by Honor* about the ethnic gang wars in California jails during the 1980s] and *American Me* [which depicts the brutality of ethnic gang life in Los Angeles with the line 'In prison they are the law. On the streets they are the power']. We have seen them so many times we know all the words. These movies are about a gang that knocks their boss and the bloke who did it gets knocked.

The gang came to believe that these movies depicted their lifestyle. In fact the movies did predict the gang's future.

By around mid 1998 the arguments over who controlled what on the streets of Kings Cross had, once again, been resolved in an uneasy truce between DK's Boys and other gangs. But the drug haze in which they lived fuelled random acts of violence and the gang began to turn on itself. They grew and sold two hydroponic cannabis crops worth nearly $100,000 but Karam kept the money for himself: the gang didn't see a cent. DK's Boys were on the road to their own destruction.

About 8 pm on Friday 17 July 1998 Kanaan and another member of Karam's gang went to Telopea Street where they met Shadi Derbas and two members of Derbas's gang. The five got into a stolen and rebirthed Mitsubishi station wagon and drove to the Café XTREME at Five Dock, in Sydney's inner west, where they discussed car rebirthing with an associate of Derbas. They were keen to expand the gang's activities beyond drugs. Several members of the gang had experience in the lucrative car theft and rebirthing racket, but they did not have the network to support their own operation.

On leaving the café, Derbas stopped the car at a red traffic light near the Five Dock Hotel. At the time Adam Wright, a grade player with South Sydney Rugby League Club, and a man named Ronald Singleton were outside on the footpath arguing. A third hotel patron, Michael Hurle, a rugby league player with the Leichhardt Wanderers, was attempting to calm them. A passenger in Derbas's car yelled out, 'Come on, fellas, punch on.' Singleton shouted back, 'Why don't you pull your head in and mind your own fucken business,' and along with Wright and Hurle ran towards the car. A fight broke out. Kanaan pulled out a .22 calibre revolver, grabbed Hurle around the throat from behind and shot him. Throwing the fatally wounded Hurle to the ground, Kanaan then fired four shots at Wright and

Singleton, fatally wounding Wright in the abdomen and wounding Singleton in the right shoulder. As Derbas tried to drive off, Singleton held on to the leg of Kanaan, who pointed his gun at Singleton's head and pulled the trigger twice, but it failed to fire—there were no bullets left.

Singleton was lucky. As they sped away Kanaan asked if everyone was okay. 'Fuck the Aussies,' he said, 'as long as we're alright. If it happened again I would do the same thing.' He then complained about running out of bullets. Told by Derbas there was another gun in the car, Kanaan responded, 'Why didn't you tell me?'

Calls were made to associates who were told to turn on their police scanners and listen for any mention of the gang or their car. Within moments they got the message, 'The car's come up on the scanner.' Derbas and his passengers returned to Telopea Street where the car was wiped down with degreaser to remove any fingerprints and DNA traces, and the door lock and ignition were scratched and damaged. The car was then dumped at Roselands and Derbas reported it stolen.

It was not long before police found the car. The gang smirked at having fooled the police once again. However, the getaway had not been completely successful. They had dropped two mobile telephones at the scene. Although bought in false names and containing pre-paid SIM cards, the telephones eventually led to Karam and his boys. Forensic examination of the car also disclosed that the damage to the door and ignition lock was inconsistent with the car having been broken into and started without keys.

The gang also had another potential problem. They had involved Neddy Smith in the shooting. His daughter, Jamie, and her husband-to-be, Nathan Wood, an international rugby league player, had been drinking in the hotel with Wright, Singleton and Hurle. When the fight broke out, Jamie had run to their assistance. Covered in blood from their wounds, she fled the scene before the police arrived.

Neddy was not happy: although a violent man himself, he had always tried to shield his family from his criminal activities. Despite his vows of revenge, Neddy was in jail and unable to do much. His health was deteriorating and a decade behind bars had robbed him of most of his connections on the outside. Had Neddy been ten years younger and free, swift and violent retribution would certainly have followed.

Not long after the Five Dock killings the TV program *Australia's Most Wanted* promoted a forthcoming show devoted to the Middle Eastern violence sweeping Sydney, and particularly the Five Dock hotel murders. Kanaan and some of his gang worried that when the show went to air they might be recognised and given up. As well as other criminals, plenty of innocent citizens would have been glad to see them locked up. Any one of them might make an anonymous call to the police. One of the gang had an idea. They couldn't stop the program being broadcast but they might be able to stop it being received in suburbs where they were known. They decided to cause a blackout by 'shooting a[n] [electrical] substation'.

On the night of the program, four of the gang jumped into a car and, armed with a machine gun, shotgun and .357 and .45 calibre handguns, drove to an electrical substation at Belfield. Pulling up beside the substation, two of the gang leaned out of the car windows and emptied their handguns into it. Nothing happened. Frustrated, they decided to mount a more aggressive attack on the area's power supply. They drove to some nearby electricity pylons and fired the machine gun and handguns at the power lines. Sparks cascaded from the pylons. Believing they had done the job, the men sped off into the night. Back at the safe house, they prepared to smoke a bit of pot. Turning on the television, the gang was horrified to find it still working. They were home just in time to watch *Australia's Most Wanted*.

By this time Karam was hated by his gang. 'We did everything for him and he treated us bad,' Rossini said. 'He threatened us by saying he would break our legs or knock us.' The gang had made well over a million dollars, but all its members knew was what Karam told them—that he had put their profits in the 'piggy bank'. The way the gang saw it, they were taking all the risks and Karam was taking all the money. They also knew that Taouil was getting preferential treatment. He was not paying 'rent' for his street sellers and had other drug and financial arrangements with Karam that were not offered to other members of the gang.

But the problems went deeper than money. Although Karam had accepted Mawas and El Assaad as gang members, he disliked them intensely because they were Muslims. He 'didn't want anything to do with them because he was a Christian', Rossini told police. Unlike the Christian members of Karam's gang, Mawas and El Assaad had not been presented with rings.

Until this point Karam had hidden his dislike of Muslims, but one night when most of the gang was sitting around smoking pot he slipped up and in front of El Assaad made disparaging remarks about how Muslims could not be trusted. Karam quickly realised what he had said and tried to laugh it off, but the damage had been done. The rest of the gang sided with El Assaad and Mawas. All now had a fierce hatred of Karam.

Media reports added to the tensions. Kanaan and Rossini became convinced that either someone in the gang or one of their associates was speaking to the police who were then passing information to the media. Karam started talking about detectives visiting his house 'once or twice a week and ask[ing] him about shootings'. They would 'come into [my] house, into [my] lounge room and drink coffee', Karam told the gang.

Such talk convinced Kanaan that Karam would sell out the gang to the police. What could they do? Leaving the gang was not an option. They knew that Karam would find and kill them. There was only one solution: Karam had to be knocked. According to Rossini, 'Mick, Rabs, Wassim and Charlie used to sit around and talk about knocking Danny about three times a week.'

It was about this time that Shadi Derbas introduced Kanaan and Rossini to 'Wally', a Lebanese man in his mid to late thirties who lived at Bankstown and was part of the Telopea Street gang. Wally was an expert at rebirthing cars. He had all the necessary contacts and could get 'blue slips, pink slips ... compliance plates [and] could have engine numbers re-stamped' through contacts in the Roads and Traffic Authority. Wally would have had a successful illegal business but for one thing: he was continually being stood over and ripped off.

Wally needed protection and he knew 'no-one fucked with Danny Karam'. Wally claimed there were about 20 people who wanted him killed. A meeting was arranged at Karam's Randwick computer shop in Sydney's eastern suburbs. It started out friendly enough, but the mood changed when

Wally unwisely said to Karam, 'Nice shop, mate, how much do you make here? ... I bet you don't make as much as I do. I make between one and two hundred thousand a week.'

Karam snapped. He pulled a .32 semi-automatic pistol from his briefcase and pushed it into Wally's stomach. Wally panicked, waving his arms in the air and screaming, 'No, no, no.'

'Get this motherfucker out of here,' shouted Karam.

Derbas laughed. He knew Wally had gone too far. Wally had a big mouth and Karam did not like big mouths.

On their way back to Telopea Street, Kanaan and the others agreed to provide Wally with protection on one condition: that he stay away from Karam. It was a condition Wally was only too happy to accept. If anyone bothered him, Wally was to give them Kanaan's and Rossini's names and mobile telephone numbers and tell them to call.

The phone rang for a while but the calls stopped coming once it became known that DK's Boys were providing the protection. Meanwhile the gang found out something that Wally had forgotten to mention: Wally was doing a lot of ripping off himself. The cost of protection went up: Wally was to 'do four cars a month' for Kanaan and Rossini. They would choose the cars they wanted and pay only $4000 for each.

A month later, Wally had not delivered the cars. Nor was he answering his mobile. Kanaan, Rossini, El Assaad and Mawas found Wally at Bankstown driving one of his rebirthed cars. They forced him over, took the car and left Wally by the side of the road. The four rebirthed cars, including a Porsche, were hurriedly delivered—at no cost. It was 'compensation' for not telling them the full story and for the problems caused by Wally's 'big mouth'. But the problems weren't over.

A few months later Rossini and Kanaan received a telephone call from Mawas, who asked them to call at his place in Lakemba. It was mid afternoon when they arrived. El Assaad was already there. Mawas's blue Magna was parked on the footpath outside the house. Wally was in the boot, his wrists and legs bound, his eyes blackened and blood around his mouth. Kanaan reached in and punched him for good measure.

None of the gang was worried about being reported to the police by neighbours or passers-by. People had learnt to mind their own business.

Kanaan and his crew jumped into the car and drove to a smash repair shop at Greenacre. It was about 6 pm and the shop was open. Wally was taken out of the boot and into the office where El Assaad and Mawas started beating him. Wally had been caught out lying and had tried to blame it on the 'Lebo bloke' who worked there. As the beating continued Kanaan pulled a revolver from the front of his trousers to show that he was not 'fucking around'. The 'Lebo bloke' pleaded for the gang to stop the beating, but their response was to give Wally another 'good kicking'. By the time the gang decided he had had enough, Wally was bleeding badly. They picked him up, threw him back in the boot, and drove out of the smash repair shop. The 'Lebo bloke'—who was also involved in the car rebirthing racket—did not report Wally's beating to the police: he knew that he could be next.

As they drove through Camspie, Kanaan saw one of his mates standing beside the road. Convinced of their impunity, the gang pulled over. Kanaan pulled down the middle section of the back seat and told his mate to have a look. Shaking his head, the man said to Wally: 'Mate, I don't know what you've done, but you've done it to the wrong people. Good luck.'

Wally was then taken to the gang's safe house in Napier Street, Paddington, where they packaged drugs for distributing to their street dealers. Blindfolded, Wally was dragged upstairs. Kanaan started belting him on the knees with a hammer. 'It was frustrating all of us that Wally was not pleading for his life,' one gang member explained. Covered in blood, Wally fell asleep on the floor. The next morning he was allowed to shower and clean himself up and was driven back to Bankstown where he was dropped off. Wally didn't give the gang any more trouble.

While Karam's gang spread violence across south and south-west Sydney, its drug operations in Kings Cross went on unhindered. But that was about to change. In early September 1998 Sam the Taxman arrived back in town and, with his mate Big Fadi, tried to 'tax' one of Danny's street dealers. The dealer resisted and was beaten up. His money and drugs were taken. Kanaan put the word out: 'Tell the other boys on the streets to keep a lookout for them [Sam the Taxman and Big Fadi] and give us a call if you see them.' Danny's Boys were heavily armed with handguns and shotguns. Kanaan wanted to send a clear message. 'As soon as we see them we'll kneecap them,' he told the gang.

For about a week the gang patrolled the streets of Kings Cross. Street runners made several sightings but by the time the gang arrived Sam the Taxman and Big Fadi could not be found. During the night of 8 September the gang received a call from one of its runners. He had just been chased by Sam the Taxman and Big Fadi who had tried to extort a 'tax' from him. The gang scoured the Cross but, once again, the pair had given them the slip.

Two nights later Kanaan received a series of calls on his mobile phone from his runners. Sam the Taxman and Big

Fadi were in the EP1 nightclub in Earl Place, Kings Cross. Runners were keeping watch outside. The nightclub was owned by the Ibrahims and Sam was on their payroll.

The gang grabbed their weapons: six shotguns and assault rifles and ten handguns—two guns for each member of the gang. Kanaan declared, 'If we spot them on the street, we all get out and shoot them, no matter where they are, no matter who's around. Even if the blueys [police] are around. They'll run. The people on the street will shit. No one will fuck with us.' He also spelled out the alternative, 'If we can't spot Fadi or Sam, we'll do a shoot up drive-by on EP1.'

With their police scanners working hard, the gang got into three cars that had been stolen for the job, put stockings over their heads and drove in convoy from Paddington to the Cross. They made a slow circuit of the Cross then went to Earl Place and parked their cars near EP1. They got out, flashing their guns. A Tongan man started to run, but he was grabbed and had a cocked shotgun pushed in his face. He was an innocent pedestrian who happened to be in the wrong place at the wrong time. He was let go and ran off yelling, 'Thanks, bro.' The gang turned their attention to EP1 and fired more than 50 shots into the nightclub.

In the chaos Kanaan accidentally fired his shotgun as he jumped back in the car, hitting a parked car and setting off its alarm. The gang raced to a prearranged spot in Woolloomooloo where they abandoned the stolen cars and escaped in others that had been left there earlier that evening. Two of the gang's street runners later described the scene after the shooting: 'Everyone is shitting themselves up the Cross and there were cops everywhere.'

Satisfied with their night's work, the gang returned to their Paddington safe house. 'Our runners had a good night that night,' Rossini recalled. 'They sold a lot of gear for us.'

The gang had several safe houses but around the middle of 1998 Karam started looking for a new one. The Paddington safe house was to be kept for the Kings Cross street dealers, while the new house was for storing and packaging cocaine and for meetings without the street dealers. They found their new safe house in Surry Hills. They chose it because of a large sign outside the apartment block which read 'Getting High in Surry Hills'.

Earlier, Karam had explained to the gang that the best way to exact punishment was to 'shoot people in the stomach and the kneecap because it causes the most pain'. Over the next few months there were at least four knee-cappings in the Bankstown and Campsie areas, all related to drugs and car rebirthing. Then, in early October, 27-year-old Elias 'Les' Elias, whose criminal record to that point was limited to traffic offences, took a liking to a 9 mm pistol being flashed around by a cousin of Wassim El Assaad and seized the gun.

The gun belonged to El Assaad, who had taken it from another criminal who had accidentally fired it in a car in which El Assaad was a passenger, putting a bullet hole in the floor. Bashed and shoved out of the moving car, the shooter considered himself lucky not to be more seriously hurt and never mentioned the matter again. Negotiations for the return of El Assaad's gun were entrusted to another member of Karam's gang, 22-year-old Jordanian-born Saleh 'Ray' Jamal. Jamal was the eldest of 12 children and had been involved in crime and drug dealing for several years. Elias trusted Jamal but refused to hand over the gun.

In a last attempt to resolve the standoff, Jamal arranged

a meeting at Greenacre on 12 October 1998. A group of eight piled into three cars and went to the meeting. In spite of Jamal's efforts to keep the peace, an argument broke out. When Kanaan intervened, Elias screamed at him, 'Who the fuck are you?'

Kanaan was standing about two metres away. 'Who the fuck am I? Who the fuck am I?' He pulled his gun and fired four shots at Elias's legs, missing with all of them. Elias grabbed El Assaad as a shield, then pushed him away and ran towards the nearby park. Now Jamal pulled a gun, laughing as he and Kanaan fired at the fleeing Elias. Frightened of being caught in the crossfire, the others ran for whatever cover they could find. Jamal, the so-called intermediary, had been anxious to ingratiate himself with Karam and knew when he arranged the meeting that Elias would come out of it worst.

Back at the Surry Hills safe house all the talk was about the shooting. 'Fuck Les, I shot him in the arse. The cops are going to shit; two kneecappings on the one day, in the same place.' Elias was shot in the legs and buttocks. The second kneecapping was an unrelated gang attack in which the victim was shot in both legs about 300 metres from the Elias shooting.

While Jamal had gone from being the go-between to one of the shooters, the next peacemaker had to be listened to. It was Raymond 'Sunshine' Kucler, a violent criminal and member of the Comancheros outlaw motorcycle gang. Kucler had been involved in the 1984 Milperra bikie shoot-out between the Comancheros and Bandidos that ended with seven dead and more than 20 wounded.

Although he had never been convicted of a serious offence, Elias was a member of a Lebanese gang headed by

Tom Atoui, a drugs and car rebirthing specialist who had spent time in jail with Karam. Kucler was known to both Karam and Atoui. With the authority and reputation of the Comancheros riding on a peace deal, the gun was eventually returned to El Assaad. In the words of *The Godfather*'s Michael Corleone, the offer made to Elias had been too good to refuse.

CHAPTER FOUR

Michael Kanaan
murders his boss

Towards the end of 1998 a series of kneecappings was happening across south-west Sydney. In October police arrested a car thief who was well known in the western suburb of Lakemba. The man was a good friend of DK's Boys, who whipped themselves into a frenzy accusing police of harassing Lebanese youths. According to Rossini, this was when 'Kanaan came up with the idea that our group should teach the police ... a lesson.' Kanaan said, 'We should do a drive-by shooting at Lakemba Police Station ... Once we've done Lakemba, Bankstown will be next.' There was even talk of blowing up police cars.

Because crime in the Lakemba area, especially drug dealing and car rebirthing, was dominated by Shadi Derbas's group, some members of DK's Boys believed—in Rossini's words—that Derbas should 'take care of any problems'.

Kanaan disagreed. 'Mick [Kanaan] considered that Derbas didn't "have the balls" to do this sort of shooting, so Mick offered the services of us to do the job.' Finally Kanaan told the gang, 'We're going to do the drive-by shooting on Lakemba Police Station. Go to Surry Hills and pick up some artillery.' On 2 November 1998 Kanaan accompanied El Assaad, Saleh Jamal and a couple of others to Surry Hills where they met Geagea, Rossini and Ghassam 'Easy' Said, a longtime criminal associate of Jamal. They gathered the weapons, including two 9 mm handguns, a .45 calibre handgun, a couple of shotguns and some SKS rifles. Several members of the gang already had their own guns. A stolen car was organised. The gang sat around the safe house, just as they had done before other shootings, smoking pot and scanning the police radio network.

Wearing stockings to cover their faces, they drove to the Lakemba Police Station and blasted away at the front of the building. The police inside threw themselves to the floor as more than 13 shots went through windows and glass doors. One officer was severely cut by flying glass and one shot shattered a computer screen where a police officer had been seated just moments before.

The gang sped away, abandoning and burning the getaway car before returning to their Surry Hills safe house. Kanaan pulled out his 9 mm handgun and re-enacted the shooting. They joked that Kanaan had almost set himself on fire as they set the getaway car alight. 'Now the cops will think twice about targeting Lebs,' Kanaan bragged, while El Assaad chipped in, 'Fuck all the coppers. Did you see that copper shitting himself and going to the ground?' Unknown to the gang, a police ballistics examination would shortly connect the bullets and cartridge cases fired at the Lakemba

Police Station with a number of other shootings and knee-cappings. The net had begun to close on DK's Boys.

About a week later Kanaan, Rossini and El Assaad were at the Surry Hills hideaway when El Assaad told them about a brawl on 3 November between Aboriginal and Lebanese inmates in the yard at the maximum security Lithgow jail. 'Rabi Kalache and Alex Ibrahim got bashed up pretty bad by the Abos,' El Assaad said. The Aboriginals and the Lebanese were the two dominant ethnic groups in the jail and Kalache and Ibrahim were known to some of Danny's Boys. Kanaan's response was immediate and predictable, 'We should do something for them.'

Later that afternoon other gang members arrived at the safe house. Warming to his plan, Kanaan continued, 'We'll get those Abos back. We'll go to Redfern and do a drive by ... This will send a message back to those fucken Abo cunts ... We should either kneecap an Abo in the street or kidnap an Abo from the street, take him for a drive, bash him then throw him out.'

The gang talked Kanaan out of this idea. Then Rossini said, 'If you want to get a message over, write something on an Aboriginal flag and toss it in the street.'

Over the next few days one of the gang made several visits to a flag shop in Rushcutters Bay, buying several flags to hide the fact that what he really wanted was an Aboriginal flag. Back at the safe house the flag was washed to get rid of finger-prints or DNA from members of the gang. Afterwards, gloves were always worn when handling the flag. They wrote: 'Fuck with our families on the inside we fuck all your families on the outside. Blood for blood! PS Lithgow gaol 2 die for.'

But when the time came for the attack, Karam argued against it: 'When the Abos hear about this it will make it worse for all the Lebos in all the jails.' In Karam's view the Lithgow jail bashings were not motivated by race but by a stand-over argument. Karam had a close association with an older Aboriginal criminal he knew from jail—one gang member described him as being the 'Aboriginal version of Karam'. The relationship was profitable and useful and Karam did not want to see it ruined by an attack on Redfern.

Kanaan pretended to listen but as soon as Karam left he set the plan in motion: the gang was going to 'shoot up Eveleigh Street, Redfern' and 'drop the flag'. The car stolen for the job was to be dumped and blown up. Another car parked at Alexandria would be used for the escape. Kanaan, Rossini, Jamal, El Assaad and Said gathered at the safe house. As usual the weapons—shotguns, assault rifles and handguns—outnumbered their handlers by two to one. The gang donned surgical gloves and headed for Eveleigh Street.

About 3.30 am on 11 November they drove down the street spraying houses and parked cars with shotgun and handgun fire. The flag was thrown from the car as they sped off. Back at Surry Hills the gang deluded themselves about another job well done. But in jail it was a different story. A meeting was held at Silverwater jail between Aboriginal and Lebanese inmates. According to Rossini, 'The Lebanese bloke representing the Lebanese was bashed because he accepted the terms of a truce that he was not in a position to do. The promise that this Lebanese bloke made was that the Abos and Lebanese should cease fighting.'

Police ballistics evidence connected the shotgun used in the Eveleigh Street raid to the one used two months earlier in the EP1 nightclub shooting and in another shooting two months before that.

*

The gang was making big profits from the Kings Cross drug trade but six months of resentment and anger towards Danny Karam was reaching its peak. Kanaan, Rossini, Geagea, El Assaad and Rabs Mawas discussed ways of murdering their boss. They decided on a hot shot of heroin. Geagea, who was supplying Karam, claimed to have access to a poison that could not be detected. He told the others, 'As soon as Danny injects he will die straight away. You can't tell the difference when you look at it.' A few days later Geagea turned up at the Surry Hills unit with the poison, a white powder. Asked how much poison he was going to mix with the heroin, Geagea replied, 'All of it.'

As he had done hundreds of times before, Geagea met Karam and gave him the heroin. All the gang could do now was wait. The phone call they eventually got was not the one they wanted. It was Karam, screaming that he wanted to see Kanaan and Rossini straight away. Although terrified, they drove straight to his Coogee home. Karam knew the heroin was bad, but Kanaan and Rossini were in luck: he blamed it on the supplier. 'Go and see the bloke that give it to Charlie [Geagea] and baseball bat him,' Karam told them.

After leaving his house they met up with Geagea. They were in a fix. They couldn't 'baseball bat' the supplier: he had powerful friends who would take revenge. In any case there was another problem: if they bashed him without killing him, the supplier would tell Karam his side of the story. It was Geagea who came up with a solution: 'I'm going to have to say I got it off a bloke at Marrickville, and that we couldn't find him.' They waited a few days and told Karam the story. Karam appeared to believe it but found a new supplier and refused to accept any more heroin from Geagea.

Despite the setback the gang were still determined to kill Karam. This time they decided to keep it simple—by shooting him. A week passed before they saw him again. Karam told El Assaad that he needed a stolen car and some guns. He inspected the arsenal stored at the unit in Surry Hills and helped himself to several weapons.

Kanaan was suspicious and wanted to know what was happening. 'I have to go and do something,' Karam told him. 'Don't worry about it.' Some of the other members offered to help but Karam rebuffed them, insisting that he didn't need their help.

Worried that Karam had found out about their plan to kill him, the rest of the gang decided to stay together. Karam cancelled the next night's meeting, further heightening their suspicions. Had he heard something? They had decided to ambush Karam the next time he visited the Surry Hills unit. According to Rossini, 'The arrangement was that all four [Kanaan, El Assaad, Geagea and Mawas] were going down to do the shooting; two on each side of the car. They were going to stand on an angle so they wouldn't get caught in the crossfire.' Fearful that the killing would prompt a police raid, the unit was continually cleaned of fingerprints and other evidence.

About 8 pm on 13 December 1998 Karam buzzed to be let in through the apartment block's security door. Kanaan, Geagea, El Assaad and Mawas grabbed their guns. Karam was getting impatient and kept buzzing. The killers ran out of the unit and down the back stairwell. Rossini and a few of the gang stayed in the unit. Let in by Rossini, Karam looked around and asked, 'Where is everyone?' Rossini told him they were out with their girls but Karam did not seem to believe him. He said he'd come to fetch a few shotguns.

After choosing two, he gave orders for them to be taken down to his car, which was parked in the laneway outside. As Karam sat down to drink coffee and smoke dope, Mawas returned to the unit. Karam seemed to sense that something was wrong, but Rossini and others calmed him. After finishing his coffee and joint, Karam left. As soon as he was out of the unit, Mawas called the waiting assassins on his mobile phone: 'He's on his way down.'

At that moment 'Rahme', a longtime friend of Rossini and several other members of the gang, buzzed the apartment from the outside security door. Shouting into the apartment's intercom, El Assaad called to Rahme, 'Get out of here. Get out of here.' But it was too late: Rahme was standing at the security door when Karam opened it. 'How are you, mate?' asked Karam as he let Rahme into the apartment building.

They were the last words he would speak. Seconds later the killers opened fire. Sixteen shots hit Karam. His car was riddled with bullets. The killers grabbed Karam's mobile phone and destroyed it, together with the SIM card, in an attempt to get rid of anything that might lead the police to the gang. The shots could be heard in the apartment. Realising what had happened, Rahme left in a hurry, anxious not to be involved.

Later Kanaan described the shooting to the gang: 'When Danny was in the car, Danny saw me and smiled at me. I pulled out the gun, smiled, nodded my head and went,' motioning with his hands as if he was shooting. 'After I shot him I went back and shot him again.' Mawas chipped in, adding, 'Fuck I shot him a lot.'

The gang had killed the boss; now they had to make sure that they were not killed in turn. Before murdering Karam the gang had organised a new safe house in the Haymarket in Sydney's central business district. This became their new headquarters. They had good reason to be scared. As well as Karam they had intended to kill his protégé, 'Little Al' Taouil, but that plan unravelled when Karam came to the apartment alone. Taouil's response to the news of Karam's death was exactly what his killers had expected: 'Don't worry, we are going to kill whoever did it.'

The guilty men needed a fall guy. Kanaan named Tongan Sam (Sam the Taxman), Sam Ibrahim's right-hand man, as one of the shooters. He was to be killed as retribution. This would show everyone that Danny's gang was still a force to be reckoned with, even without Danny.

Still fearful of reprisals, several gang members did not attend Karam's funeral. The Karam family and some of Karam's friends were offended. Taouil was suspicious.

Over the next few days the gang learned why Karam had wanted the extra guns. He was planning to rip off two major drug dealers for four kilos of cocaine. The dealers were mates of Russell Townsend. Karam had not intended to share the spoils with the rest of the gang. While this news reinforced their view that they were justified in getting rid of Karam, it didn't make them feel any safer.

Meanwhile they were facing another problem: on hearing of Karam's murder, most of the gang's street dealers had panicked and run off. Money slowed to a trickle. They had to get dealers back on the streets—quickly.

The search for Tongan Sam was on: Kanaan, Mawas, El Assaad, Mark Chiekh and Rossini were constantly armed, expecting a shootout. Between them they carried a total of 15 handguns, automatic rifles and shotguns. Kanaan wanted a crowd around when they found and killed Tongan Sam. Kings Cross had to know that Kanaan was the avenger of Karam's murder and that he was the gang's new boss. Rossini passed the message to Karam's family: 'We are going to look for Tongan Sam. We are going to shoot all of Danny's enemies.' Karam's brother, Norm, liked the idea so much that he grabbed Rossini by the chest and, looking into his eyes, told him, 'Do me a favour, bring back the guy's shirt with his blood on it.'

Kanaan, Rossini, Mawas, El Assaad and other gang members searched the streets of Kings Cross. They gathered five of their runners at Rushcutters Bay and Kanaan gave them the message, 'Tongan Sam is going to get it tonight ... we'll get them back for Danny ... Go and find Tongan Sam for us.' But he was nowhere to be seen. The search was repeated night after night.

During the early hours of 23 December 1998 Mark Chiekh, Rossini, Kanaan and El Assaad were roaming Kings Cross and Rushcutters Bay, following the same route they had taken each night since their hunt began, when they were spotted by a police patrol car. When they saw the police car do a U-turn, the gang panicked. Kanaan and El Assaad lay on the floor, screaming, 'Go, go, go,' and the car sped off, chased by the police. They hurtled around the back streets trying to lose their pursuers, but ended up in Alma Street, a dead end in Rushcutters Bay. Leaping out of the car, they ran into the Weigall Sports Ground, chased by police.

Ignoring calls to stop, Rossini climbed a high wire fence and escaped but the other three did not make it. One of the police, Senior Constable John Fotopoulos, tackled El Assaad to the ground. Pulling out his gun, Kanaan took aim and started firing. The second police officer, Constable Chris Patrech, was hit twice and fell to the ground with wounds to the arm and leg. Still struggling with El Assaad and with his partner bleeding beside him, Fotopoulos drew his gun and fired at the muzzle flashes. In the exchange that followed, Kanaan fired about seven times, wounding El Assaad. Five of the 12 shots fired by Fotopoulos hit Kanaan. Forensic examination of the guns seized in the park confirmed that one of the three 9 mm pistols had been used to kill Karam a few weeks earlier.

Kanaan survived but his injuries confined him to a wheelchair. He was charged with two counts of attempted murder, shooting to avoid apprehension, possessing and discharging a firearm. At first bail was refused, although it was granted later. El Assaad was charged with breaching a previous bond for concealing a serious offence, affray and possessing ammunition.

On bail Kanaan resumed control of the former DK's Boys and their drug network. For the next six months he ran the gang from his wheelchair—money was now desperately needed to cover legal fees. During this time about a quarter of a million dollars worth of cocaine was sold on the streets of Kings Cross.

After the shootout Kanaan's behaviour changed. He became increasingly paranoid. Believing his Belfield home and his wheelchair were bugged, he went around shouting his innocence and claiming to have fired at the police in self-defence. He gave orders to the gang only in writing, burning the notes after they had been read.

For the rest of the year the biggest threat to the gang came not from their rivals in the drug trade, but from the police.

On 25 April 1999 Mawas was arrested at Sydney airport as he tried to leave Australia for Lebanon. Bail was refused.

In September 1998 Strike Force Lancer had been set up as a joint operation between Crime Agencies (later renamed the State Crime Command) and the Bankstown region command to investigate the wave of violent crimes in Sydney's south-west. For months it had been using undercover police to make drug buys from the gang's Kings Cross dealers. In May 1999 six were arrested and charged with a series of cocaine supply charges. Four were under the age of eighteen. Some of those arrested rolled and agreed to assist police. On 1 June El Assaad, Rossini and other gang members were arrested in police raids across south and south-west Sydney. About 11.30 am the same day police attempted to arrest Kanaan at his Belfield home but Kanaan, his mother, brother and three associates refused to come out of the house. Kanaan shouted to police that he was 'prepared to die for his cause', claiming that he and the others had knives and would 'stab in the neck any police officer who attempted to come into the house'.

Special Weapons police surrounded the house; roads were blocked and nearby residents evacuated. Electricity, water and the landline phone to the house were cut off. Spotlights were shone into the house. The police were in control of the situation; their aim was to make those inside as uncomfortable and unsettled as possible. Police arranged a telephone hook-up so that Kanaan could speak to his lawyers—Winston Terracini SC and Peter Sitz—but Kanaan refused to surrender. The hours dragged by. There was little negotiation since those in the house refused to talk. Sensitive listening devices picked up whispered conversations. Dr Michael Diamond, a forensic psychiatrist experienced in negotiation situations, analysed every contact and advised specially trained negotiators on tactics. After 32 hours it was time to make a move.

Heavily armed police in bulletproof armour approached

the front of the house. A window was smashed and a smoke bomb thrown in to create a screen as police lobbed a mobile phone—contained in a steel ball about the size of a soccer ball—into the house. Known as a racal phone, it is practically indestructible. The intention was to provide an avenue to reopen communication with those in the house, while at the same time showing that the police were in charge. The response was not the one the police had expected. Amid the confusion caused by the darkness, the shattered window and the smoke bomb, Kanaan and the others panicked, mistaking the racal phone rolling across the timber floor for a bomb that signalled the start of an armed police attack in which they would all be killed. Their surrender was quick and unconditional. Kanaan was back in jail—and this time there would be no bail.

Three months later detectives began the next major phase of arrests. They cleared up the two Five Dock murders, the drive-by shooting of EP1, the kneecapping of Elias Elias, the drive-by attack on the Lakemba Police Station, the Eveleigh Street shoot-up and the murder of Danny Karam, as well as breaking the gang's cocaine distribution networks.

By late 1999 Danny's Boys and the short-lived Kanaan gang had been wiped out. During the 12 months that followed Karam's murder more than 50 people associated with the gang were arrested and charged with more than 100 offences including murder, shootings and drug trafficking. But it was not the end of the story.

Saleh Jamal was one of those arrested. He was convicted of supplying cannabis and jailed for 12 months. Jamal was also among those charged with the 1998 drive-by shooting of the Lakemba Police Station and spent two years in jail before being granted bail in 2001. In jail he came under the influence of radical Islamic teachers and after his release he associated with extremist Muslims in Lakemba.

In March 2004, while on bail, Jamal fled Australia on a false passport. Two months later he was arrested for terrorism offences while attempting to flee Lebanon. A year later he was convicted of possessing weapons and explosives, using a forged Australian passport, forming a terrorist group and planning acts that endangered state security. He was sentenced to five years' jail with hard labour. A year later the Lebanese Court of Appeal overturned Jamal's conviction on terrorism charges and he was extradited to Sydney. On 17 August 2007 he was sentenced to nine years' jail on nine counts of shooting at a person with intent to cause grievous bodily harm (including the kneecapping of Elias Elias) and another related offence of discharging a firearm in a public place. In November 2009 Jamal was convicted of the drive-by shooting of the Lakemba Police Station.

In September 1999 Charbel Geagea fled Australia before he could be arrested for the murder of Danny Karam and of another man outside a 7-Eleven store in Lakemba on 20 May 1999. In the second case 21-year-old Pierre Anthony Drouby was dragged from a car by three men who bashed him about the head. During the bashing one of his attackers shot him four times in the chest and stomach; Drouby died that night while undergoing emergency surgery at St George Hospital. The driver of the car and another passenger were unhurt. If Geagea thought he'd escaped justice he was mistaken. Four years later, in May 2003, Geagea was sentenced to 20 years' jail by a Beirut court which found him guilty of the murder of Danny Karam in Sydney. Geagea holds dual Australian and Lebanese citizenship and under local law a citizen can be tried for crimes committed in another country.

In 2001 Kanaan was convicted of the murders of Wright and Hurle at Five Dock and given two life sentences. He was also given 25 years for the malicious wounding of Singleton. Derbas pleaded guilty to hindering the discovery of evidence connected with the murders and was sentenced to five years' jail with a three-year non-parole period.

In 2002 Kanaan was convicted, together with El Assaad and Mawas, of the murder of Karam. For Kanaan, it was another life sentence. Mawas and El Assaad were sentenced to 25 years and 24 years respectively. There were threats to bomb the court; a prison van carrying Kanaan was run off the road and the Crown's star witness, Rossini, wore a bulletproof vest while giving evidence, surrounded by four security guards. The sentencing judge described the killing of Karam as a deliberate, cold-blooded assassination carried out under the leadership of Kanaan. A 2005 appeal against their conviction to the New South Wales Court of Criminal Appeal was dismissed, but El Assaad's sentence was reduced to 22 years.

A year later Kanaan was sentenced to a maximum ten years for shooting Constable Patrech, eight years for shooting at Constable Fotopoulos and seven years for shooting to avoid arrest. Kanaan and El Assaad were acquitted of the drive-by shooting of the Lakemba Police Station.

In 2007 Kanaan was convicted of the kneecapping of Elias Elias and sentenced to ten years' jail. The sentence meant little to Kanaan: he was already serving three life sentences.

Saleh Jamal's longtime criminal partner Ghassam Said also fled Australia while on bail. He is believed to be overseas, living in Saudi Arabia, and is wanted over the drive-by attack on the Lakemba Police Station, the Eveleigh Street shoot-up and other crimes of violence.

For the two police involved in the December 1998 Weigall Sports Ground shootout, the nightmare didn't end with the arrest of Kanaan and El Assaad. At the committal hearing the magistrate, Ms Pat O'Shane, had dismissed the charges against Kanaan of shooting with intent to murder, shooting with intent to inflict grievous bodily harm and firearm offences. She also found that Constables Patrech and Fotopoulos had harassed Kanaan and the other three men by chasing them. 'Despite it later becoming clear that the group had some criminal intent that night, police had no lawful reason to stop them at the time,' Ms O'Shane said. Constable Fotopoulos, she went on, had led his junior colleague into an 'extremely dangerous situation' for no good reason. 'That was stupid, reckless, foolhardy.'

There was a public outcry. The police executive and the Police Association criticised Ms O'Shane's comments. The police and the government sought a review of her findings. The Director of Public Prosecutions overruled Ms O'Shane and filed indictments against Kanaan. A judge and jury also disagreed with Ms O'Shane.

Constable Chris Patrech recovered from his wounds and returned to work.

Almost immediately after the shootout Fotopoulos ceased active duty. In March 2002, nearly three and a half years later, Fotopoulos resigned from the police 'medically unfit'.

With Kanaan safely in jail, the police executive appeared to change its view of Fotopoulos's and Patrech's actions. In a 2005 article 'A broken police hero lives on $300 compo',

Sunday Telegraph journalist Neil Mercer quoted transcripts from Fotopoulos's 2005 Supreme Court action for compensation. In the transcripts counsel for the police suggested to both Fotopoulos and Patrech that they should never have followed the car that night as they had no legal power to give chase without some other basis for suspicion.

During his time in the witness box Constable Patrech was reduced to tears. Constable Fotopoulos's mental and physical condition had deteriorated to such an extent that one doctor said of him, 'he appears barely able to look after himself on a day-to-day basis. He may never be able to resume a normal lifestyle.' A psychiatrist described him as suffering post-traumatic stress disorder and panic attacks. Fotopoulos was unable to deal with the proceedings and walked out of the court and away from his compensation action, telling the *Sunday Telegraph* that since the Weigall Sports Ground shooting 'Everything has changed in my life. It's like the person that was there that night had died. Now there is a new person ... and I don't like the new person very much.' Costs of $250,000 were awarded against Fotopoulos. He was a broken man, mentally and financially, living on a workers' compensation pension of less than $300 a week.

The police department's attack on Fotopoulos is all the more difficult to understand when, at the same time it was criticising him in the courts, the police commissioner was preparing to award him a Valour Medal for his actions in the shootout. Seven years later the medal had not been presented to him. On 3 June 2005, Police Commissioner Ken Moroney wrote to Fotopoulos, who had asked that his award be posted to him: 'It is my decision as Commissioner of Police that all awards under my hand and seal are presented with the ceremony and dignity befitting the award, showing respect to the recipient.' The commissioner went on to extend a 'personal invitation' for Fotopoulos to accept the award in person. 'John,' he wrote, 'this is a special award which you thoroughly deserve.'

Twelve months after Moroney wrote to Fotopoulos, Justice Latham, in sentencing Kanaan over the Weigall Sports Ground shootout, commended Fotopoulos for saving Constable Patrech, wounding Kanaan and arresting another gang member. Constable Fotopoulos had tested positive to having used cannabis before the shooting, but expert testimony at the trial was that the amount of cannabis was so minuscule that it would not have impaired Fotopoulos's reactions.

Neddy Smith never followed up on his threat to kill whoever was involved in the Five Dock shooting as punishment for endangering his daughter, Jamie. When Neddy and Kanaan eventually met in jail they were both in hospital. Smith was suffering from Parkinson's disease and Kanaan from injuries inflicted in the Weigall Sports Ground shootout. They got along, which surprised quite a few of Neddy's old mates, both in and out of jail. Others knew better. 'He was all mouth,' said one. 'Neddy never did anything unless he was pissed, and he couldn't get a beer in jail.'

CHAPTER FIVE

The Darwiches, the Razzaks and the Telopea Street Boys

In the three years following the Wood Royal Commission the Danny Karam and Michael Kanaan gangs brought unprecedented violence and chaos to the drug trade from Kings Cross to Bankstown, but neither Karam's murder nor the jailing of Kanaan brought any relief. Sydney's underworld was changing and it wasn't just the usual suspects who were trying to take advantage. A new generation of criminals was making its presence felt across an arc of Sydney's southern and south-western suburbs.

Many of these new kids were Lebanese Muslim teenagers whose parents had arrived and settled in south-west Sydney during the mid 1970s and early 1980s. These teenagers were untouched by the investigations of the Wood Royal Commission: like the Vietnamese street gangs in Cabramatta, they had no alliances with police, corrupt or otherwise, and no intention of forming any. They treated the police exactly as they treated anyone else who got in their way: with violence.

Around the mid 1990s a group of teenagers—including Gehad Razzak and his brother Ziad, or 'Ziggy', and their cousins Bilal (known as 'Bill'), Mohamed and Samear Razzak; Haissam Hannouf and his brothers Ahmad, Rabbi and Wahib; 'Moukhtar'; Ahmed Fahda, his brother Hussein and Ali Hamka—was involved in the theft and rebirthing of stolen motor vehicles. From there they progressed to large-scale insurance frauds relating to vehicles they had stolen and rebirthed or bought in false names, and other insurance scams. Some extended their business to standing over shopkeepers in Punchbowl for protection. By the late 1990s they were operating drug 'runs' in and around Bankstown and looking for ways to expand their drug operations.

On the streets they became known as the Razzak crew. The gang was led by Gehad, who was regarded as its strongest member. Gehad's influence was such that he was able to maintain control during significant periods he spent in jail during the 1990s. The crew instilled fear, even among their associates, and had a reputation for behaving 'like gangsters'. By the early 2000s Ahmed Fahda was proclaiming himself to be 'the king of Punchbowl' while 'Moukhtar' always carried $10,000 to $20,000 cash, spending it on lavish dinners and visits to brothels and massage parlours with his 'workers'.

But the Razzak gang was not alone in terrorising the streets of south-west Sydney. It had a rival in the larger

Darwiche crew, headed by Adnan 'Eddie' Darwiche. Evolving from an earlier teenage gang, the crew included Darwiche's brothers Abdul and Michael; Ali 'Biggie' Osman and his brother Abass; Ramzi 'Fidel' Aouad; Naseam 'Sam' El Zeyat, also known as 'Erdt' (which is Arabic for 'the monkey'); Khaled 'Crazy' Taleb; Khaled El Assaad; Mohammed 'MT' Touma; Ahmed 'Gary' Awad; Ghassam 'Easy' Said, and half a dozen others. Sam El Zeyat, Easy Said and Khaled El Assaad's brother Wassim had been members of Danny's Boys and Kanaan's gang, while several other members of the Darwiche crew had run off these earlier gangs, doing business with and for them.

The Darwiche gang emulated the Razzak crew in progressing from motor vehicle theft and rebirthing to protection, standover rackets and drugs, but by beating the Razzaks to the drug trade they were able to establish a bigger and more profitable network of drug runs across Sydney's south-west. The runs were well organised, with local dealers phoning in their orders to a runner who would obtain supplies from the Darwiches before delivering to the dealers at prearranged drop-off points, stopping only momentarily to hand over the drugs and collect the cash. Several drop-offs could be made in one suburb and several suburbs could be covered in a single run. Each runner had his or her own territory and network of dealers. Their operations were protected by Eddie Darwiche.

The Darwiche crew were obsessed with guns and accumulated a large arsenal. Eddie paid for all the guns, allowing others to use them but always retaining 'ownership' himself. Various relatives had gun licences and legally-held firearms. These legal firearms enabled gang members to use local gun clubs for shooting practice. The gang's stockpile ranged from handguns to military assault rifles.

Darwiche had a rule that when a gun was 'dirty'—that is, had been used in committing a crime—it had to be disposed of, either by 'on-selling' or by being cut up or melted down. This reduced the risk of police linking crimes and linking the gang to those crimes. But, as with the Karam and Kanaan gangs, the rule was not always followed. Sometimes favourite weapons were hoarded. Over time this mistake would allow the police to tie the Darwiche crew to a variety of crimes.

Biggie Osman and Sam El Zeyat always carried guns and wanted everyone to know they were willing to use them. While having their hair cut at the hairdresser's shop at Lakemba, the pair would pull pistols from the front of their pants and place them on the counter as though preparing for a shootout. No one who saw the guns said anything: they knew what would happen if they did. By the late 1990s even the Razzak crew envied the power and reputation of the Darwiche gang.

On 15 April 1997, while negotiating the sale of a pistol, Eddie Darwiche looked every bit the professional gangster—until he started playing with the gun, accidentally firing three shots. 'Fuck, I got shot,' he screamed as a bullet entered his chest. Admitted to hospital under the name Adnan Alkhair, Darwiche made up a false story and declined to help police. The next day he discharged himself from the hospital. The bullet remained in his chest but, according to Khaled Taleb, 'it came out by itself a few months later'. It was not the last time a member of the Darwiche or Razzak crew would be involved in an accidental shooting.

Money wasn't enough for Darwiche: he wanted to be acknowledged by his rivals as the number one gangster. By late 1997 he was spoiling for a fight. In January 1998 he and a few of his crew became involved in a pushing and screaming match with a gang from Punchbowl. Both sides pulled guns. The rival gang was led by Ahmad Nagi and the confrontation ended when he and his group stormed off.

A few days later Eddie Darwiche's brother, Abdul, was waiting at traffic lights in Punchbowl when some of Nagi's gang pulled alongside and gave him 'a dirty look'. That was enough for Abdul, who took offence and told his brother. Eddie demanded the Nagi gang meet him in Punchbowl Park. Screaming into a phone, he told Nagi: 'If you want to fuck with us, fuck you. Let's meet up.' Eddie and some of his crew went to the park, but the Nagi gang did not come. To Eddie Darwiche, not turning up simply added insult to injury. He went looking for them.

On the evening of 14 January Darwiche found Nagi outside his home at 21 Victoria Road, Punchbowl. Nagi wasn't alone: word had gone around that Darwiche and some of his crew were on their way and 20 to 30 friends were there for support. But it was too late for Darwiche to pull out, even if he'd wanted to. There was shouting and several shots were fired from the house. Soon both sides were firing at each other. After Nagi had been shot in the leg, Darwiche and his crew ran out of bullets and fled.

Meanwhile neighbours had reported the shootout. A fleet of police cars and ambulances converged on the scene. At first Nagi cooperated with police. An arrest warrant was taken out for Darwiche but before it could be executed Nagi withdrew his statement and identification of Darwiche. It was the usual story: money for peace. Darwiche had paid Nagi to keep his mouth shut. No arrests were made.

By the late 1990s Shadi Derbas, the small-time car thief,

rebirther and drug dealer (see Chapter 3), had also established himself in the drug markets of Lakemba and Punchbowl. His gang—a combination of experienced criminals and local youths, some as young as 12—became known as the Telopea Street Boys. The Derbas gang were advertising up to 20 cars a week for sale to the public through the *Trading Post* and weekend newspapers. One of their main customers for rebirthed cars was Danny's Boys. According to the rollover Alan Rossini, Derbas's group dominated the drug trade, car rebirthing and general crime in the Lakemba area.

Derbas and his Telopea Street network continued to expand and by 1999 he was openly operating a 'drive-through' drug market from the footpaths at the eastern end of the street. On 17 October 1998, 14-year-old Korean boy Edward Lee and a few mates went to Telopea Street to attend a school friend's party. They accidentally went to the house of one of the Telopea Street Boys where one of a group of youths screamed out, 'What the fuck are you looking at?' An exchange of words escalated into a fight during which Lee was stabbed by 15-year-old Moustapha Dib. Dib yelled, 'the fucking Asian deserved it' and shots were fired, shattering a window of the car in which Lee and his friends were attempting to escape. Lee died soon afterwards from knife wounds. More than 20 people stood and watched but none came to the aid of Lee and his friends.

The gang became more reckless. The local police radio network was intercepted and death threats and abusive calls were made against police. Threats were made to bomb a police station. The drive-through drug market continued unabated. The police had lost control.

Sydney was hopelessly unprepared for the violence that was about to explode on its streets. It began in early January

2000 and continued for two months. During that time there were more than a dozen shootings in the Bankstown–Punchbowl area—the result of turf wars, 'family' business, hatred towards the police and, in some cases, of someone simply 'looking sideways' at the wrong time and at the wrong person. The shootings included kneecappings, the drive-by shootings of a brothel, houses and cars, and the abduction of a prostitute.

About 8.30 pm on 13 February four people were standing on their veranda when a car, stolen a few hours earlier, was driven slowly past the house. Two balaclava-clad gunmen leaned out of the car windows. As the shooters were about to fire, the driver lost control and the car smashed into a parked car. The noise of the crash caused people in the target house and neighbouring houses to run out and see what had happened. In the confusion that followed, the shooters got off their shots and hit two people, but their car was now jammed against the car they had collided with. In their panic, they crashed into the parked car twice more before they were able to make their escape.

The gunmen were not impressed with their driver. Eddie Darwiche described him as a 'fucking idiot' and gave him a belt across the back of the head as he drove off. The car was dumped a few streets away and burnt. The bungled shooting was payback for an assault on one of Eddie's younger brothers a few days earlier, but amid the chaos they had shot and injured two innocent people.

In another case a week later, a carload of young men pulled up in Punchbowl Road, Punchbowl, and became involved in an argument with two men on the footpath. One of the men from the car pulled a handgun and started firing. The men on the footpath were shot, one in the leg and the other in the stomach. As an ambulance raced one of the wounded men to Liverpool Hospital it was chased by the car involved in the shooting. During the pursuit the men in the car shouted obscenities and one of them pointed a handgun at the ambulance and its driver. Several times the ambulance was forced to take evasive action to avoid being hit or run off the road by the car. It was not until the ambulance reached the hospital that the car broke off the pursuit and sped away.

At midnight two days later, the McDonald's restaurant at Punchbowl was blasted with shotguns as four staff and three customers ducked for cover. No one was injured.

Police formed Strike Force Ranger under Detective Chief Superintendent Bob Inkster, who had led the earlier investigations into Danny's Boys and Michael Kanaan's gang.

On 9 March shots were fired near a uniformed police car as it patrolled Telopea Street close to the spot where drugs were being sold. The next day more than a hundred police, supported by the Air Wing and heavily armed members of the State Protection Group, swooped on Telopea Street. Panicked dealers threw away their drugs as they fled. Four houses in the street were searched. A large cache of drugs of all types was found scattered on the ground, hidden in a Telstra junction box, in various other places along the street and in several backyards. All were in easy reach of the dealers who ran the street's drive-through drug trade. As well as drugs, police found several handguns and more than 200 rounds of ammunition.

The Telopea Street Boys learned quickly from their mistakes, formalising roles and responsibilities within the network and bolstering security arrangements. Lookouts were posted at both ends of the street and at different points in between, watching for the police as well as opposing gangs. Musclemen provided protection to ensure that dealers were not ripped off. Guns were stashed where they could be useful in a fight but abandoned in the case of a police raid.

Over the next nine months police conducted a series of covert operations and raids. Undercover police infiltrated the street's drug buyers, slowly establishing themselves as familiar faces to whom the street dealers were willing to sell. Undercover police bought drugs from dozens of sellers. Seventeen telephone intercepts were put in place and more than 25,500 calls were intercepted and monitored. A covert operations post was established to enable ongoing observations of activities in the street and to provide protection for the undercover police.

Using these methods police discovered not just the size of the Telopea Street drug operation but how it worked. Around 300 drive-through drug transactions were carried out each day. Orders for drugs were taken and money was collected. While the cash was quickly moved away from the street, the order was passed to the central dealer who supplied the street dealers. The buyers themselves never got out of their cars. Only a small quantity of drugs was held by any one dealer so as to reduce the charge and likely penalty if they were arrested. Stocks were constantly replenished by 'backroom' organisers. The gang controlled the flow of buyers into and out of the street, even closing off the street if the dealing became too congested. Street thugs could be seen openly playing with their guns.

Two months into the operation, the police made their first major swoop. In early May 2000 more than 200 officers, including heavily armed members of the State Protection Group, hit Telopea Street while police helicopters hovered

Lennie McPherson in 1969.

Frank Hakim arriving at St James' Court in 1987. He was jailed for six and half years for bribing Labor corrective services minister Rex Jackson to secure the early release of prisoners. (Courtesy of News Limited)

In 1976 George Freeman was charged by Commonwealth police with obtaining and using a false passport.

Louis Bayeh was charged in 2000 over a shootout outside a restaurant at Narwee in Sydney's south. (Courtesy of NSW Police)

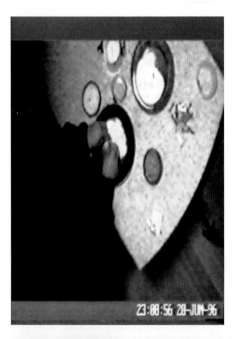

Covert picture of Bill Bayeh's 1996 drug den, where heroin and cocaine were cut and packaged for sale.

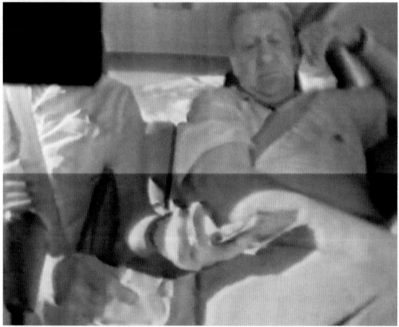

Covert picture of Detective Trevor Haken paying a bribe to chief of detectives Graham 'Chook' Fowler.

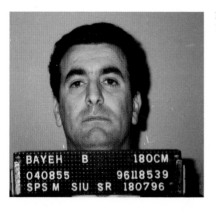

Bill Bayeh was charged with drug offences in 1996. (Courtesy of NSW Police)

Danny Karam on steroids and lifting weights in Long Bay jail, c. 1985.

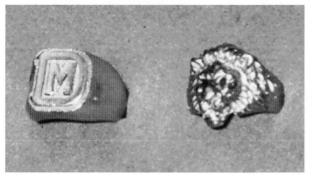

Rings given by Danny Karam to his gang. *Left:* The gang member's initial 'M' (for Michael Kanaan) is inside the letter 'D' for Danny. *Right:* The tiger head is the gang ring.

Top: Five Dock Hotel, scene of the 1998 shooting murder of Michael Hurle and Adam Wright, and the wounding of Ronald Singleton.

Middle: The burnt-out car used in the drive-by shooting of the Lakemba Police Station by members of the Karam gang in 1998.

Left: A computer with a bullet hole in the screen. A police officer had been at the computer only seconds before.

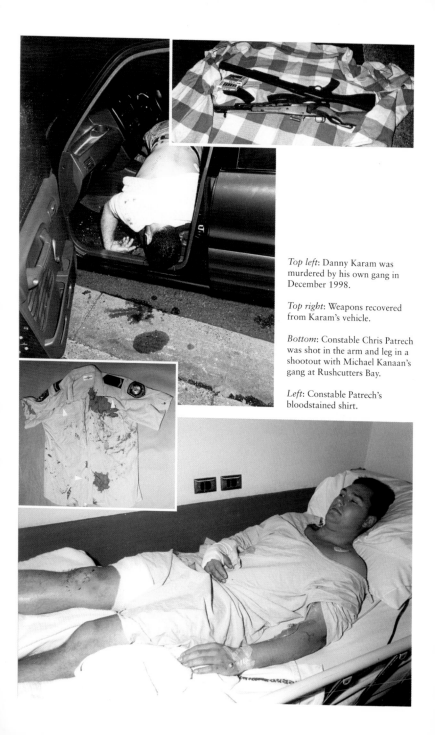

Top left: Danny Karam was murdered by his own gang in December 1998.

Top right: Weapons recovered from Karam's vehicle.

Bottom: Constable Chris Patrech was shot in the arm and leg in a shootout with Michael Kanaan's gang at Rushcutters Bay.

Left: Constable Patrech's bloodstained shirt.

Adnan 'Eddie' Darwiche, head of the Darwiche crew. (Courtesy of NSW Police)

Abdul Darwiche, older brother of Adnan. Police claimed Abdul took control of the Darwiche family crime syndicate. He was murdered at Bass Hill on 14 March 2009. (Courtesy of NSW Police)

After the murder of Abdul Darwiche, his brother Michael was arrested and charged with firearms and other offences. When arrested, he had the names and addresses of several members of the Fahda family. (Courtesy of NSW Police)

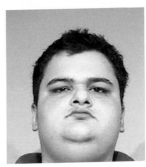

Darwiche gang member Ali Osman was jailed for eight years over a shooting at Narwee and for ten years on drug charges. (Courtesy of NSW Police)

Darwiche gang member Abass Osman was jailed for 27 years for his part in the murder of Ahmed Fahda. (Courtesy of NSW Police)

One of ten rocket launchers and rockets stolen from the Australian Defence Force and sold to the Darwiche gang.

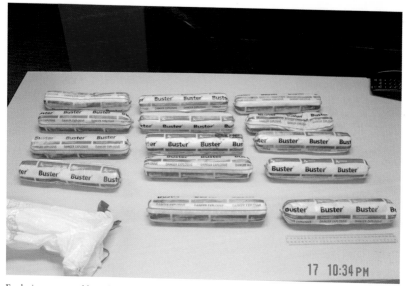

Explosives recovered by police along with one rocket launcher and rocket.

Gehad Razzak, convicted drug dealer and head of the Razzak crew, survived several attempts on his life. (Courtesy of NSW Police)

Gehad's cousin Mohamed Razzak, who was jailed for contempt of court. (Courtesy of NSW Police)

Gehad's brother Ziad Razzak, who was shot dead in the war with the Darwiche gang. (Courtesy of NSW Police)

Samear Razzak, another cousin. (Courtesy of NSW Police)

Bilal Razzak, another cousin, who was shot and severely wounded during the war with the Darwiches. (Courtesy of NSW Police)

Ahmed Fahda, self-proclaimed 'king of Punchbowl', was shot dead in 2003. (Courtesy of NSW Police)

Razzak ally Mohammed 'Blackie' Fahda, who was charged with the 2009 murder of Abdul Darwiche. (Courtesy of NSW Police)

Hussein Fahda, brother of Ahmed and 'Blackie', was jailed for firearms offences. (Courtesy of NSW Police)

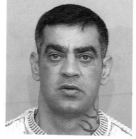

Top left: Fadi Ibrahim was shot five times in June 2009 as he sat in his black Lamborghini in Castle Cove. (Courtesy of NSW Police)

Top middle: Sam Ibrahim, standover man, protector of Kings Cross drug dealers, and former Nomads and Notorious gang leader. (Courtesy of NSW Police)

Top right: Michael Ibrahim, now in jail for manslaughter. (Courtesy of NSW Police)

Left: Todd O'Connor, drug dealer and associate of the Ibrahims, was murdered at Tempe in 2008. (Courtesy of NSW Police)

Sam Ibrahim (front right) leads the now-defunct Parramatta chapter of the Nomads on a ride, followed by one-time national president Scott Orrock.

Colours of 18 of the estimated 35 outlaw motorcycle gangs in Australia.

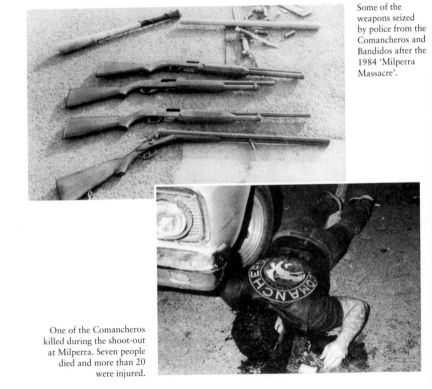

Some of the weapons seized by police from the Comancheros and Bandidos after the 1984 'Milperra Massacre'.

One of the Comancheros killed during the shoot-out at Milperra. Seven people died and more than 20 were injured.

A brick barbecue hides the entrance to a secret amphetamine laboratory in the grounds of a bikie clubhouse.

Inside the secret drug laboratory.

Bandidos at the grave of Rodney 'Hooksey' Monk, president of the Sydney chapter, who was shot dead in 2006 by former sergeant-at-arms Russell Oldham.

The Nomads clubhouse at Granville in 2004.

Nomads member Mahmoud Dib leaves the Granville clubhouse in September 2004 as police execute a search warrant.

Members of the Nomads' Parramatta chapter in 2006. Sam Ibrahim is centre, with white T-shirt, leather jacket and sunglasses.

The drink dispenser at a Nomads clubhouse contained a cache of illegal weapons.

Weapons seized from the drink dispenser.

Illegal firearms seized by police in a raid on another Nomads clubhouse in 2000.

The Hells Angels' clubhouse at Petersham was firebombed on 4 February 2009. Shots were fired into a nearby tattoo parlour.

Police and other equipment seized in a 2009 police raid on a Comanchero house in Kogarah.

Hydroponic cannabis crop seized in 2007 from the Tweed Heads' clubhouse of the Lone Wolf outlaw motorcycle gang. *Inset*: The concealed entrance to the underground hydroponic cannabis crop at Tweed Heads.

The Rebels' national president, Alex Vella, leads the funeral procession for Edin 'Boz' Smajovic, a fellow Rebel killed in a shootout at Campbelltown in 2009. (Courtesy of Fairfax Media)

Mazen Touma pleaded guilty in 2008 to a terrorism-related charge and was jailed. (Courtesy of NSW Police)

Moustafa Cheikho was found guilty in 2009 of conspiring to commit acts in preparation for a terrorist act or acts. (Courtesy of NSW Police)

Mirsad Mulahalilovic pleaded guilty in 2008 to a terrorism-related charge and was jailed. (Courtesy of NSW Police)

Khaled Cheikho was found guilty in 2009 of conspiring to commit acts in preparation for a terrorist act or acts. (Courtesy of NSW Police)

Shane Kent pleaded guilty in 2009 in Victoria to making a document connected with the preparation of a terrorist act and was jailed.

Bassam Hamzy is serving a jail sentence for murder and other crimes. He was found to be converting jail inmates to radical Islam.

overhead. Around a dozen dealers were arrested, including senior members of the gang. The raid served its primary purpose by stirring things up. Dealing and consequently cashflow were disrupted. Replacement drugs and dealers had to be found. The telephones ran hot. Face-to-face meetings were necessary. In the course of regrouping, the network exposed itself and became more vulnerable to police action.

Three months later, on 2 August, around 250 police, again supported by helicopters and members of the State Protection Group, carried out the next phase of the operation. Thirteen search warrants were executed. Fifteen people were arrested and charged with a range of drug, firearm and other offences. High-calibre handguns, including a machine pistol, were seized, together with ammunition, a bulletproof vest and a portable police radio. This time police broke the back of the network. The Telopea Street drug market was shut down. Over the coming weeks local police increased their patrols of Telopea Street without fear of reprisal. At last the residents, Muslim and non-Muslim alike, felt able to walk along their own street in safety.

In August 2000 Shadi Derbas was charged with being an accessory after the fact to the 1998 murders of Michael Hurle and Adam Wright and the wounding of Ronald Singleton by Michael Kanaan and Bassam Kazzi at Five Dock. The charges were later dropped when Derbas pleaded guilty to hindering the discovery of evidence connected with the murders and was sentenced to five years' jail.

Moustapha Dib was charged with the murder of Edward Lee. He pleaded guilty to manslaughter and in 2003 was sentenced to ten years' jail. Moustapha's older brother, Mohammed Dib, and Michael Kanaan were sentenced to three years' jail for being accessories after the fact to the murder of Lee. Narwas Refai, a friend of Dib and Kanaan, was given a two-year suspended sentence. On the night Lee was killed Kanaan, Mohammed Dib and Narwas Refai had fabricated an alibi for Moustapha by driving to Queensland, ordering a pizza in Moustapha Dib's name and booking a hotel room.

Two years after the murder of Edward Lee and while on bail for the murder, Moustapha Dib was charged with the murder of Anita Vrzina and the attempted murder of Telopea Street Boy Ahmad Banat on 23 November 2000. Moustapha had pulled alongside a car being driven by Banat with his wife, Vrzina, and their two-year-old child as passengers, and started firing. Vrzina was shot in the stomach and died almost immediately while Ahmad was shot in the neck and lived. The child was not injured. Six months earlier Banat had rolled over to police and implicated Moustapha in the killing of Edward Lee. At Moustapha's trial Banat changed his mind and refused to cooperate with the prosecution, which declared him a hostile witness. The jury was later discharged and a new trial set, but by then Banat had fled the country with his child. He is believed to be living in Jordan, having been threatened and paid off. A warrant is out for his arrest.

The gun fired at Lee and his friends was recovered by police at the scene of a home invasion and attempted murder at Oak Flats, near Wollongong, south of Sydney. It was dropped by one of the offenders as they fled. Seven offenders were later arrested over a series of home invasions in southern Sydney and the Illawarra and sentenced to long jail terms: they were all from the Punchbowl–Bankstown area of Sydney.

*

Since the mid 1990s a simmering turf war over drugs had existed between Derbas and Joseph Attallah, the owner of the Eternity Escorts brothel in Bankstown. Attallah was a longtime heroin trafficker and user. In the early 1990s he had been jailed for several years for selling heroin. He was also involved in illegal gambling clubs in the inner-city suburbs of Campsie and Marrickville. His drug network supported the habits of his prostitutes and others working along Canterbury Road, as well as the street drug markets of Bankstown and nearby suburbs. Its success had eaten into Derbas's profits.

A 1997–98 inquiry by ICAC—'Report on the Investigation into the Department of Corrective Services: First report: The conduct of Prison Officer Toso Lila [Josh] Sua and matters related thereto'—found that during the early and mid 1990s Attallah had been involved in corrupt conduct with a prison officer. While Attallah was in jail on remand for supplying heroin, a prison officer, Toso Sua, had smuggled contraband into the jail for Attallah and another prisoner, Kostas Kontorinakis, a well-known member of the Kings Cross underworld who had featured prominently in the Wood Royal Commission (see Chapters 1 and 9). While on bail Attallah hired the prison officer as protection for his prostitution and drug businesses. ICAC described Attallah as 'a parasite. For no other motive than financial gain he fed off and promoted the drug habits of prostitutes in the Canterbury–Bankstown area of Sydney. It is hard to imagine that their day-to-day existence was other than miserable.'

After his release from jail Attallah dived straight back into drugs and prostitution. He was untouched by the May 2000 Telopea Street raids, but one month later his Bankstown brothel was sprayed with bullets. It was the second time the brothel had been the target of a drive-by shooting. Six months later, on 9 November, police stopped Attallah while he was driving his car in Greenacre. Seventy bags of cocaine were found. He was arrested and charged. Attallah was sentenced to two life sentences for trafficking around $3 million worth of cocaine and heroin. On appeal his sentence was reduced to 24 years' jail.

Attallah had loaned his longtime colleague Cliff Rahme and Rahme's adult sons, John and Charbel, $180,000 of his drug and prostitution profits to renovate their brothel at Banksia, near Rockdale in Southern Sydney.

In June 2005 Charbel pleaded guilty to receiving money from child pornography and controlling premises used in an act of child pornography. He was sentenced to three years on each count. He beat several related charges.

As a result of the police raids on Telopea Street more than 60 people were arrested and charged with more than 300 offences, including drug supply and conspiracy, illegal firearms, car theft, car rebirthing and fraud. Dozens of others were arrested in related operations. More than 70 other people of interest were identified, many of whom were arrested in later police operations. Around $3 million in assets was restrained.

Commenting on the operations, Detective Superintendent John Kerlatec declared, 'Drug dealing in Telopea Street, Punchbowl, was the norm in 1999–2000 [but by 2004] was totally eradicated.' Perhaps he should have added, 'for the time being'.

On 14 August 2009 Moustapha Dib, now 26 years old, was released from Goulburn jail, having served eight years and three months of his ten-year jail sentence for the killing of Edward Lee. A month before his release, his father, 53-year-old Abdulrahim; his mother, 59-year-old Fatme; and brothers, 31-year-old Mohammed, 24-year-old Ahmed—both of whom had served time in jail over the Lee killing—and 20-year-old Omar, were among 14 people charged with running a major motor vehicle rebirthing racket involving almost 50 cars. Of those arrested, at least eight (all members of the Fahda family of Punchbowl, and Minkara family of Wiley Park) were related to the Dibs.

CHAPTER 6

The Darwiche– Razzak war

A deceptive calm followed the break-up of the Telopea Street Boys. The Darwiche crew expanded to fill the void. At first they met no resistance, but a bitter rivalry with the Razzak crew simmered just beneath the surface. The Darwiche drug network now stretched from Bankstown through the southern suburbs of Hurstville, Sutherland and Miranda to Brighton-Le-Sands. The Razzak crew watched enviously as the Darwiche crew's power and profits grew. It wasn't long before the Razzaks made their move.

Bilal Razzak started ripping off Adnan 'Eddie' Darwiche's drug runners. In retaliation the Darwiche crew started leaning on dealers in Razzak territories to change sides. Threats and counter-threats quickly turned to violence as both sides embarked on a spree of drive-bys and kneecappings.

As the two gangs feuded over drugs and drug runs, a

savage argument broke out between members of the Razzak crew. It was caused by the theft of a four-wheel drive vehicle from Ahmed Fahda's lawyer. Fahda accused the Hannouf brothers of stealing the vehicle and demanded compensation. The Hannoufs denied stealing the vehicle and wanted to know whether it was covered by insurance. Fahda shouted back, 'I don't give a fuck if he [the lawyer] got paid or not ... I still want the money.' Fahda demanded $50,000 compensation and threatened to kill the Hannoufs if the money was not paid—perhaps he was simply looking for a way to pay his legal fees. The argument blew over without any money changing hands, but the ill-feeling would continue to fester.

On 18 October 2000 Eddie Darwiche ordered a knee-capping as payback for a rip-off on one of his drug dealers. Haissam Yassine was lured to Punchbowl Park by some of his cousins. They had received a promise from Darwiche that Yassine would not be killed. As he struggled and squirmed on the ground, the shooter complained, 'He keeps moving his legs. I don't want to fuck it up or Eddie will spew.' Accidentally killing Yassine would be a 'fuck up', but so would missing him altogether. Eventually the punishment was carried out. Shot in the back of both legs behind the knees, Yassine was left bleeding in the park while the assailants rang 000 and called for an ambulance. Yassine declined to assist police. He knew that next time it wouldn't be his legs that were shot.

As part of their move on Darwiche territory, the Razzaks organised a hit on Khaled Taleb, one of the main Darwiche enforcers, whose drug operation in Peakhurst the Razzaks had long coveted. In late February 2001, before the hit could be carried out, Darwiche and Taleb bumped into members of the Razzak crew. There was an argument followed by the usual pushing and shoving, but no guns were drawn. A few days later Darwiche's younger brother Mohammed, known as 'Ali', and some of his mates had a fight with Bilal Razzak. Then Eddie Darwiche's home was sprayed with bullets during a drive-by.

Darwiche had had enough. He called Taleb: 'I need you, come over, someone drive by'd [sic] my house, bro.' Summoning other members of his crew, Darwiche handed out guns. 'We'll do the same to them, we'll blast their houses. First we'll get Bill [Bilal].' They drove to the block of units at 46–52 Sir Joseph Banks Drive, Bankstown. Eddie Darwiche and Khaled Taleb both had handguns. After identifying what they thought was Bilal Razzak's unit, they peppered the building with gunfire. Two days later Darwiche collected other members of his gang and drove to the home of a Razzak-aligned family in Padstow. They fired more than 40 shots into the house before speeding off. No one was injured.

A few days later they learned that their celebrations over the Razzak unit shooting had been premature. They had shot up three units in the block, but none of them belonged to Razzak. Angry and determined to do the job properly next time, the men drove to Bilal Razzak's parents' home in Bouvardia Street, Punchbowl—and waited. They had been told that Razzak was using his cousin Samear's Subaru WRX. It wasn't long before they spotted the car. As the Subaru pulled up, Taleb emptied his Glock pistol into it before speeding off. But it was another cock-up. The driver wasn't Bilal Razzak but Samear. Despite the number of shots fired, Samear escaped injury.

After two botched shootings and a warning drive-by, Bilal Razzak wasn't going to sit back and wait for another attack. A few days later, on 7 March, he left the country for Lebanon, where he would stay for the next two months.

On 28 May 2001, 27-year-old Michael Collins's badly decomposed body was found in his Roselands home. He had been shot several times with a .32 calibre handgun as he lay in his bed, apparently asleep, and had been dead about a week. Collins worked for Eddie Darwiche. His rented home had been used as a drug safe house for runners pushing drugs into Hurstville, Rockdale and Brighton. He was a 'supervisor' responsible for collecting drug profits from the dealers he supplied, and he had been ripping off his employer.

Two weeks later, on 12 June, a 26-year-old Lakemba man, Bassam Mansour, was stabbed several times in the chest and thigh by two men at Long Jetty, a small town on the central coast. Although he was rushed to a nearby medical centre, Mansour died from his wounds. Mansour was a drug dealer with a long criminal record. He had ripped off several dealers, including some who worked for Darwiche.

Holed up in Lebanon, Bilal Razzak had been getting regular reports about the situation in Sydney. At the start of May he judged it was safe to return—but he was wrong. On 17 June, just six weeks after his return, two masked men—one of them Eddie Darwiche—burst into Razzak's Bankstown home and shot him four times as he lay in his bed. Darwiche later told gang members, 'His old man [was there], he didn't do anything and Samear [Bilal's cousin] did nothing either.'

To everyone's surprise Bilal Razzak survived, but he spent several months in hospital, losing a kidney and suffering bowel damage and nerve damage to both legs. Both the Razzak and Darwiche families declined to assist police.

They would deal with their problems in their own time and in their own way.

The immediate cause of the shooting was the breakdown in the marriages of Eddie Darwiche's sister Khadije to Ali Abdul Razzak, and Ahmed Fahda's sister Donna to Ramzi 'Fidel' Aouad. The Fahda family were close to the Razzaks while Aouad was an associate of the Darwiches. The next three months were a waiting game: who was going to strike first? At one point Eddie tried to negotiate a truce over the telephone with Gehad Razzak. The conversation degenerated into a screaming match with Eddie shouting, 'I'm gonna put holes in your head motherfucker, you and your whole family, you're fucking dead.'

Gehad and his brother, 24-year-old 'Ziggy', had recently been released from prison. Both had served long jail sentences for drug dealing and both were now on parole. A family gathering was to be held to celebrate. Their release made the Razzak crew stronger and more determined to increase its territory at Darwiche's expense. Violence between the two gangs was inevitable.

On the night of 22 September 2001 Darwiche called members of his crew together, including his brother Abdul, as well as Khaled Taleb, Ali Osman and Ramzi Aouad. 'It's on,' Eddie told them. 'Go get the guns.' He took Abdul, Taleb and Ramzi and ordered the rest to wait for their return.

The Darwiche crew headed for the Razzak family home in Cornelia Street, Punchbowl. Two carloads of the Razzak crew were gathered outside the house, but that didn't worry Darwiche. As they drove along the street, disaster struck. The stolen car's steering wheel locked up and they did not have the car keys to release it. Darwiche and his crew were suddenly trapped in the middle of the road. They made frantic attempts to break the steering lock before they were seen and attacked by the Razzaks. They were lucky: the lock broke and they sped from the scene. It was yet another botched job. Eddie Darwiche was livid.

The crew changed cars—they had other stolen cars hidden away—and began preparing for another attack. Near Eddie's house their suspicions were aroused by the sight of an unfamiliar a car parked at the top of the street. As they approached the car they recognised the occupants as two of the Razzak crew. They pulled up alongside, pointed a rifle at the driver and called out, 'What are you doing here?'

The Razzak car sped off with the Darwiches in pursuit, heading for the Razzak home in Punchbowl. But at the intersection of Punchbowl Road and Bouvardia Street the pursuers suddenly became the pursued when the car did a handbrake turn and opened fire. The Razzak crew in the car had rung ahead. Suddenly other members of the gang who had been hiding behind cars and in front yards leapt out and opened fire. The Darwiche crew was under attack from three sides. They had been lured straight into an ambush. Eddie and Taleb returned fire but they were sitting ducks. All they could do was flee for their lives. During a search of the area, police found 11 high-powered rifles and handguns that had been thrown into nearby yards and other weapons hidden in vehicles.

Police anticipated a revenge attack but instead there was a precarious calm. The Razzaks wanted a truce. Surprisingly, the Darwiche camp was receptive to the idea. Gehad and Eddie agreed to peace terms which included a payment of around $15,000 to Bilal as 'compensation' for being shot. Over the next four years 'blood money', or 'compensation', was regularly demanded—and, on occasions, paid—in return for a temporary peace.

Around the same time Ahmed Fahda's father, Abdul, tried to ease the growing tension between his family and the Razzak-aligned Hannouf family. The two families had been friends for a long time and Abdul hoped that the older generation could sort out the problems caused by their children. As the two fathers drank *gowhwa*—short black coffee made in the traditional way—in the kitchen of the Hannoufs' home in Juno Parade, Greenacre, discussing their children and lamenting how they showed their parents no respect, Ahmed and Hussein Fahda turned up and started screaming. They forced their way into the house and in the argument that followed shots were fired, leaving bullet holes in the walls of the hall, the kitchen and the lounge. Ahmed and Hussein eventually ran from the house, chased by the Hannoufs. Having failed in his demand for compensation over the theft of his lawyer's four-wheel drive, Ahmed now wanted $50,000 from the Hannouf family to leave them alone. The two fathers had been right—their sons were out of control.

Around this time Eddie Darwiche told Taleb and Aouad, 'That's it. I've had enough. I don't want to do it anymore.' He could certainly afford to walk away from crime, having made millions of dollars out of the drug trade—enough to buy property in Lebanon and invest in property developments in Sydney. The recent death of his father had made Eddie rethink his life. He grew a beard and took to wearing 'religious' clothing. He attended the Lakemba mosque daily. The mosque's leaders, including the controversial muslim cleric Shiek Taj El Din Al Hilaly, had from time to time acted (with limited success) as mediators trying to arrange peace between the warring families and gangs.

Vowing to break with his criminal past, Eddie handed over control of the drug business to 'Crazy' Taleb and 'Fidel' Aouad, but they were in charge for only a few weeks before the truce with the Razzaks was put at risk. About 2 am on 24 December 2001 Bassam Darwiche drove his friend Wahib Hannouf to Bankstown Hospital where he was admitted with bullet wounds to his legs, right arm and stomach. He claimed to have been the victim of a drive-by shooting while walking near the local Pizza Hut. But there was something odd. For once no one was bragging about the shooting. There were no threatening or abusive telephone calls. Even within the gangs nobody seemed to know what had really happened.

It wasn't long before the truth came out. Wahib and Bassam had visited Youseff, a local drug dealer and friend of Bassam, in Bankstown. While they talked Youseff had pulled out a silver pistol and started playing with it. The gun went off, accidentally hitting Wahib. Wahib said that doctors at the hospital told him he had been shot four times—in the stomach, hand and legs—but he 'didn't say anything to them even when I knew that was not true. I only [heard] one bang before I was shot and I was certain that Youseff had done this by mistake and I still believe this. The only way I could think that I had so many wounds was because the bullet may have hit the concrete wall behind me or something like that, to break the bullet up.'

As 'compensation' Wahib received $5000 and an apology from Youseff. A short time later Youseff was arrested and jailed for supplying drugs.

A month after Wahib Hannouf was accidentally shot, Taleb and Aouad sold the drug business to Abass and Ali Osman and Khaled El Assaad for $100,000. The territory they 'bought' stretched from Bankstown to Campsie,

Peakhurst, Mortdale and Lakemba, in Sydney's south-west. As part of the deal Taleb and Aouad handed over three mobile phones used by the dealers to communicate with their suppliers as well as the necessary contact numbers.

Eddie Darwiche's 'retirement' wasn't as complete as he made out. After relinquishing the business, he offered to provide the Osmans and El Assaad with any weapons they wanted. Crucially, he also gave his word that in the event of trouble with the Razzaks, he would take their side.

The truce between the Razzaks and the new owners of Darwiche's former drug runs continued through most of 2002, though it was always brittle. In mid 2003 it finally broke over a dispute about a car thief who had been supplying stolen cars to the Darwiche-aligned crew only to switch sides when he received a better offer from the Razzaks. The Darwiches showed their annoyance by abducting and bashing a Razzak peace negotiator, 'Gary', then leaving him to be picked up by the Razzaks at a Greenacre service station.

A few weeks later, on 13 July 2003, Eddie Darwiche, his brother Abdul and Mohammed Touma left Sydney for the Hajj in Saudi Arabia, a pilgrimage that would keep them away for a month. With Eddie off the scene, the Razzak crew saw the chance for a payback attack. On 30 July two gunmen wearing balaclavas walked into a halal butcher shop in Bankstown and shot Khaled Taleb five times. Taleb survived the shooting but spent the next three weeks in hospital. It would be another six months before he was able to stand unaided and several months more before he was able to walk. He still has to use crutches. Before the shooting, Taleb had led a charmed life with only a minor criminal record to show for years of drug dealing, murders and shootings.

News reached Eddie in Saudi Arabi that Taleb had been shot. Eddie rang for news and was given a blunt message by his old colleagues: he was needed back in Sydney. Cancelling his pilgrimage, he returned at once and visited Taleb in hospital. He wanted answers. Taleb had lied to the police investigating the shooting, insisting that he couldn't identify the shooters because they wore balaclavas. 'I'm pretty sure it was Ziggy and "G" [Razzak],' he told Eddie.

Eddie's reply left no one in doubt that he was back in business. 'We're gonna make sure, and if it was them ... they're dead ... This is it. I'm either gonna die or spend the rest of my life in jail.' This time they were determined to wipe out the Razzaks. Over the next six months there were 18 shootings across south-west and west Sydney. Six people were murdered and five others wounded. Tit-for-tat reprisals were quick, violent and sometimes spectacular.

In late August Eddie called together his brother Abdul, Ramzi Aouad, Mohammed Touma, and Taleb. He told them he had tracked down Gehad and Ziad Razzak to a Razzak home at 106 Yanderra Street, Condell Park. 'This is what's gonna happen. Fidel [Ramzi Aouad] can drive down the road and shoot at their house. When they come out to see what the fuck happened, me and Abdul [Darwiche] will be standing on the corner with the SKS's and blast them.'

Two days later, around 9.30 in the evening, a gunman fired more than ten shots from a .40 calibre handgun into a car parked out the front of 106 Yanderra Street. As those in the house ran to the front door to see what was going on, two more gunmen opened fire with 7.62 SKS military rifles. Bullets went straight through the walls of the house and hit four neighbouring houses. Amazingly, no one was injured.

Two days later, around 1.30 pm, 34-year-old father of four Ali Abdul Razzak, Gehad and Ziad's uncle, was executed as he left the Lakemba mosque after a prayer session with about 300 other worshippers. As he walked to his car in Koala Road, Lakemba, a small black car pulled up and three gunmen wearing balaclavas got out. One walked over to Abdul Razzak and fired 15 shots, killing him instantly. More than 30 worshippers witnessed the murder. Abdul Razzak was estranged from his wife, Eddie Darwiche's sister, and there was a dispute over property and custody of the children. He had also been part of the Darwiche–Razzak drug feud. That afternoon Eddie told Taleb he had shot Abdul Razzak: 'I waited. When he got in the car I unloaded a magazine on him. I saw one bullet hit him just above his eyebrow. I saw him take his last breath.' According to Eddie, killing Abdul Razzak was a favour to Taleb: 'See what I done for you,' he kept saying.

Reprisals were swift. Around 1.30 am the next morning more than 30 shots were fired into 37 Boundary Road, Lurnea, where Taleb was living. No one was injured. This was the second attempt on Taleb's life in a month. Just half an hour later the Lurnea home of another Darwiche associate, Ramzi Aouad, was hit with more than 50 shots.

Darwiche fought back. During the early hours of 14 October four gunmen stood in a line outside 5 Lawford Street, Greenacre. Using both military assault rifles and handguns they blasted the home with more than 100 shots, 75 of which penetrated the walls. Ziad Razzak was inside, together with 22-year-old Mervat 'Melissa' Nemra and her partner, Ali Hamka. Melissa was killed as she slept by bullets that penetrated the walls and struck her in the neck. Ziad Razzak was hit in the back of the head and died of his wounds. Darwiche had brought two rocket launchers to use in the attack. His plan had been to use one but he changed his mind when he learned that not all the Razzaks were inside. The second rocket launcher was to be used against police in the event of a chase.

Meanwhile, Haissam and Wahib Hannouf went looking for weapons. They spoke to 'Gus', an Australian of Lebanese background, who was offering weapons to anyone who could pay for them. He had home-made machine guns for between $5000 and $7000 each and claimed to be able to get 'kilos of C4' explosives. 'Gus' was in the security business, providing protection to nightclubs, while his bouncers supplied ecstasy, speed and coke to patrons inside (see Chapter 7).

Haissam and Wahib Hannouf inspected one of 'Gus's home-made machine pistols—it looked like an Uzi. They sat in Haissam's Honda Civic as 'Gus' guaranteed the reliability of the weapon and showed them how to use it. There was a loud bang. For a few moments there was panic and Haissam thought he had been shot. But it was another accidental shooting: the gun had gone off by mistake, shattering the windscreen and putting a bullet hole in the dashboard. Haissam was furious. He was trying to sell the car and had a prospective buyer, but the bullet in the dashboard had almost certainly put an end to the deal.

Taleb had not been allowed to take part in the Lawford Street shooting: he couldn't walk, let alone run. If they were chased by police he was bound to be caught. Taleb's nickname was 'Crazy' but he was smart enough to realise he was not going to live long if he stayed in Sydney. He could see Darwiche becoming paranoid and irrational and worried that Darwiche might be setting him up. Taleb had always been loyal to Darwiche but now Taleb was a liability. Taleb knew that Darwiche would not simply cut him loose: the risk of his rolling was too great. He also knew that if Darwiche decided he had to go, he wouldn't stand a chance. Without telling anyone in the gang, Taleb collected his parents and drove to Melbourne. On 18 October 2003 he left Australia for Lebanon. His parents followed a few weeks later.

The shootings and drive-bys continued until 30 October when 25-year-old Ahmed Fahda was shot dead at a Punch-bowl petrol station by two hooded men as he filled a car with petrol. At point blank range the two assasins fired around 30 shots from Glock pistols. Fahda had had a foot in both camps. He was a former enforcer and ally of murdered drug dealer Ziad Razzak but his sister was married to a close associate of Eddie Darwiche. Fahda and two other men had been charged with the 1997 attempted murder of a man shot in the head in Avoca Street, Yagoona, but the charge was dropped by the Director of Public Prosecutions on the basis that Fahda had acted in self-defence. He was convicted of discharging a firearm without regard for the safety of others and served 20 months' periodic detention.

On 7 November Haissam and Wahib Hannouf went to 'Moukhtar's panel-beating shop in Condell Park, to fetch some equipment used to manufacture amphetamines. The Hannoufs had known 'Moukhtar' for at least ten years. Like them, he was a member of the Razzak crew and moonlighted in both drug dealing and car rebirthing. Double-crosses were all part of a day's work. 'Moukhtar' and the Hannoufs took the equipment to Wahib's unit in The Boulevarde, Punch-bowl, before driving to an area behind the Hurstville Aquatic Centre where the Hannoufs drew Glock pistols and pistol-whipped the unsuspecting 'Moukhtar'. 'You're a dog, we're going to pop you,' Wahib shouted as Haissam shoved his pistol in 'Moukhtar's mouth and threatened to kill his family. A passing police car probably saved 'Moukhtar's life: the Hannoufs panicked and fled the scene.

The next day Haissam, Wahib and Abass Osman went to the Condell Park panel-beating shop looking for 'Moukhtar', but he wasn't there. Haissam threatened 'Moukhtar's father: 'Your son is supposed to be doing something with us today. He doesn't come today, I shoot him. Do you care if I shoot him?'

'Moukhtar's younger brother, 22-year-old 'Habib', was taken hostage with the threat that he would be shot if they did not get $20,000 which they claimed 'Moukhtar' owed them. That night Haissam, Wahib, Abass and two other men took 'Habib' back to the repair shop. They took two cars and a go-kart as payment. They also kept 'Moukhtar's car, a Toyota Rav4. With the debt now repaid, 'Habib' was released. What the Hannoufs did not know was that 'Moukhtar's family had gone to the police and rolled. The police were now monitoring the Hannouf family's every move and conversation.

Less than a month later, during the afternoon of Sunday 7 December 2003, several of Eddie Darwiche's associates were having a drink in the Kings Head Tavern at Hurstville. Naseam El Zeyat and Ramzi Aouad left the hotel and were standing in the carpark when two members of the Razzak crew opened fire. Aouad and El Zeyat drew guns and returned fire. The gangsters stood just a few metres apart, exchanging shots in a crowded suburban shopping centre. Bystanders dived for cover as bullets flew among the parked cars. One passed through a car window narrowly missing the driver and her young child.

A .40 calibre Glock pistol with a 30-round magazine, used in the shootout, was recovered from a nearby industrial waste bin. It was one of 31 Glocks that had been stolen three months earlier from a private security firm at Chester Hill. As Detective Chief Superintendent Bob Inkster—the officer leading the investigation—later quipped, 'They certainly lived up to their name, "Obliging Security".' In what many would see as irony, Aouad and El Zeyat, 'victims' of the shootout, were arrested and charged with shooting with intent to cause grievous bodily harm to their attackers. They were later charged with several other shootings and murders committed during the war with the Razzaks.

A few hours after the Kings Head Tavern shootout 59-year-old Sayed Franeigh's daughter, Elizabeth, arrived at Bristol Street, Merrylands, to see two men sitting in a parked car outside the family home. The men, both of Islander appearance with stockings over their heads, leapt out of the car and started firing at Elizabeth as she ran to the house. Sayed heard his daughter's screams and ran out to investigate. As he opened the front door he was shot once in the chest. Sayed died at the scene. This was the second shooting at the house. Three months earlier gunmen had opened fire with a M1 .30 calibre carbine semi-automatic and a Norinco .45 calibre semi-automatic pistol. On that occasion no one was hurt. Each time the getaway car was found burnt out in the same location in a nearby suburb.

The Franeigh shootings were a distraction to the police in their investigation of the Darwiche–Razzak war. Raymond Franeigh, Elizabeth's brother, had been arrested and charged with drug offences in 2001. He was sentenced to a total of two years and eight months' jail and released in March 2003—six months before the first shooting. Raymond was still arguing with the New South Wales Crime Commission over assets it had confiscated while he was in jail. Needing money, Raymond had arranged to sell his BMW through Ken Tan, a man police describe as being 'a crime wave'. Tan sold the car, but the money never reached Raymond, who reported the matter to police. They recovered the BMW from a storage container on 25 September. On hearing of the seizure, Tan immediately organised the drive-by shooting of the Franeigh's house, telling the shooters to 'shoot in front of the house and just scare him'. Tan made sure that he was seen gambling at Sydney's Star City Casino while the shooting was carried out.

The dispute between Tan and Raymond Franeigh didn't end with the September drive-by. On 7 December the two men saw each other in Granville and started screaming abuse and threats. Suddenly Franeigh rammed the Subaru WRX in which Tan was a passenger and which was being driven by his brother, Anthony. Tan's two-year-old son was in the back seat. This time it was Tan who dialled 000. That night Ken Tan ordered the shooting that led to the death of Sayed Franeigh.

Tan was later charged with commissioning both shootings. In November 2006 he was found guilty of the first shooting and sentenced to four years and four months' jail. In 2009 Tan pleaded guilty to the manslaughter of Sayed and on 17 July was sentenced to 12 years and four months' jail. Several of Tan's colleagues were also charged over the shootings and jailed.

On 9 January 2009, 23-year-old Edin Smajovic, a member of the Southern Highlands chapter of the Rebels bikie gang, and an associate visited Anthony Tan at his Campbelltown car yard, Macarthur Auto Centre. A gunfight broke out. Tan was shot in the neck. Smajovic was killed by a single bullet wound to his heart. More than 300 members of the Rebels, including their national president Alex Vella, attended Smajovic's funeral at the Auburn Mosque in south-west Sydney. Following his recovery from the wounding, Anthony Tan fled to Vietnam where he is now believed to be living. At the time of writing no person had been charged over the shooting.

Meanwhile the Darwiche–Razzak war raged on. On 19 December 2003 Ahmad and Rabbi Hannouf were at their home in Newbridge Road, Chipping Norton, when it was sprayed with gunfire. Not content with having given the Hannoufs up to police and collaborating with the police to catch them, 'Moukhtar' had decided to take revenge into his own hands.

Five days later four young men aligned with the Razzak crew parked their car illegally outside the Bankstown Police Station. There were police standing nearby and the two groups eyeballed each other. It seemed a bizarre thing to do—parking illegally outside a police station, in full view of police on the footpath. The men got out of the car and two walked into the station. They were on bail and their bail conditions required them to report to police. The two other men stood beside the car. The police approached and searched the two young men and their vehicle. A full 30-round magazine clip was found in the car and a loaded six-shot Smith and Wesson revolver was found stuffed down the pants of 20-year-old Mohammed Fahda, whose brother Ahmed had been murdered seven weeks earlier. Mohammed and 23-year-old Waleed Mhaich were arrested and charged with firearms and traffic offences. Seeing police searching the car, the two men who'd reported for bail started walking briskly in the opposite direction. When police came after them, the pair broke into a run. After chasing them through the streets, police finally caught up with the men—only to find there was nothing they could charge them with.

Amid the shootings the Darwiche and Razzak crews were

still raking in money from their drug networks, but each day was bringing the police a little closer. On 29 December 2003, a week after Hannouf's Chipping Norton home had been shot up, Ahmad and Rabbi Hannouf gave an amphetamine sample to an undercover cop at Star City Casino. He agreed to a $40,000 buy. The deal was done the next night when he took 354 grams of amphetamine from them. The scene was now set for the final police sting.

On 15 January 2004 Ahmad and Rabbi Hannouf met the undercover cop to complete a $178,000 amphetamine deal. As the deal was being finalised, the police raided 13 homes and businesses owned by members of the Hannouf family in south-western Sydney. The four Hannouf brothers and their cousin, 20-year-old Bilal Hannouf, were arrested. The brothers were charged with 18 counts of manufacturing and supplying drugs, armed robbery, demanding money with menaces, kidnapping, and possessing illegal firearms and ammunition. Their cousin was charged with possessing precursors for the manufacture of amphetamines and $47,000 in cash. Ostensibly unemployed and living on the pension, the brothers had accumulated more than $2 million in assets and taken long and costly visits to Lebanon.

Just after 6 pm on 1 February 2004, 20-year-old Mark Nicholls was shot once in the head and four times in the body while standing in the Condell Park smash repair shop of his friend 'Moukhtar'. 'Moukhtar' told police he was out the back of the repair shop when he heard gunfire and the screech of car tyres. He found Nicholls dead on the floor and dialled 000. It looked like a case of mistaken identity— 'Moukhtar', after all, was a police informant who would soon be testifying against the Hannouf crime family—but

18 months later 'Moukhtar' was arrested and charged with Nicholls's murder.

Though Nicholls had no criminal record, he had been 'Moukhtar's partner during a two-year crime spree that included robbing the National Australia Bank at Paddington of nearly half a million dollars, the theft of money from several automatic teller machines and the theft of five Glock pistols from a Bankstown security firm. The pair was also involved in car rebirthing and drug trafficking. While employed as a guard by a well-known security company, Nicholls worked for the amphetamine syndicate set up in early 2000 by Ahmad Hannouf and the Razzaks. 'Moukhtar' had been using one of the spray booths at his smash repair business to cook up amphetamines. It was Nicholls's job to drive around Sydney buying the cold and flu tablets from which they extracted pseudoephedrine to make amphetamines. Large quantities of Sudafed packages were also acquired through one of 'Moukhtar's relatives who worked in a factory where 'damaged' Sudafed packages were discarded. Distributors included 'John' in Wollongong, who sold one to one and a half kilograms of amphetamines each week for the syndicate.

On 8 May 2004 Mustapha Darwiche was shot outside his Condell Park home. Up to five men opened fire as they drove past, shooting him twice in the leg. Days later an arsenal of handguns, automatic rifles and a shotgun were seized by police during a raid on a Razzak home in Bankstown. One of the guns was linked to the attack on Mustapha Darwiche. It turned out to be one of the last acts of the Darwiche–Razzak war.

Strike Force Gain had been set up in October 2003 to tackle the explosion in street violence in the Punchbowl–Bankstown area and neighbouring suburbs. Its primary targets were the Darwiche and Razzak crews. By February 2004 the core members of both crews were either dead or in jail, remanded on charges ranging from murder and shootings to possession of firearms and drugs. Within a year 1100 arrests and 2400 charges had been laid for crimes ranging from murder to traffic violations, while drugs with an estimated street value of $3.5 million had been seized. Six people had been charged with offences including murder, attempted murder and conspiracy to murder.

Darwiche crew members arrested and refused bail included Abdul and Eddie Darwiche, Ramzi Aouad and Naseam El Zeyat. Members of the Razzak crew in jail included Gehad Razzak, Hussein Fahda and the four Hannouf brothers, Ahmad, Haissam, Rabbi and Wahib. In mid 2005 they were joined by 'Moukhtar' who was charged with the murder of Mark Nicholls, supplying 12,000 pseudoephedrine pills, conspiracy to supply amphetamines and providing false information to obtain an Australian passport.

In jail, the Hannoufs rolled. Speaking in the New South Wales Legislative Council on 5 April 2005, Peter Breen said:

> There is strong evidence the Hannoufs are serious criminals involved in extortion, kidnapping, car rebirthing and drug trafficking, yet the Crime Commission decided that the Hannoufs would be much more useful as witnesses than as defendants ... Apart from no billing the Hannoufs, the Crime Commission returned property to be confiscated as the proceeds of crime, including a factory at Bankstown, a petrol station and house in Halden Street, Lakemba, a property in Newbridge Road, Moorebank, and another property in Chiswick Avenue, Greenacre.

The Hannoufs gave evidence in a number of trials and have been relocated with their families to another state.

By late 2006 Eddie Darwiche, Naseam El Zeyat and Ramzi Aouad had been convicted and given separate life sentences for the 2003 murders of Ziad Razzak and Mervat Hamka at Greenacre. As they were sentenced in the Supreme Court they laughed and joked and shouted, 'God is great!' El Zeyat screamed abuse and profanities at the trial judge, Justice Bell, as he was led from the court. Abdul Darwiche yelled at reporters that his brother Eddie was innocent. Aouad and El Zeyat were each given a third life sentence for the murder of Ahmed Fahda. Abass Osman, who drove the others to the shooting, was convicted and sentenced to 27 years' jail. Two and a half years earlier Osman had been extradited to New South Wales after being detained by Customs at Melbourne's Tullamarine Airport as he attempted to board a flight to Lebanon using a false passport in the name of David David.

Eddie Darwiche was convicted and sentenced to 18 years' jail for the attempted murder of Farouk 'Frank' Razzak at Condell Park in 2003 and eight years' jail for the 2001 shooting of Bilal Razzak, despite Bilal reneging on his deal with the prosecution to give evidence against Darwiche. Warned by the judge that he could be jailed for refusing to cooperate, Bilal's only response was, 'Sweet'. As a result of his refusal—which constituted a contempt of court—Bilal was jailed for 15 months. The sentence came on top of a minimum four-year jail term he was already serving over a 2001 stabbing outside Star City Casino. Bilal's brother, Mohamed, was also jailed for nine months for contempt. Like Bilal, he refused to give evidence against Darwiche. There was a hung jury in Darwiche's trial for the murder of

Ali Abdul Razzak at Lakemba in 2003 and Darwiche was acquitted of the charge of being an accessory before the fact to the murder of Ahmed Fahda. Eddie Darwiche's declaration to his crew three years earlier that 'I'm either gonna die or spend the rest of my life in jail' had proved prophetic. He will spend most if not the rest of his life in jail.

In mid 2005, as police investigated the year-old murder of Mark Nicholls, 'Moukhtar' was arrested in Canberra and charged with possessing stolen property and drug trafficking. In court, police noted that 'Moukhtar' operated under 48 different names and had 17 different driver's licences. Despite the aliases, 'Moukhtar' was granted bail. At the time of writing the Canberra matters remain outstanding.

A few months after his Canberra arrest, 'Moukhtar' was arrested and charged with Nicholls's murder. In June 2009 he was acquitted by a jury. It was 'Moukhtar's third trial for the murder. His 2007 trial had been aborted after several months and the jury could not agree at his 2008 trial. During the third trial, 'Moukhtar's brother, 23-year-old 'Zyad' (not his real name), was charged with contempt when he threatened a Crown witness at the Supreme Court, saying 'I'll smash you.' 'Zyad' was given a nine months' suspended jail sentence.

Ali Osman was arrested in April 2004 and charged with the shooting of Tal Arnaout outside the Wadi El Arayesh nightclub at Narwee on 11 May 2003. He was convicted and sentenced to eight years' jail for the shooting and up to ten years' jail for a variety of drugs charges. The shootout was not the first outside the nightclub. Three years earlier, on 2 July 2000, when it was known as the El-Bardowny, there had been a wild shootout during which the underworld boss Louis Bayeh and others were wounded.

Ahmad 'Gary' Awad, who was alleged to have been involved in several shootings, fled Australia as the Darwiche crew broke apart and is believed to be living in Tripoli. He is said to have demanded money from Darwiche for his silence.

Several of those who rolled on their former partners-in-crime have done quite well for themselves. Three years after fleeing Australia to escape both Eddie Darwiche and the police, Khaled 'Crazy' Taleb was tracked down in Beirut. Detective Inspector Russell Oxford and Detective Robert Tuckerman of the New South Wales Homicide Squad persuaded Taleb to roll. In a secret police operation he was returned to Sydney in early 2006 and given immunity for all his crimes. Taleb gave evidence against Darwiche and several of his crew in a number of murder trials. He is currently living in an unknown location.

In March 2007, during an appearance before the New South Wales Administrative Decisions Tribunal, where he was appealing against the police's refusal to grant him a tow truck driver's licence, Darwiche complained that a witness against him in criminal proceedings—'Crazy' Taleb—had received two million dollars, a boat, a new identity and a pension for life; that seven members of his family had been brought from Lebanon and given Australian citizenship and pensions for life; and that Taleb had been indemnified on 17 attempted murders and four murders. Darwiche was partly right: the benefits he listed were close to those demanded by Taleb for his cooperation, but he did not get everything he asked for. It is true, however, that Taleb was indemnified for several murders and attempted murders and was handsomely rewarded in financial terms.

Another rollover, Tony Haddad, had extensive experience in the theft and rebirthing of stolen motor vehicles. In the early 1990s he was selling stolen cars to Haissam Hannouf for rebirthing and at other times the pair rebirthed stolen cars together. Haddad had 'an Asian guy' in the New South Wales Roads and Traffic Authority who provided 'receipts for stolen car parts' and the 'official paperwork' necessary to have rebirthed cars registered. This arrangement continued for almost ten years. By the early 2000s Haddad was in the habit of carrying a gun when doing business. He joined Danny's Boys on a number of their shooting sprees, including the September 1998 shoot-up of the EP1 Kings Cross nightclub. On 1 June 1999 Haddad escaped the net when police raided properties across Sydney, including the Belfield home of Michael Kanaan. It was Haddad's wedding day and he left his wife and guests standing at the altar. Four months later he was arrested and charged over the EP1 shooting.

Facing a possible life sentence, Haddad rolled. In November 2004 he pleaded guilty to perjury—he had lied in order to beat a home invasion charge—and was sentenced to one year and eight months' jail. By making a deal with police, Haddad won indemnity against a decades-long career of serious crime that included the EP1 nightclub shooting, several murders and attempted murders, kidnappings, motor vehicle theft, supplying drugs, possession of guns, fraud, robbery, larceny, money laundering and assault. In 2006 he gave evidence against his former colleagues Ramzi Aouad and Naseam El Zeyat for the murder of Ahmed Fahda and against Eddie Darwiche for inciting El Zeyat to murder and for being an accessory after the fact.

During cross-examination Haddad admitted to driving a $200,000 convertible Ferrari and having his rent, living expenses and lawn mowing bill paid by New South Wales authorities in return for his evidence at trial. He confessed to committing a $300,000 drug rip-off while negotiating his indemnity from prosecution, to having been jailed for perjury, and to having lied to police for more than ten years. He told Darwiche's defence counsel, '[I have] years and years of practice ... I was born a liar.'

Several members of another criminal family also rolled. They made statements that were used in various court proceedings and gave evidence against several members of the Razzak crew. Charges against them were dropped and they were allowed to keep their assets. Their deal included other financial incentives, assistance for overseas relatives to move to Australia, and relocation to another state. Once there, however, the family returned to its criminal ways, setting up an elaborate operation for the theft and rebirthing of motor vehicles in their new state. The subsequent crime wave caused severe embarrassment for New South Wales and federal authorities.

Eddie Darwiche's older brother, Abdul, was acquitted at trial of the 2003 shooting at the home of Frank Razzak, and beat a charge of attempting to murder Bilal Razzak at Bankstown in 2001 when the Office of the Director of Public Prosecutions declined to proceed on the matter. In March 2007, in a matter before the New South Wales Administrative Decisions Tribunal, police gave evidence that 'Abdul Darwiche has now assumed control of the Darwiche Family Criminal Syndicate, maintaining drug distribution networks established in the south west of Sydney.'

Abdul Darwiche's time as head of the family didn't last long. On the afternoon of 14 March 2009, six years after the killing of Ahmed Fahda at a Punchbowl service station, 37-year-old Abdul took his family and two friends of his children to a fast-food restaurant at the corner of the Hume Highway and

Miller Street, Bass Hill. Leaving the others in the restaurant, he came outside to speak to 21-year-old Mohammed 'Blackie' Fahda, a younger brother of Ahmed Fahda. The two men argued and Abdul is reported to have said, 'What are you going to do? Kill me in front of my fucking family?' Blackie shouted back, 'I don't give a shit where I kill you.'

For six years 'Blackie' Fahda had blamed Darwiche for his brother Ahmad's death. Now, investigating police allege, he pulled a gun and shot Darwiche in the body. As Darwiche tried to escape in his black utility, Fahda is alleged to have fired through the windscreen, hitting Darwiche five more times, once in the head and four times in the body. In September 2009, seven months after the shooting of Abdul Darwiche, Blackie Fahda was detained in Tonga for being there illegally and deported to Australia where he was charged with Darwiche's shooting. At the time of writing his case was still before the courts.

Within days of the shooting, *Sydney Morning Herald* journalist Dylan Welch reported that Eddie Darwiche had sent a message from Goulburn's Supermax jail to his brother's killer. The message said, 'I'm going to kill you, even if it's kids, I don't care.'

A few days after Abdul Darwiche's alleged murder, another brother, 40-year-old Michael Alin Darwiche, was arrested in a blue BMW driven by a friend, 36-year-old Michael Darwick. Underneath the rear passenger seat police found a Glock 23 pistol and ammunition, a street directory, and the names and addresses of the Fahda family. Darwiche and Darwick were charged with eight offences, including unlicensed possession of an unregistered firearm and being armed with intent to commit an indictable offence.

CHAPTER SEVEN

Drugs, guns and rocket launchers

The Lebanese crime network established by Frank Hakim under the protection of Lennie McPherson and George Freeman was predominantly Christian. Membership of the Danny Karam and Michael Kanaan gangs was also overwhelmingly Christian Lebanese. While Karam tolerated Muslims in his gang, he never hid his dislike and distrust of them, and this gradually became a source of tension within the gang. The Christian Lebanese domination was broken by the Telopea Street Boys and the Darwiche and Razzak crews. All three gangs were Muslim Lebanese but the networks within which they operated were a United Nations of crime, unrestricted by religion or race.

Mark Nicholls, a cook and major player in both the Hannoufs' amphetamine network and the Razzaks' drug and car rebirthing operations, was a Caucasian

Australian. Nicholls's partner, 'Gary', was another Caucasian Australian.

'Mark' and 'Peter' were amphetamine cooks for the Razzaks, while 'Greg' assisted the Razzaks in their frauds on finance companies. All three were Australian-born Caucasians.

'Pit', a Caucasian who lived in Sydney's inner west, was an amphetamine cook and supplier to 'Moukhtar' and the Razzak gang.

'Samir', a Pakistani, provided the gangs with false identification papers, credit cards, Medicare cards and other papers including tax returns.

'Jamie' was a South American who also provided false identification documents and dealt in drugs.

'James' was Chinese. His brother ran a large Asian drug importing and trafficking syndicate that operated in Australia and dealt in ecstasy, ice, heroin and cocaine. 'James' used to work on the door of the Love Machine at Kings Cross in the late 1990s and later owned a brothel in Canberra.

'George', who was Greek by birth, helped the Hannoufs in frauds relating to car rebirthing.

'Jeff', a Greek from Liverpool, was a junkie who stole and stripped cars for 'Moukhtar' and, from time to time, helped in 'Moukhtar's insurance frauds.

'Ali' was a Turk who supplied fake driver's licences.

'Matt', a Caucasian Australian, lived in Canberra and produced false identification and documentation for use in car rebirthing, as did an 'Asian lady at Croydon Park'.

Then there was 'Tony', an Italian whose connections with the Philippines, Malaysia, China and Indonesia were invaluable in his work as a middle-man for an Asian amphetamine syndicate.

'John' was a Greek from Wollongong who was involved with the Hannoufs in drugs and car rebirthing. At times he was buying nearly one and a half kilograms of amphetamines a week from them.

Most of the runners for the Darwiche and Razzak drug networks, both male and female, were Caucasians.

The networks trading in firearms were no less diverse. Like the Telopea Street Boys and the Darwiche and Razzak crews, Karam and Kanaan had virtually unlimited access via at least eight suppliers to weapons ranging from handguns to military-style assault weapons.

Glenn Aranzamendez was a Philippine citizen who lived in the eastern Sydney suburb of Randwick and sold various types of handgun, along with explosives and hand grenades. His source was Cabramatta's 5T gang. In late April 2000 Aranzamendez and a Vietnamese teenage gang member were arrested while planning an armed robbery. Aranzamendez was also charged with another Vietnamese gang member with insurance fraud. He pleaded guilty to all charges and was given a two-year suspended sentence and fined $1000.

George Farid Abouhaidar of Beverly Hills was another source of weapons. He was also selling block cocaine imported from Bolivia. In late July 2000 Abouhaidar was stopped by police who searched his car and found two 60 gram bags of cocaine. A follow-up search of his home found almost half a kilogram of marijuana. Abouhaidar was arrested and the following year was sentenced to three years' jail on two counts of supplying prohibited drugs. A decade earlier Abouhaidar had been found in possession of cocaine and jailed for five years.

Abouhaidar's source was Peter Robert Madison, also known as Robert Gordon, David Gordon, David Andrews and Peter Graham, who lived in Lakemba. Madison has a long criminal record in New South Wales and Victoria going back to 1972. He has convictions for property crimes, rape and other sexual offences, violence, drug supply and firearms offences. In December 2000 Madison was arrested and charged with 26 counts of supplying heroin and cocaine and firearms offences. While several charges were dropped, Madison was convicted and given jail sentences of up to six years. He had sold both drugs and handguns with ammunition to an undercover police officer. Through Abouhaidar he supplied guns to the Telopea Street Boys.

The gun used by Kanaan in the Weigall Sports Ground shootout with police was traced back to a licensed Tasmanian firearms dealer and gun collector operating illegally in New South Wales. William Francis Watson bought 21 pistols from the licensed New South Wales gun trader Kenmax Special Products Pty Ltd and then sold them on the black market for around $5000 each. Few of the guns were traced or recovered. In September 2000 Watson was convicted of ten firearms offences including possession of a prohibited weapon, possessing a firearm without a licence and failure by an unauthorised person to surrender a firearm. He was sentenced to 18 months' periodic detention.

The Nomads outlaw motorcycle gang, which had strong ties to Lebanese crime gangs through Sam Ibrahim, was an important firearms supplier. The Rebels also supplied firearms and had drug dealings with Lebanese gangs.

Police investigating the trade in illegal weapons had an important breakthrough with the rollover of a Darwiche gang member given the pseudonym Ahmad Hassan. In September 2006 the New South Wales Police and Australian Federal Police terrorism investigations units and the New South Wales Crime Commission set up Strikeforce Ridgecrop into the theft and distribution of rocket launchers. Within weeks one rocket launcher that had been bought by Adnan 'Eddie' Darwiche was recovered in a controlled operation. It was an L1A2-F1 rocket launcher armed with an A3 rocket warhead assembly. Australian Defence Force (ADF) records revealed that it was one of several rocket launchers that were to have been destroyed five years earlier at a military facility in outer Sydney. ADF experts describe that type of launcher as having an effective range of 200 metres for a stationary target and 180 metres for moving targets. However, they can fire a warhead up to 1100 metres. The rockets can penetrate armour and concrete. If a rocket hit a motor vehicle it would almost certainly kill all the occupants.

Further information came from another rollover, code-named Harrington. A member of the Darwiche gang and former bikie, Harrington told police that he'd first heard rocket launchers mentioned around mid 2001 when he was visited in jail (he was serving a sentence for drug offences) by his wife and a man he had not met before, 31-year-old Dean Taylor, together with Taylor's then wife, Catherine. Harrington claimed that Dean Taylor 'offered to get me rocket launchers, grenades, bulletproof vests and night vision goggles. He offered me other military stuff but I can't remember them all.' According to Harrington, he and Taylor discussed the supply of military weapons again some months later, when Harrington was on work release. Taylor named the supplier as Shane Della-Vedova, his former brother-in-law. Both men were former members of the Australian army. As an ammunitions technical officer and ordnance special-ist, Della-Vedova had been responsible for the disposal of weapons that were to be decommissioned.

Harrington claimed he still wasn't sure whether Taylor was genuine. The next week Harrington spoke to 25-year-old

Milad Sande: 'I contacted Milad because I was aware that he was widely connected throughout the criminal community and I thought that he would be able to find a buyer for the weapons ... Milad told me that he was interested in buying the weapons but he wanted to start by buying one rocket launcher.'

Harrington claimed in evidence that he obtained one rocket launcher from Taylor and sold it to Sande for $20,000. A few days later he obtained a second launcher, but Sande was not interested. According to Harrington, 'Whoever he had sold the rocket launcher to was not happy with it. They didn't realise that it was only a single shot weapon.' Sande returned the first rocket launcher. Harrington was to reimburse Sande out of subsequent weapons sales but the debt was never paid.

With Milad Sande no longer involved, Harrington turned to Taha Abdul-Rahman as a potential buyer. Twenty-nine-year-old Abdul-Rahman had a criminal record that included convictions for robbery, stealing and assaults. He regularly sold weapons to the Darwiche gang and was keen to buy.

In late 2002 Harrington met Taylor at Taylor's Mount Annan home, about 60 kilometres south-west of Sydney, where Harrington claimed they discussed the supply of rocket launchers, hand grenades and explosives. Harrington said that Taylor gave him a piece of paper with the following words on it:

(1) 10 x M66 ready to rock,
(2) grenades,
(3) explosives.

According to Harrington, 'explosives' referred to five kilograms of power gel. He said Taylor also gave him a 'terrorism handbook' which contained information 'on the acquisition, storage and use of chemicals, propellants and explosives, as well as chemical recipes. The manual included references to the construction of projective weapons, rockets and rocket bombs.' Harrington agreed to buy more weapons from Taylor.

Harrington told Abdul-Rahman what sort of weapons were available and how much they would cost. Abdul-Rahman met one of Eddie Darwiche's lieutenants, a man to whom police gave the pseudonym Ahmad Hassan. A deal was quickly struck for the sale of one rocket launcher. According to Abdul-Rahman, he later 'drove to Liverpool and he [Hassan] was there and Eddie [Darwiche], Eddie was waiting around the corner in his car and I went and picked it [the rocket launcher] up from Harrington and then gave him the money. He gave me the rocket launcher and I went and drove around the corner and gave it to Eddie.'

Around this time Harrington's alleged contact with Taylor stopped—Taylor was going through a messy divorce—so Harrington contacted Della-Vedova direct. They met and agreed to the sale of another six or seven rocket launchers. According to Harrington:

> I got in touch with Shane [Della-Vedova] and I organised to pick up [the other] rocket launchers. Shane said that they would be put in the boot of a white Ford Laser that was parked on the grass where Catherine was living at Casula. The car belonged to Dean Taylor but was being used by Catherine Taylor. Shane said he would leave the key to the Laser on the front tyre so that I could open the car ... I drove to Catherine Taylor's house and backed up to the white Ford Laser. I opened the car with the key and I popped the boot and saw two dark garbage bags.

I picked up the bags and I remember that they were not
of equal weight and I thought that there were four rocket
launchers in one bag and three in another.

On 9 October Abdul-Rahman drove to a house in Claymore
in Sydney's outer west where Darwiche gave him the cash
to buy the rocket launchers. Abdul-Rahman then drove to a
nearby street where he met Harrington. According to Abdul-
Rahman, Harrington 'opened the boot of the car which was
a Commodore; I opened the boot [of mine] and he passed
them over—passed the rocket launchers over into my boot.
They were in two garbage bags. I gave the money to him at
the same time.'

Harrington thought he received 'about $70,000' from
Abdul-Rahman for the rocket launchers, of which 'I kept
around $10,000 [as commission]'. Abdul-Rahman, on the
other hand, remembered being given $60,000 by Darwiche
and giving $55,000 to Harrington, having pocketed $5000 as
commission. After handing over the money Abdul-Rahman
then drove back to the house in Claymore where Darwiche
and Hassan were waiting, and delivered the weapons.

Four years later, on 15 December 2006, police raided the
Leumeah home of Abdul-Rahman. They found ammunition
but did not charge him. The next day he appeared before the
New South Wales Crime Commission, refusing to cooperate
with authorities unless he was paid a large amount of money.
On leaving the commission Abdul-Rahman made a call to
an associate on his mobile phone, saying, 'They fucked me
bro ... about those things that fly ... that dick [the man
known as 'Hassan'] has spoken man.' He continued, 'Yeah,
plus the supply of the seven other big ones.'

A month later Abdul-Rahman was arrested and charged with two counts of buying and two counts of receiving Australian Defence Force rocket launchers and possessing ammunition. He rolled, admitting his involvement and implicating others in the receipt and supply of one rocket launcher on 30 September 2003 and the receipt and supply of 'either four or six' launchers ten days later. (Harrington thought there were seven.) All were bought from Harrington for between $12,000 and $15,000 for sale to Eddie Darwiche. Abdul-Rahman received a 'commission' of around $1000 for each rocket launcher.

Worried that they would be caught up in the widely publicised police investigation into the rocket launchers, Della-Vedova and Harrington met Taylor on 27 March 2007 at Mount Annan. During this conversation Harrington revealed that Darwiche had on-sold the rocket launchers to people involved in terrorism: 'It's my stupid fucking mate ... I sold them to my mate [Darwiche] and he sold them to these fucking dickheads ... Terrorists have got 'em now it's a fucking drama.'

Among the 'terrorists' Harrington referred to was 41-year-old 'Hussein', one of nine men arrested in anti-terrorism raids in Sydney during November and December 2005 and charged with conspiring to make explosives in preparation for a terrorist attack against the Sydney Harbour Bridge and the Lucas Heights nuclear reactor. As part of the same police operation, 13 people were arrested in Melbourne and charged with terrorism-related offences (see Chapter 10).

A week later 46-year-old Della-Vedova was arrested and charged in relation to the theft and possession of ten rocket launchers and rockets. He pleaded guilty to these charges on 28 November 2007 and six months later was sentenced to ten years' jail.

On the same day Della-Vedova was arrested, police arrested Taylor and charged him with possession of two rocket launchers and five hand grenades, and one count of receiving stolen property (the rocket launchers and hand grenades). In July 2008 a jury deliberated for just two hours before acquitting Taylor of all charges.

Harrington was not charged with any offence relating to the rocket launchers. He was indemnified against prosecution in return for giving evidence.

In *Dead Man Running*, by Ross Coulthart and Duncan McNab, a convicted criminal, former bikie and police informer who uses the name Steve Utah (but appears on television and in pictures without disguise) claims to have seen Della-Vedova sell five rocket launchers to a senior member of the Bandidos in February 2005, three years *after* the offences for which Della-Vedova was convicted. However, senior police who investigated the theft and sale of the rocket launchers have dismissed Utah's claims. In the words of one officer who had dealings with Utah:

> There's no doubt he was around the edges of the Bandidos and was involved in the amphetamine trade, but he claims he was with them for ten years and was at the centre of the action, including being an accessory to a murder, but was never made a patched member. That says a lot: it means they didn't trust him and he was never a big-time player.

Close allies of the Razzaks told of two further sources of illegal weapons. 'Imad' (not his real name) is said to have imported firearms from the US to Australia in containers.

He is also said to have imported several B7 rocket launchers hidden in cars (including five Mustangs and one Dodge Viper) and to have arranged for handguns to be sent to Australia in the post using fake names. The runners who picked up the parcels were given false identification papers to match the names on the packages. Over two years during the late 1990s 'Imad' made at least 20 trips to the US—often travelling first class—to organise the importation of weapons into Australia. In 2002 'Imad' was offering ten .45 calibre pistols for sale. Ahmed Fahda stole the guns from 'Imad' and this caused bad blood. Fahda then kidnapped 'Imad's brother and demanded $100,000 for his return. He finally accepted 'Imad's offer of $50,000 and some hand grenades.

A year later 'Imad' went to Lebanon. He bought weapons in America and smuggled them into Lebanon in cars. He also bought weapons in Lebanon and, using his contacts in Australia, obtained false Australian passports for members of the Hezbollah. At least some of these passports were used to visit Australia. 'Imad' was arrested in Lebanon with several false Australian passports but was released after the Hezbollah corruptly negotiated his release.

On his return to Sydney 'Imad' claimed to have rocket launchers, Uzi machine guns, M16 grenades, Glocks and other handguns for sale to the Darwiche crew. Several of the weapons were shown to gang members.

Though 'Imad' was aligned with Darwiche he also did business with the Razzaks. As one source said, 'he used to supply everyone [with weapons]. He was everyone's friend and everyone's enemy: to ['Imad'] it was just business.'

Another major weapons supplier was 'Gus', a Lebanese Australian in his mid 30s who lives with his family in a southern Sydney suburb. He had spent several years in the Australian army. Using his connections with the army, 'Gus' was able to offer weapons to both crews. He manufactured his own machine guns, which he offered to the gangs for $7000 each, and claimed to be able to get 'kilos of C4' explosives with remote controlled or timer detonation devices. 'Gus' also sold drugs: 'eckies, speed and coke'.

Despite their easy access to weapons and despite Darwiche's own rule that the crew had to get rid of a gun once it was 'dirty', Darwiche himself held on to certain guns, either because they were favourites or because they were too expensive to throw away. The 9 mm pistol used to shoot up a home unit in Bankstown on 26 February 2001 was used two days later in a drive-by of another home at Padstow, and was one of the weapons used in the double murder of Ziad Razzak and Melissa Nemra at Greenacre two and a half years later. Two military assault rifles used to kill Razzak and Nemra had been used two months earlier to shoot up a car parked outside Frank Razzak's home at Condell Park.

Mistakes like these were instrumental to the success of the police task force that finally broke up the Darwiche and Razzak gangs and put their leaders behind bars. After half a decade of untrammelled violence, relative calm has returned to the streets of Sydney's south-west. But while the gang leaders are in jail, the criminal networks they built are still largely in place. New gangs and new networks have begun to form—just as they did in Kings Cross after the upheaval of the Wood Royal Commission. There are still drive-bys and shootings as rivals look for a foothold in Sydney's voracious market for illegal drugs. Limitless profits are—and will continue to be—a recipe for limitless violence.

CHAPTER EIGHT

The traffickers

For nearly a century Kings Cross has been a magnet for illegal drugs, and for the traffickers who sell them. In the 1920s, according to Larry Writer's book *Razor*, 'police estimated there were around 5000 drug addicts in Kings Cross, Darlinghurst and Woolloomooloo. People smoked marijuana and opium, injected heroin and morphine ... and drank paraldehyde ... But cocaine—or "snow"—was Sydney's drug of choice.' Drugs and dealers have come and gone but the allure of Kings Cross, with its mix of squalor and glamour, sex and money, its long tradition of police corruption and its lucrative proximity to the naval dockyards of Woolloomooloo, has stayed constant for traffickers and users alike.

The Lebanese involvement in the Kings Cross drug trade, which began with Frank Hakim and reached a homicidal peak with the gangs of Danny Karam and Michael Kanaan, spanned a period when the Cross was unchallenged as

Australia's drug capital. Its pre-eminence went back to the late 1960s when thousands of US soldiers and sailors arrived in Sydney on rest and recreation leave from the Vietnam War. These cashed-up servicemen flocked to the bars and brothels and strip clubs of Kings Cross, bringing with them—as Alfred McCoy wrote in *Drug Traffic*—'their taste for cannabis and heroin'. Local criminals, protected by corrupt police, quickly entered the drug trade, both as importers and distributors. During the next three decades the exploding market for illegal drugs transformed the business of organised crime.

In the early 1970s the trade in heroin and cannabis was mostly in the hands of relatively small-time entrepreneurs using couriers. Importations could be as much as a few kilos at a time but the operations were often makeshift and poorly planned. Many of the couriers were themselves heroin addicts and while the organisers made big profits, they showed little inclination to invest for the future.

By the mid 1970s the sheer amount of money to be made from illegal drugs began to draw in larger and more sophis-ticated operators. One of these was Michael Moylan, whose father owned the infamous 33 Club in Darlinghurst and had long been involved in illegal gambling. Moylan lacked the old man's business nous and the contacts necessary for protection. After his father's death, Moylan was forced to close the club. An unsuccessful but compulsive gambler, he was in desperate need of money. In 1975 he was introduced to the international drug trade when a solicitor organised for him to bail several couriers charged with smuggling cannabis and opium. Over the next 12 months the Moylan syndicate used couriers to bring in 24 shipments of cannabis, totalling more than 350 kilograms. On another occasion they imported more than a tonne of cannabis hidden inside large cylindrical batteries, but were double-crossed—not for the first time—by an associate who kept the proceeds after telling them that the shipments had been intercepted by Customs.

Two prominent members of the syndicate were Murray Riley and Richard 'Snapper' Cornwell. Riley was a former New South Wales police officer with a reputation as a criminal 'heavy'. Moylan was attracted by Riley's American connections, which he hoped to use in his plan to smuggle heroin into the US. Cornwell was a regular gambler at the Moylans' gambling club and already a successful cannabis importer when he was invited to join the group. Moylan and Cornwell used several of the club's employees, including Cornwell's then girlfriend, as couriers.

The syndicate collapsed after a year when a number of couriers were arrested and rolled to law enforcement agencies. Michael Moylan and his wife fled to England, but six months later Moylan and others were arrested and charged with importing cannabis into England. Moylan was still serving his sentence when, along with his wife, he was extradited to Australia to face more drug importation charges. He died in jail of a heart attack in 1980.

After the collapse of the Moylan syndicate in Australia, Riley set up his own operation and Cornwell joined him. During 1976 Riley's group imported more than 50 kilograms of heroin into Australia. Riley also explored the feasibility of trans-shipping heroin through Australia into the US, but the operation never got off the ground.

The following year Riley joined forces with an old partner in crime from the 1960s, William Sinclair, a political fixer who dabbled in SP betting and heroin dealing. Sinclair also owned the Wings travel agency which, over just two years, organised more than 200 itineraries for criminals and drug smugglers.

Warren Fellows had already smuggled hashish from India and was involved in a heroin syndicate with Sinclair and a Sydney publican when he joined Riley. The notorious criminal Arthur 'Neddy' Smith also joined Riley, operating as both the syndicate's muscle and its principal distributor. In his memoir *Neddy*, Smith claims that he and Riley sold several million dollars' worth of heroin during 1977 and that he had ten distributors working for him, largely in Sydney's eastern suburbs. Much of the heroin ended up on the streets of Kings Cross.

The same year Riley loosened his ties with both Cornwell and Smith. Through contacts in the Chinese triads, Riley approached Thai drug suppliers with an order for five tonnes of cannabis. At the same time, Balmain criminal Wayne Thelander was preparing to import two tonnes of cannabis into Australia. By chance, Riley and Thelander hired the same man, a New Zealander named Graham Lyall Cann, to transport shipments to Australia. Cann was a member of the Mr Asia heroin syndicate.

In late March 1978 Cann loaded both consignments in Thailand and sailed for Australia. When the vessel developed engine trouble Cann dumped the cannabis overboard at Polkington Reef, between Papua New Guinea and the Solomon Islands, to be retrieved later by boat or seaplane.

Working together, the two syndicates bought a yacht, the *Anoa*, which sailed to Polkington Reef to recover the cannabis. While it returned down the coast to New South Wales, the *Anoa* was watched by the federal Narcotics Bureau. Over the next six weeks police arrested most members of both syndicates and recovered the bulk of the cannabis. Two tonnes were never found. Riley and Thelander were sentenced to ten years' jail (the maximum penalty at that time) over the importation.

Neddy Smith, William Sinclair and Warren Fellows continued importing heroin after the split with Riley until Sinclair, Fellows and Paul Heyward were arrested in Bangkok with 8.5 kilograms of heroin in late 1978. A few days later police in Sydney arrested Neddy Smith, seizing two kilograms of heroin and almost $400,000 cash. Fellows and Sinclair were sentenced to life while Hayward was sentenced to 30 years in a Thai jail. Four years later Sinclair was pardoned. In 1988 Fellows and Hayward were pardoned. Smith spent two years in jail before gaining his release on bail. Six months later he beat the charge.

By now the Mr Asia syndicate had couriers regularly bringing heroin into Australia. At least 200 kilograms of heroin was imported between late 1976 and 1979. While much of it was sold in Sydney, some was distributed as far afield as Melbourne and Perth.

By the start of the 1980s another large-scale drug importer, Daniel 'Danny' Chubb, had switched from cannabis to heroin. His network included Neddy Smith—back on the streets having beaten the 1978 drug charges—and Melbourne criminal Michael 'Mick' Sayers. Chubb and Sayers were among the first victims of the gang war that erupted in Sydney in the mid 1980s, provoked in part by rivalries over the Kings Cross drug trade.

Around the same time cocaine began to flood the streets of Kings Cross in competition with the existing heroin trade. Some suppliers, such as Bill Bayeh, welcomed the cocaine as being more profitable than heroin.

Having split with Riley, Cornwell was now importing huge quantities of cannabis, heroin and cocaine. Ships brought the drugs to agreed locations off the Queensland and New South Wales coasts where they would be transferred to local pick-up boats. In August 1982 two principals in Cornwell's network, Terrence Basham and his partner, Susan Smith, were found shot in the head on their horse stud near Murwillumbah on the far north coast of New South Wales. According to Melbourne criminal Alan Williams, the killer was Christopher 'Rent-a-Kill' Flannery—apparently acting on Cornwell's orders. Eight days later, Cornwell fled Australia for a year. After years of investigation by the National Crime Authority, Cornwell was eventually arrested and charged with importing two tonnes of cannabis and conspiring to import a second shipment. In 1987 Cornwell was sentenced to 18 years' jail. The courts eventually confiscated $6.9 million from Cornwell's estimated assets of $23 million.

In July 1988 the National Crime Authority's Chinese liaison officer was reported as saying that the Chinese had been linked to every major seizure of heroin in the previous two financial years. Three years later the Australian Federal Police (AFP) estimated that Chinese crime groups were responsible for the importation of 'perhaps 80 per cent of all heroin being imported into Australia'. In a 1994 submission to parliament, the AFP declared: 'Stability in the price of heroin and its quality in Australia indicate the importation of heroin into Australia is well organised and dominated by Chinese Organised Crime groups. Heroin is routed through Bangkok, the Malay Peninsula, Hong Kong and the People's Republic of China.' The view of ethnic-Chinese domination in the importation of heroin was supported by the New South Wales Crime Commission.

But if the ethnic Chinese played a dominant role in importing heroin into Australia, other groups controlled its distribution inside Australia. In 1991 the Criminal Environment Assessment Unit in the Commonwealth Attorney-General's Department described the Chinese as operating 'a heroin wholesale business, with little evidence of ... further involvement downstream into retail distribution'.

Other criminal groups were only too happy to seize opportunities spurned by the Chinese. Prominent among these criminal groups were Lebanese gangs whose roots went back to the original Lebanese 'godfather', Frank Hakim, and the Calabrian Mafia, known as the `ndrangheta, based in the New South Wales town of Griffith.

By the early 1980s Milad Sande, a professional thief turned drug trafficker (and uncle of the Milad Sande who bought the rocket launcher), controlled a drug network that extended from Kings Cross to the Fairfield–Cabramatta area in Sydney's outer west. WS14, a police rollover to the Wood Royal Commission, admitted regularly receiving bribes from Sande from the early 1980s and said that Sande had paid bribes of up to $35,000 to other police to beat charges. According to WS14 Sande was 'one of the major distributors of heroin in the Sydney area ... [in the late 1980s and during the 1990s] ... [H]e was dealing direct with Chinese people to get his heroin ... [and was dealing in] large amounts ... like, pounds.'

WS14 told the commission that while he was at the Drug Squad it was common for him and other police to have their lunches bought by Bill Bayeh, Louis Bayeh and Milad Sande. Another regular at these lunches was Morris George, who in 1986 was sentenced to five years for conspiring to bribe Rex

Jackson, the then Labor minister for corrective services, to obtain the early release of prisoners from jail. Morris George's partner, Harry Lahood, was a major supplier of heroin and other drugs to Kings Cross and other parts of Sydney, usually with the help of corrupt police.

In 1985 Independent South Coast Member of Parliament John Hatton, was given six pictures taken six years earlier at the engagement party of Benito 'Benny' Esposito. Hatton passed the pictures to the New South Wales Police and the National Crime Authority. In 1990 he told the Legislative Assembly that among the people depicted in the pictures were 'Harry Lahood, Dominic Sergi, Pat Sergi, with Lahood and [name deleted] identified as close associates of [Frank] Hakim ... Judge Foord ... Benny Esposito [and] Frank Sergi. ... The reputation of many of these people would be known and must have been known to former Judge Foord.'

At the time the picture was taken the Woodward Royal Commission into Drug Trafficking (1977–80) was investigating the activities of the Sergis and others in connection with the large-scale cultivation and distribution of cannabis and the murder of Griffith anti-drugs campaigner Donald Mackay. According to Hatton, the person who gave him the pictures was then serving a jail sentence at Long Bay and had told him that he, the inmate, 'was involved in the marijuana and heroin industry and that former Judge Foord was a vital part of that industry. The prisoner said that he [the prisoner] was a courier of money from Griffith to Pat Sergi.'

Within months of the engagement party pictures being taken the then Fairfield alderman John Newman was guest of honour at Esposito's wedding. Toasting the bride and groom, he said: 'I can't think of a more significant event in my lifetime than coming along tonight to celebrate Benny's wedding.' The following year Esposito was charged with possessing $350,000 in forged American banknotes. He was given a bond—largely on the basis of a glowing reference from Newman. In 1986 Esposito was sentenced to ten years' jail for conspiring to cultivate 6000 marijuana plants valued at $6 million. One of Esposito's co-conspirators—also jailed—was Cabramatta Senior Constable Claude Swan.

The same year, Newman became the state Labor member for the seat of Cabramatta. On 5 September 1994, in the presence of his fiancée, Newman was assassinated in the driveway of his Cabramatta home on the order of his political rival Phuong Canh Ngo. After several trials, Ngo was sentenced to life in jail, never to be released.

Pasquale 'Pat' Sergi (born 1 January 1946 in Plati, Calabria), who married into the Trimbole family, is the brother of Antonio (born 25 September 1944). He is a cousin of Antonio 'Tony' Sergi (born 29 October 1935), the then owner of the House of Sergi, now known as Warburn Wines. The Woodward Royal Commission found that Pat Sergi and his brother Antonio had acted as 'dummies' for Tony Sergi in business transactions and that both Pat and his brother had 'acted in concert with Trimbole' and were 'under the immediate control of Robert Trimbole', distributing cannabis and 'channelling ... finance back to the Griffith end of the [drug] operation'. The commission found that Tony Sergi ran the growing side of Trimbole's cannabis operation and was a senior member of the 'ndrangheta.

In the lead-up to the 1995 state election the Labor Party decided to nominate Pat Sergi for the Sydney seat of Fairfield—he was a longtime financial supporter of the party and for many years had been able to bring the Calabrian vote to Labor. But according to a secret New South Wales police report, the plan 'may have been terminated when a "police probe" was conducted' and threatened exposure of Sergi's connections to Robert Trimbole and the `ndrangheta's drug network and money-laundering operations.

On 25 September 1981, four months after Robert Trimbole fled Australia to escape a police dragnet, 21-year-old Francesco Mittiga of Fairfield in Sydney's west was arrested and charged with conspiring with Trimbole and others to obtain false passports used by the Mr Asia syndicate between 1979 and 1981. Mittiga's home was searched and a piece of paper with the name 'Bob' and a silent telephone registered to Trimbole was found. A home at Cabramatta where Trimbole had lived was also searched and an address book containing the name 'Frankie' and personal particulars that corresponded to Francesco Mittiga was found.

Mittiga was a clerical assistant with the Department of Foreign Affairs and was Trimbole's contact in the Passports Office. At first he pleaded 'not guilty' to all charges but during committal hearings at Sydney's St James Court of Petty Sessions Alison Dine gave evidence against him. The former lover of Mr Asia boss Terrence Clark, Dine had been a principal heroin courier and recruiter of couriers for the syndicate. She was also an accessory after the fact to the murder of syndicate member 'Pommy' Lewis, whose body was found in bushland near Port Macquarie on the mid north coast of New South Wales in May 1978. Dine had been given indemnity from prosecution. She said that Trimbole had given her two false passports—using false documentation provided by her—and that she had used the passports.

Dine said that Trimbole had told her 'I have a book of blank birth certificates [and] a contact in the Passport

Office ... [He] will get us a Passport within 24 hours and he will scrub all the documents so there is no trace.' Dine got each of her passports within two days. The court also heard that Mittiga had 'obtained Trimbole's file from the department archives. The file has not been accounted for since.' Evidence was also given that a book of 100 blank birth certificate forms went missing from the Griffith registry of births, deaths and marriages in 1972.

In September 1983 Mittiga was committed for trial. Six months later he pleaded guilty before Judge John Foord in the District Court to conspiring with Trimbole and others to defeat the *Passports Act*. On 5 March 1984 Mittiga was fined $2000 and placed on a $1000 three-year good behaviour bond. In sentencing Mittiga, Judge Foord said that it was 'alarming' to see the way in which the Clark organisation had used passports to carry out its illegal operations. Clark himself, Judge Foord said, had spoken of 'using passports like confetti'.

Around this time an Australian Federal Police officer, Sergeant John Franklin, recorded a meeting with Mario Cannistra and John Commisso, who had been arrested in Canley Vale, a suburb in Sydney's west, along with five others, in possession of around 250 kilograms of cannabis worth about half a million dollars. The meeting is described by Roderick Campbell, Brian Toohey and William Pinwell in their book *The Winchester Scandal*. Franklin later told the Winchester Inquest, which ran from 1989 to 1991, that Cannistra and Commisso wanted to grow 'a quick crop' to enable them to beat their charges or at least gain a light sentence. It would cost about $200,000 to get them off lightly. Franklin said they told him, 'the going rate was $60,000 each [to get off the charges] ... and the balance of $80,000 was to go into a Labor [Party] slush fund'. Although Franklin recorded and reported the meeting and intended corruption to his senior officers, the AFP failed to investigate.

In 1986 Shadow Attorney General John Dowd questioned Judge Foord's connections with Trimbole 'and other members of the Sydney based mafia' and the judge's handling of a number of major drug cases involving, for the most part, people of Calabrian origin. Dowd told the New South Wales parliament, 'In 1984, [Judge] Foord also heard the case against Francesco Mittiga, who was associated with Trimbole in producing false passports. Foord's three-year bond and $2000 fine was replaced on appeal by a custodial sentence of 12 months.' The Court of Appeal did impose a 12-month sentence but due to delays in hearing the appeal ordered Mittiga to serve one month and then be released on a $1000 two-year good behaviour bond.

Dowd described the allegations concerning Foord's relationship with crime figures and court decisions as 'some of the worst allegations involving organised crime'. He went on, 'These allegations were all the more disturbing because of the number of members of that organisation, including close associates of Trimbole, who had come before Judge Foord and received light sentences.' Earlier, Leader of the Opposition Nick Greiner had told parliament, 'For several years a light sentence before Judge Foord was one of the most lucrative rackets in town, being offered by that class of touts and conmen who thrive on the edges of the law.'

In November 1984 Judge Foord was charged with two counts of attempting to pervert the course of justice in relation to the committal proceedings and trial of Morgan Ryan, a solicitor, old friend and wheeler and dealer for the Labor Party. A year later Foord was acquitted of the charges.

In September 1986 Professor Tony Vinson released a report, commissioned by the government, into allegations concerning the sentencing of drug cases in the District Court between 1980 and 1982. Vinson found that Foord had exercised leniency in dealing with clients of the solicitor Morgan Ryan. Foord immediately stood down from the District Court and resigned on medical grounds.

On 30 April 1996 Joe Tripodi made his inaugural speech in the Legislative Assembly, thanking several people for his success in winning the seat of Fairfield. 'It is with a great sense of pride that I stand in this place as part of a Carr Labor Government,' he said. 'During my election campaign I made many new friends in the local Italian community who assisted me, namely, [names deleted] Tony Mittiga and Pat Sergi. These people are friends I intend to keep for a long time.' Pat Sergi is the person identified by the Woodward Royal Commission as being a drug trafficker and money launderer. The Tony Mittiga referred to is an older brother of Francesco Mittiga, the man convicted of providing Trimbole and the Mr Asia syndicate with false passports. Tripodi later insisted that he had been unaware that Sergi had been named in the royal commission until well after the election.

Pat Sergi's fellow engagement party guest, Harry Lahood, shared his interest in the cannabis trade. In September 1983 the Australian Federal Police received a tip-off from the Dutch police that a major drug syndicate in Amsterdam was planning large-scale cannabis importations into Australia. The Australian buyer was Lahood. According to Bob Bottom in his book *Bugged*, Lahood had visited Amsterdam and been shown 'a cache of 15 tonnes of cannabis in a warehouse'. The Dutch syndicate 'arranged to ship from Pakistan' but kept 'several tonnes [of cannabis] here [in Amsterdam] in stock in case the political situation changes'.

Federal police monitored Lahood and the planned importations. In December 1983 and April 1984 the federal police intercepted cannabis importations totalling 298 kilograms. As the syndicate moved to sell the April consignment—which had been replaced by police with blocks of plaster—they met at Kings Cross where they were arrested.

Lahood pleaded guilty to conspiring to import cannabis resin into Australia between 1 May 1983 and 21 June 1983 and had two other importations—one carried out in December 1983 and the other in April 1984—and a number of charges relating to the supply of the drug taken into account by the court. He was jailed for 24 years. The importations involved 420 kilograms of cannabis resin that had a street value at the time of more than $4.5 million. Lahood was also ordered to forfeit $180,000 under the Commonwealth proceeds of crime legislation. He unsuccessfully challenged the order, arguing that $130,000 in bribes paid to New South Wales police was a cost incurred in financing the importation and should be deducted when considering any profit he might have made from crime.

While Lahood was in jail, a major state drug operation kept surveillance on meetings between members of his family and known 'ndrangheta members in north-west New South Wales.

Lahood was released from Silverwater jail in September 1993. Two and a half years later he was described at the Wood Royal Commission into the New South Wales Police Service as a major drug trafficker with an extensive network that included corrupt police.

Former police detective WS4 said that drug dealer WS1 had told him he was buying heroin from Lahood for $6000 an ounce. Another police rollover, WS14, admitted to being offered $40,000 by Arthur Haddad (the brother of Joe and associate of the Bayehs and Morris George) to assist him and Lahood avoid Customs detection of the 1983 importation. WS14 described how he introduced Haddad and Lahood to Drug Squad detectives, but said the arrangement fell through when the importation was detected by federal police.

WS14 was asked by counsel assisting the commission, Ms Bell, whether he had given evidence at court on behalf of Haddad 'that he [Haddad] had been trying to assist police as an informant' and was not involved in the importation. He answered, 'That's right.'

Ms Bell: 'And you knew that defence to be a complete fabrication?'

WS14: 'Yes.'

Haddad had been arrested at Kings Cross in 1984, along with Lahood and eight other men, by the Federal Police and charged with importing 200 kilograms of cannabis. All received lengthy jail sentences. Haddad was sentenced to 16 years' jail, Lahood to 24 years'.

In late 1997 Harry Lahood, his son Jabour Lahood and Joseph James Melham were arrested and charged with supplying heroin. Jabour Lahood was jailed for four years and Melham was placed on a two-year bond. Harry Lahood beat the charges.

In July 1999 Harry Lahood, his 25-year-old son Anthony, 38-year-old Glenn Anthony Baker, 46-year-old Penny Rompel, and 61-year-old Morris George, all from south-west Sydney, were arrested with others when police seized large quantities of drugs including ecstasy, heroin and amphetamines from houses across western Sydney. The charges arose from a police investigation into the manufacture of methyl-amphetamine in western Sydney and the distribution of drugs across Sydney and Perth. Court records alleged that George and Rompel 'acted as "middle-men" who introduced the [West Australian] purchaser [Anthony] Labianca to various suppliers being Harry Lahood and Glenn Baker ... they also assisted in providing a pick-up point for the movement of the drugs between the source and the couriers.'

In 2001 Morris George was sentenced to four years' jail for supplying a commercial quantity of methylamphetamine. Two similar offences were taken into account in sentencing. George's de facto wife, Ms Penny Rompel, was jailed for three years for similar offences. In 2002 Glenn Anthony Baker was jailed for two years for supplying methylamphetamine. The trial against Labianca did not proceed because he was serving a sentence in Western Australia. Harry Lahood and his son Anthony beat all charges.

In June 2006 *Sydney Morning Herald* journalists Greg Bearup and Kate McClymont reported that Eddie Hayson, 'one of the nation's most controversial punters', was in business with Lahood. According to Bearup and McCly-mont they were partners in Stiletto—'one of Sydney's most successful brothels'. In a later article McClymont and James Pandaram identified the manager of Stiletto as Harry's son Jamelie Lahood. Hayson's stable, Bearup and McClymont wrote, included horses named Sign Nothing, Backstabber, Tampered With, Get to Work and Ring the Police, while Lahood's 'included the colourful runners Federal Agent and Forensic'.

The involvement of a major Lebanese heroin trafficker such as Harry Lahood in the sale of methylamphetamine drew attention to the growing importance of other drugs and other players in Australia's increasingly complex illegal drug trade. As new opportunities arose, new alliances were formed.

Milad Sande, identified during the Wood Royal Commission as a major drug trafficker who dealt directly with Chinese importers, had close ties to both the Bayehs and the Ibrahims. A nephew, Danny Sande, was president of the Bandidos' Blacktown chapter. Another nephew, also named Milad Sande, was an associate of the same outlaw motorcycle gang.

While the influx of US servicemen during the Vietnam War had massively increased the market for heroin in Kings Cross, the flood of Vietnamese migrants after the war had its own effect on the city's illegal drug trade. Vietnamese criminals began by obtaining heroin from Chinese importers but gradually widened their sources of supply to buy from the Barry McCann–George Savvas network and Vietnamese including Sarin 'Mummy' Long and Duong Van Ia (known as Van Duong and called Brother Number Six by his buyers).

By the mid 1990s Cabramatta's Vietnamese street gangs had made it the country's undisputed drug capital. Its streets were awash with heroin and the surplus continued to feed Kings Cross. From the traffickers' point of view Cabramatta had an important advantage over the Cross: neither the suppliers nor the vicious gangs that pushed heroin to the streets formed alliances with corrupt police. As a result Cabramatta was largely ignored both by the Wood Royal Commission into the New South Wales Police Service and by the distracted police executive in Sydney. The easy flow of heroin to Cabramatta continued until a Crime Agencies crackdown in 1999 effectively dismantled the street gangs.

The nationwide heroin shortage, which took hold in 2001, finally choked off the trade in Cabramatta. In doing so, it proved to would-be heroin traffickers the mistake of over-reliance on a single drug. The world of illegal drugs had changed. The market had both expanded and diversified and there was a new generation of consumers hungry for so-called 'party drugs'. New traffickers were entering the market and the old ones would have to learn new tricks.

CHAPTER NINE

Bikies Inc.

Outlaw motorcycle gangs first emerged in the United States during the late 1940s. As they spread across the country, violence usually followed. About 20 years later, they began to appear in Australia. Like their American counterparts, Australian bikie gangs fought ruthlessly for territory and for dominance over rival gangs. Since the mid 1980s there have been more than 100 bikie murders around Australia, together with hundreds of non-fatal shootings and violent attacks on gang clubhouses.

The Comancheros were formed in the western suburbs of Sydney in 1966. The following year saw the arrival of the Hells Angels, also in Sydney. Three years later they were joined by the Rebels, the Nomads, the Gypsy Jokers and the Finks—all in Sydney. The next few years saw the emergence of the Coffin Cheaters in Western Australia and the Black Uhlans in Queensland. By the mid 1990s there were around

50 outlaw motorcycle gangs with 120 chapters spread across Australia. In 2007, internal disputes saw the Nomads split and the emergence of Notorious, a new breed of bikie gang in which not all members rode bikes.

Traditionally, bikie gangs have operated with strict hierarchies at the level of local chapters and less formal hierarchies at the state and national level. In this way the structure resembles a system of tightly controlled franchises rather than a national syndicate. Gangs such as the Bandidos, Gypsy Jokers and Hells Angels are closely aligned with and follow the rules of their US parent gangs.

By the mid 1980s outlaw motorcycle gangs were showing an increasing interest in crime, especially illegal drugs. Violence became not merely a tool of prestige but of profit. In their efforts to increase territory and power, big gangs took over smaller rivals, often by force, and relaxed their traditional membership rules, all in the interests of business. They introduced informal mechanisms in an attempt to mediate quarrels between chapters and gangs.

During the early 1980s tension within the Comancheros led to the creation of a new chapter in the inner Sydney suburb of Birchgrove, but a number of tit-for-tat acts of violence followed. The Birchgrove chapter broke away from the Comancheros and formed the Bandidos. The violence between them only increased. On Father's Day, 2 September 1984, the Comancheros and Bandidos confronted one another at the Viking Tavern at Milperra, in Sydney's southwest. When the shooting was over four Comancheros, two Bandidos and a 15-year-old girl—an innocent bystander—were dead. Another 20 people were injured.

Eventually 31 Comancheros and Bandidos were charged over what became known as the 'Milperra Massacre'. Their trial lasted a year, finishing in mid 1987. As the verdict was announced almost 40 uniformed police sat in the court-room while around 60 heavily armed Tactical Response Group police patrolled the court perimeters. All the accused were convicted of crimes ranging from multiple murders to manslaughter and affray, and all were jailed.

While on remand before the trial several Bandidos teamed up with 33-year-old Arthur Joseph Loveday, who was also doing time in Parklea jail. Loveday had a history with bikie gangs going back to at least the early 1970s when he had been arrested several times for relatively minor offences as a member of the Vikings. Soon, the Bandidos were part of Loveday's crew and Loveday was a Bandido.

Beyond his bikie history, Loveday had a long and violent criminal record that included kidnapping, rape, armed robbery and supplying drugs. In the 1970s he was jailed for several years for armed robbery. A few years later he cut his way through the roof of a prison van taking him from Long Bay to Parramatta jail and escaped. He committed at least two armed hold-ups, netting about $70,000, before being recaptured. A few months later Loveday again tried to escape, but the attempt failed when warders opened fire and Loveday surrendered. In September 1983 he and two other prisoners were found guilty of the May 1981 murder of Parramatta jail inmate Stephen Shipley. All three were given life sentences. Shipley had been serving 20 years for armed robbery and escaping from custody. He had been bashed over the head with an iron bar.

Loveday and his accomplices belonged to a group of around ten inmates known as the Death Squad who, for several years, inflicted a reign of terror on other prison-ers, dispensing 'justice' to those they judged to be guilty of some 'offence'. Loveday remained a jail enforcer until his release. Seven years after his conviction and following several unsuccessful appeals Loveday produced new evidence which resulted in a judicial review of the conviction. The original Shipley case relied heavily on the evidence of another inmate, Allen Cohen, but now there was another inmate whose evidence supported Loveday and discredited Cohen. In 1992 Loveday was granted a pardon for the murder but he still had time to serve on his original sentences.

During the mid 1990s Loveday became friendly with former detective sergeant Roger Rogerson while both were serving sentences in Berrima jail. Rogerson was doing time for perverting the course of justice by giving misleading information to police about the source of money deposited in two bank accounts under false names in 1985. These charges arose out of the reinvestigation of the 1984 shooting of Detective Michael Drury. The introduction had been arranged through a former police colleague of Rogerson's, Raymond 'Chopper' Johnson, who had been pensioned out of the police in 1987 and was now a senior member of the Bandidos.

Ironically, it was another of Rogerson's old colleagues, former detective sergeant Bill Duff, who had been instrumental in securing Loveday's 1983 conviction for the murder of Shipley. (In a further twist, Duff and Loveday had gone to school together in Sydney's south-west.) Later Duff became involved in drug production with a network of amphetamine cooks tied to the Bandidos and other bikie gangs.

Rogerson was released from jail in December 1995. Loveday was released six months later. Less than 15 months after Rogerson's release, police intelligence indicated that he was involved in brokering a deal between Kings Cross crime figures and the Nomads for control of the local drug trade and protection of the pornography and sex industry. One of the criminals was Bandidos associate and longtime criminal Tony Vincent who, along with his two sons and others, was arrested in 2004 after a major police undercover operation and charged with supplying drugs. The then 64-year-old's involvement in organised crime went back to Kings Cross during the 1970s. It was claimed that his various strip joints and sex clubs, including Lady Jane in Market Street in Sydney's central business district, were fronts for his crime activities. At the time of Vincent's arrest, Superintendent Ken McKay of the State Crime Command described him as the leader of a major drug syndicate trafficking large amounts of cocaine in the city centre. McKay called him the patriarch of one of Sydney's biggest crime families.

Twelve months after his arrest Vincent and ten others were charged with an international $150 million super-annuation fraud. In February 2007 Vincent was sentenced to ten years' jail for drug supply. A year later he pleaded guilty to a lesser charge relating to the superannuation fraud and was sentenced to three years' jail.

A 'consultant' to Vincent's Lady Jane club was longtime Kings Cross associate Kostas 'Con' Kontorinakis. In the mid 1990s during the Wood Royal Commission it was alleged that Kontorinakis had been paying police protection money for his strip clubs. On 18 May 1997, not long after the Wood Commission closed its doors, Kontorinakis and two other well-known criminals were sitting outside a café near his club when three Asians in a car they had just stolen at gunpoint pulled up outside the café and fired six shots at the trio. Kontorinakis was not injured but one of his companions was hit in the arm by a bullet that ricocheted off the footpath.

Two years later Kontorinakis and other criminals were targeted by Operation Oslo, a Police Integrity Commission investigation into the payment of protection money to police and former police. Kontorinakis admitted to being the owner of the Eros Cinema in Goulburn Street, Sydney, which ran private peep shows as a front for its illegal activities, and to being a 'consultant' at Lady Jane's. For three years from 1996 Kontorinakis had been paying Rogerson $500 a week protection money.

Rogerson's old Bankstown workmate 'Chopper' Johnson also figured prominently in the inquiry. The commission found that Johnson had been involved in criminal activities with Rogerson and others; that in 1998 they had conspired to break into a property at Austral and steal; that in 1998–99 they had discussed a plan to cultivate cannabis; and that Johnson had leaked confidential information to Rogerson about an inquiry by ICAC into kickbacks to an employee at Liverpool Council.

A few years earlier Johnson had been arrested and charged with amphetamine trafficking. While he was on remand two people found a pistol and more than a quarter of a million dollars in cash and jewellery hidden beneath a rockery in his backyard. They handed their find to police and became witnesses against Johnson.

Although acquitted by a jury of the amphetamine charges, Johnson and two Bandidos were found guilty of intimidating witnesses (two well-known crime figures) and sentenced to jail. However, an appeal quashed the conviction of Johnson and one other—the third did not appeal his sentence. In unrelated proceedings in 2002 Johnson was convicted of assault and possessing a prohibited weapon and sentenced to four months' jail.

The Police Integrity Commission also found that in January 1999 Rogerson and Boris Link, also known as Boris Katic, had driven to Peats Ridge to inspect a property for the purpose of growing a cannabis crop. (Rogerson claimed they had intended to grow vegetables.) Link had plenty of experience in the cultivation of cannabis. Five years earlier he had been jailed for his part in a major drug operation in which large amounts of cannabis were cultivated in rented houses across Sydney.

Rogerson was also found to have tampered with evidence in ICAC hearings and—along with his partner, Anne Melocco—to have given false evidence to the Police Integrity Commission. Both were charged with giving false evidence to the commission. In 2005, five years after lying to the commission, Rogerson was sentenced to two and a half years' jail. His partner was sentenced to two years' periodic detention.

In December 1995, the month Rogerson was released from jail, former detective Bill Duff was introduced to Richard Simpson, an amphetamine 'cook for hire' of more than 15 years' experience, by 34-year-old Craig Haeusler, a longtime eastern suburbs cocaine and amphetamine dealer. Simpson's services were in big demand from bikie groups. At the time Duff was on bail on a charge of supplying heroin. He had been arrested on 14 January 1994 when police pulled over his car and found him in possession of 57 grams of heroin worth an estimated $40,000 and more than $17,000 in cash.

On bail, broke and facing a certain jail sentence, Duff persuaded Simpson to teach him the tricks of the trade. The site for the cook was a workshop at Bankstown Airport controlled by the Bandidos bikie gang. Duff was the organiser. Using precursors provided by Haeusler, Duff and Simpson produced five kilograms of pure methylamphetamine which, when cut, broke down to around 50 kilograms, worth about $5 million on the street. As they prepared for their second cook, Simpson, who was standing his trial for an earlier cook, was convicted and sentenced to jail.

In November 1997 Duff was found guilty of the 1994 heroin supply charge and sentenced to three years. He was on parole in May 1999 when the Special Crime and Internal Affairs branch of the New South Wales Police executed search warrants on a network of suspected amphetamine labs across west and south-west Sydney, including the Bandidos' workshop at Bankstown Airport. Chemical tests confirmed the workshop had been used as an amphetamine laboratory. A large cache of Bandidos weapons, including semi-automatic military rifles, handguns and ammunition, was also seized. Duff was charged over the lab but five years later the charges were dropped.

Another former police officer arrested during the 1999 raids on the drug labs was Bill El Azzi, who had also become an apprentice cook to Simpson. El Azzi had been introduced to Simpson by Duff three years earlier. El Azzi's career in the police was short and colourful. He was a close friend of the Lebanese 'godfather' Frank Hakim and used to call him 'uncle' out of respect. During the Sydney gang wars of the mid 1980s El Azzi was charged with conspiring with Victor Camilleri and Kevin Theobold to murder Michael John Sayers and later with possessing cannabis and importing heroin into Australia, firearms and related offences. He beat all charges. In 1987 he was dismissed from the police for misconduct, only to be reinstated on appeal 18 months later.

El Azzi's luck finally ran out with his arrest on drug charges in 1999. Four years and more than 40 court appearances later he was convicted of conspiring to manufacture amphetamines and sentenced to seven years' jail.

Simpson and the other 'cooks' with whom Duff and El Azzi had become involved were part of a loose confederation of 'cooks for hire', often to bikie gangs. The syndicate had used around 50 different laboratory sites, most of which were located around Sydney. It is estimated that this confederation, which was largely broken by the 1999 raids, had over the previous decade been responsible for producing and distributing more than 200 kilograms of pure methylamphetamine, which translated to 2000 kilograms of street-quality 'meth' worth around $200 million.

On his release from Berrima in June 1996, Loveday became a Bandidos enforcer and president of the gang's New South Wales north coast chapter. His power base increased in February 1998 when he married Catherine Vella, a cousin of the multimillionaire national president of the Rebels outlaw motorcycle gang, Alex Vella. Among the wedding guests was Roger Rogerson. The marriage cemented the partnership between the two gangs.

Vella had taken over the leadership of the Rebels in 1972 at the age of nineteen. A bricklayer by trade, Vella was driving a Rolls Royce by 1990. The car, he explained to the *Sun-Herald*, was 'a wedding gift from a lot of friends'. The gang itself had also prospered. Its clubhouse complex at Austral in Sydney's west was set on three hectares. It had cabins for visiting club members, a bar, an auditorium and a swimming pool.

Vella has a long police record but few convictions. His

only drug conviction relates to about $15,000 worth of marijuana found in his house in 1990. Vella claimed the drug did not belong to him. It had been left there by a friend who had been minding the house, he said, but the jury did not believe him and in 1995 he was convicted of possessing a trafficable quantity of marijuana and sentenced to two nights a week in jail and two days a week of community service at the Eastern Creek raceway for 18 months.

Vella had millions of dollars in assets seized by the National Crime Authority and New South Wales Crime Commission in the mid 1990s but was allowed to get them back by paying a $650,000 settlement to the commission.

His connections and influence were not limited to outlaw motorcycle gangs. In April 2001 Graham 'Croc' Palmer died and was buried at the Forest Lawn Memorial Garden Cemetery in Leppington, 55 kilometres south-west of Sydney. More than 500 mourners attended his funeral. Members of the Rebels motorcycle club wearing full colours escorted his coffin to the graveside. Vella was one of the speakers. He read a poem he had written about Palmer. Among the mourners was Roger Rogerson.

During the 1960s and '70s Palmer—who featured in a number of inquiries and reports into organised crime and drug trafficking—had been a well-known illegal casino operator and associate of Lennie McPherson and George Freeman. Like many involved in the world of illegal gambling, Palmer's luck changed with the closure of the casinos. By the early 1980s he had joined others in the importation of seven tonnes of hashish through Darwin. At the time it was Australia's largest importation. The organiser was Danny Chubb, who was murdered in November 1984 in a hit arranged by Arthur 'Neddy' Smith at the start of Sydney's gang war. A year after Chubb's murder, Palmer and others were arrested and jailed over the importation.

Arthur Loveday consolidated his large and growing crime network by making the `ndrangheta's Francesco 'Fat Frank' Barbaro the godparent of his twin children, thereby establishing a working relationship, based on family ties, between the Bandidos and Rebels and the Calabrian Mafia. Several Italian crime figures have since been admitted to the Rebels as patched members.

In 2002 Loveday and Barbaro were arrested for trafficking in ecstasy tablets. In 2006 Barbaro was convicted and sentenced to four years' jail. Loveday escaped conviction when the prosecution did not proceed with the charges.

Loveday was not the only Bandido cementing relationships with the Calabrian Mafia's Fat Frank. Since at least the 1990s Loveday's colleague, 32-year-old Rodney 'Hooksey' Monk, president of the Sydney chapter of the Bandidos, had been involved in large-scale amphetamine deals with Barbaro. Monk made lots of money with Fat Frank but that didn't stop him taking advantage of other opportunities when they arose. He became a major cocaine distributor for Shayne Hatfield and worked as a standover man for Michael Hurley's Coogee Mob and for other drug traffickers in Sydney's eastern suburbs. During the last six months of 2004 alone, Monk acted as middle-man in the sale of 25 kilograms of cocaine by Hatfield to a network of around 12 buyers for the Bandidos.

On the evening of 20 April 2006 Monk was shot dead in a laneway in East Sydney by Russell Oldham, the 39-year-old former sergeant-at-arms for the Bandidos. Oldham was a murderer and drug trafficker. More than 150 Bandidos and members of other outlaw motorcycle gangs wearing full colours attended Monk's funeral. Speaking at the funeral, Arthur Loveday described himself as Monk's protégé. Three weeks later Oldham walked into the water at Balmoral Beach on Sydney's north shore and shot himself in the head.

By the late 1990s other bikie gangs had emulated the Bandidos by forming alliances with the Calabrian Mafia. The Romeo branch of the 'ndrangheta was closely tied to Adelaide chapters of the Gypsy Jokers and Hells Angels, and through them to chapters in Western Australia, Victoria and New South Wales. Another South Australian 'ndrangheta crime family, well known to law enforcement agencies, developed close links with the Gypsy Jokers, Rebels, Finks and Hells Angels. These alliances revolved around the drug trade—amphetamines, in particular.

In extending their criminal operations, the bikies cultivated other groups besides the Calabrian Mafia. At the height of the drug turf wars of the early 2000s, the Comancheros demonstrated their authority with Lebanese crime gangs by negotiating a peace deal between the Karam gang and the smaller gang of Tom Atoui. In December 2005, in front of Sydney's assembled media, the Comancheros and Maroubra's infamous Bra Boys met and called for (some say declared) peace after race riots and revenge attacks in Cronulla and other beachside suburbs.

The Comancheros were able to intervene in the Karam gang feud and the Cronulla riots because for a decade they had been actively recruiting criminals of Middle Eastern backgrounds as members. With the Bra Boys presenting themselves as Australia's most 'multicultural' surfer group, the Comancheros could point to the high proportion of Lebanese in their gang.

On 8 February 1995 the National Crime Authority (NCA), Queensland Police and Victoria Police raided a number of drug labs near Brisbane and a disused one at Wallan East near Melbourne. The NCA described it as the world's biggest amphetamine bust, announcing that more than 300 kilograms of 'speed' (a form of methylamphetamine also known as 'goey' or 'whiz') worth around $500 million on the streets had been produced at the labs. Six people received sentences of up to 20 years, while dozens more were arrested in the coming months in a crackdown on the broader network. The labs had been providing speed to the Hells Angels and truckies, mostly in Victoria. The principal, Garry Maguire, was not a bikie, but the Hells Angels provided him with protection and muscle and knew him as 'the old bloke'. Maguire knew what the Angels expected in return—a reliable supply of high-quality speed and financial support for gang members who were jailed for their part in the operation.

Maguire's business came undone when the NCA stumbled across it while investigating links between the Hells Angels and Melbourne and Griffith-based members of the `ndrangheta. A Calabrian mafioso had sold the Angels as many as 300 untraceable mobile telephones.

In July 1996 the national president of the Bandidos, former Nomad Mick 'Chaos' Kulakowski, flew to the US to take part in peace talks between the Bandidos and Hells Angels. As part of the Bandidos' international leadership team the 40-year-old Kulakowski had brokered an end to a gang war over drug and prostitution networks that saw 11 Scandinavian members murdered. Among the arms used by the feuding gangs were missiles and anti-tank weapons.

Twelve months later Kulakowski and two other Bandidos

were shot in the head and killed in the basement of the Black-market Café nightclub in Redfern by two members of the rival Rebels outlaw motorcycle gang. A fourth Bandido was wounded. The cause of the shooting was the discovery that a woman had been sleeping with two bikies—not usually a problem, but in this case one was a Bandido and the other was a Rebel. Forty-two-year-old Bruce Malcolm Harrison and 36-year-old Constantine Georgiou were eventually convicted of the murders and jailed.

The late 1990s and early 2000s witnessed an upsurge in violence by outlaw motorcycle gangs across Australia with more than 20 murders, bombings, arson attacks, disappearances and shootings in 20 months. The murder of Don Hancock, the 64-year-old former chief of the Western Australian Police Criminal Investigation Branch, was the most sensational.

Two years earlier Hancock and a mate, 63-year-old Lou Lewis, had been killed when a bomb planted in Hancock's car exploded in a Perth street. The noise was heard more than eight kilometres away. Hancock had retired from the police in 1994 and moved to Ora Banda, a small town about 70 kilometres north-west of Kalgoorlie, where he bought a pub. On 1 October 2000 he confronted several drunken Gypsy Jokers and ordered the gang out of the pub after one of them started swearing at his daughter, Alison. An hour later Billy Grierson was shot dead as he sat next to 33-year-old Gypsy Jokers sergeant-at-arms Graeme 'Slim' Slater at the gang's nearby camp site. The Jokers accused Hancock of killing Grierson and vowed revenge. After his pub was blown up and his home gutted in an arson attack, Hancock fled with his family back to Perth. But even in Perth he was kept under close surveillance by the Jokers.

Gypsy Joker Sidney 'Snot' Reid pleaded guilty to the murder of Hancock and Lewis and was sentenced to life with a minimum of 15 years' jail. He rolled and gave evidence against Slater. Reid admitted planting the bomb under the front passenger seat of Lewis's station wagon, claiming that Slater had given him the ammonium nitrate for the bomb and had later used a mobile phone to detonate it—whispering 'Rest in peace, Billy' as he did so. The problem for the Crown was that Reid was a self-confessed liar, drug dealer and thief and had knowledge of explosives. The jury didn't believe him and acquitted Slater of two wilful murder charges and the lesser charges of murder and manslaughter.

Despite Slater's acquittal, Hancock's murder was a Gypsy Jokers' hit: Hancock was the target, his friend Lewis an innocent bystander. In sentencing Reid, Justice Anderson described the murders as:

> ... a savage, terrorist-style crime, carefully and meticulously planned, involving many days of surveillance and a very considerable amount of preparation, including the manufacture of a powerful bomb capable of being detonated remotely. It was a cold-blooded, premeditated, planned bomb attack intended to take the life of one man for reasons of revenge without regard for who else might be killed or maimed in the process.

Earlier in the year Reid had been the key witness in the Perth murder trial of Gary White, an associate of the Gypsy Jokers. In that trial White was jailed for life for murdering an amphetamine user whom he claimed owed him money.

On 20 February 2000, in an attempt to stem rising

violence and territorial disputes between South Australia's Bandidos and Gypsy Jokers, a meeting was convened on neutral territory. Around ten representatives of each gang flew into Sydney airport for a meeting in the Qantas Domestic Lounge Captain's Room. Gang 'security' patrolled the airport, keeping an eye out for the police.

The meeting was businesslike. A 'retired' Bandidos president from Queensland had flown down as chairman. He argued that the markets for crime in New South Wales were big enough for everybody. In South Australia, however, the markets were much smaller and they would have to reach agreement on territory and profit sharing. Conflict was bad for business, he told them: it attracted increased police attention, destroyed market opportunities, reduced profits and put the gangs themselves at risk. He emphasised that the gangs were running businesses, and the purpose of those businesses was profits and survival. There had to be discipline.

They discussed tactics for undermining police investigations by making them so expensive that they would be shut down. Take your time, create suspicion that forces the police to commit additional resources, particularly after 5 pm when they have to pay overtime, and then 'just run them around for a few weeks'. The 'bean counters' will step in and stop the operation and then you can go about your business. It was a tactic, said the chairman, that had served him well in the past.

The meeting went on to discuss the extent to which the warring gangs were armed and the weapons they had in their possession, including rocket launchers and other military-style firearms. As described in Chapter 7, a few years later the Lebanese crime gangs in Sydney's south-west also acquired rocket launchers which had been stolen from the Australian

Defence Force and sold through the Rebels. In 2006 a bikie source claimed that the Hells Angels in the Northern Territory were manufacturing home-made rocket launchers.

A peace agreement was reached and the Bandidos returned to Adelaide on the next available plane. Not so the Gypsy Jokers, who broke out the cocaine, sniffing lines off the table in the Captain's Room at the airport. Two Gypsy Jokers were arrested in possession of an ounce of cocaine and more than $25,000 in cash.

During the late 1990s and early 2000s there were several strikes on bikie gangs across New South Wales. After the arrest of Pyrmont chapter president Felix Lyle, the State Crime Commission kept more than $3 million worth of Bandido assets in Sydney. Over an 18-month period around 30 bikie amphetamine laboratories were raided and members of the Bandidos, Nomads, Gypsy Jokers and Life and Death gangs were arrested.

In late 1998 Crime Agencies and Hunter Region police began an investigation into the Newcastle chapter of the Nomads and its then president, 36-year-old Brett 'Alvey' Taylor. Taylor learned of the investigation when a confidential police document was accidentally sent to him by a federal agency. Police responded by raiding the gang's clubhouse and several homes in the area, uncovering valuable evidence of the chapter's involvement in the drug trade and the scale of its distribution networks. A pound of methylamphetamine was seized and confiscation proceedings over significant assets were begun by the New South Wales Crime Commission, but the investigation stalled as the Nomads took extra precautions to thwart police surveillance.

The police waited two years before relaunching the investigation. This time results came quick and fast. Twenty-eight-year-old Richard Walsh, the chapter's sergeant-at-arms, was identified as the head of the network, actively supported by his partner Melinda Love. In addition to running a major drug network for the gang (his most profitable criminal activity), Walsh was also implicated in possessing and supplying weapons, stealing and rebirthing motor vehicles and earth-moving equipment, and handling stolen property. He was buying a pound of 'pure' amphetamine every three weeks, which was cut by Love to produce ten pounds. This was then sold to middle-men and on to street dealers. Walsh sold mostly to local chapter members and to the Nomads' Sydney chapter, while Love's network of about 75 buyers comprised non-bikie dealers spread across Newcastle. The source of the amphetamine was 33-year-old Todd Little, a senior member of the Gold Coast chapter of the Nomads.

Over several months the supply and distribution of amphetamines was monitored by police. On 24 September 2001 Walsh and 29-year-old Robert Zdravkovic, another Newcastle Nomad, were arrested at Murwillumbah. They had just bought another pound of amphetamine and were returning to Newcastle. Little's home at Terranora near Tweed Heads was raided. A quantity of amphetamines, $145,000 in cash and multiple packets of Glucodin used for cutting the amphetamines were seized, together with several loaded guns. Storage sheds at nearby Murwillumbah, leased by Little in a false name, were raided and found to have been used as the laboratory for manufacturing the drug. Bulk quantities of amphetamines in various stages of production, and with a street value of around $55 million, were seized. At another storage shed in Tweed Heads, also leased by Little, police seized a quantity of precursor chemicals and a large quantity of weapons including handguns and military rifles and silencers. Explosives and detonators were also seized.

Walsh's Newcastle home, a storage shed and business premises used by him to conduct his drug deals were raided. Several guns were seized along with other evidence that confirmed his drug operations. Walsh, who was only one of Little's distributors, had been a major trafficker since around 1997. During that time, police estimated he had supplied about 450 kilograms of speed with a street value of around $200 million. At the time of his arrest Walsh was using up to $6000 worth of the drug each week and gambling away another $10,000 to $20,000.

As well as seizing around $7 million in assets, the police operation resulted in the arrest of 52 people, of whom around 20 were principals in the drug network. Love rolled and was given immunity from prosecution in return for giving evidence against her colleagues.

In May 2002 Brett Taylor, on whom the original 1998 investigation had centred, was extradited from Queensland and charged with supplying amphetamines over a four-year period up to September 2001. Two years later a jury acquitted Taylor of the charge.

In 2005 Walsh was sentenced to 32 years' jail for supplying speed. He was also convicted of numerous other crimes, including firearms offences, for which he was sentenced to a concurrent 13 years and eight months' jail.

Little was sentenced to 22 years' jail for manufacturing and supplying speed.

In September 2001 the Commonwealth, South Australian and Western Australian governments had issued a media release agreeing to a crackdown on outlaw motorcycle gangs in South Australia and Western Australia. 'The lawless activities of outlaw motorcycle gangs in our two States pose a significant risk to public safety and security', the release said.

Commenting on outlaw motorcycle gangs in its 2001–02 Annual Report, the New South Wales Crime Commission noted:

> OMCGs are now more likely to involve professional associates, such as accountants, and are increasingly involving themselves in diverse 'legitimate' business interests. They are also now more likely to involve other criminal networks, and there has also been a move towards multicultural membership, which was previously contrary to club rules. Associations with Asian and Australian/Lebanese gangs, for the supply of drugs and firearms, are now more common.

Over the next five years police recorded dozens of violent crimes, including several murders, involving bikies.

In May 2004 police raided 28 properties across New South Wales, South Australia and Queensland, arresting 21 members of outlaw motorcycle gangs. They seized guns, ammunition, other prohibited weapons, amphetamines and chemical precursors, as well as evidence of clandestine drug laboratories. The network, which cultivated and trafficked in cannabis and manufactured and sold amphetamines, involved the Hells Angels, Gypsy Jokers, Rebels, Nomads and Finks, and netted amphetamines and cannabis worth $23 million. Drugs worth several times that amount are believed to have been sold by the network.

The operational centre of the drug network was the country city of Dubbo in the central west region of New South

Wales. Located at the intersection of the Mitchell, Newell and Golden highways, Dubbo was an ideal distribution point for an interstate drug network. As Detective Superintendent Ken McKay observed, 'Dubbo is on the main route where these drugs were being transported to and from South Australia and Queensland.' The drugs were sold to and distributed by truck drivers operating on routes linking these states.

In its 2005–06 Annual Report the Australian Crime Commission described Australia's outlaw motorcycle gangs as being involved in:

> ... a large number of serious and organised criminal activities designed to generate income and protect gang interests. Such offences include murder, firearms, illicit drug supply and production, extortion and prostitution, serious assault, sexual assault, arson, robbery, theft, vehicle rebirthing, receiving stolen property, fraud, money laundering, corruption and bribing officials and perverting the course of justice.

In the same report the commission warned that the involvement of outlaw motorcycle gangs in outwardly legitimate business enterprises 'is potentially [having a severe adverse effect] on a number of key market sectors in Australia, including finance, transport, private security, entertainment, natural resources and construction'.

Around the same time, South Australian Premier Mike Rann announced that the four-year police crackdown on bikies in that state had resulted in almost 3000 arrests, the seizure of 300 firearms, large quantities of cannabis, amphetamines, ecstasy and fantasy, as well as assets worth around $2.7 million. But while justifiably celebrating the achievement of taking 300 firearms off the streets of South Australia, the premier failed to mention that in 1999 more than 500 weapons, including large-calibre handguns, were stolen during the home invasion of a firearms dealer at Peterborough, 250 kilometres north of Adelaide.

Nor was South Australian Attorney General Michael Atkinson as confident about the bikie crackdown as the premier. He told the *7.30 Report* that, according to police, 'eight out of ten licensed venues in the [Adelaide] central business district [still] have crowd controllers supplied to them by companies associated with outlaw motorcycle gangs.' The security was believed to be a front that provided protection for the sale of drugs inside the clubs.

In mid 2005 a series of assaults, shootings and arson attacks accompanied the Rebels' attempt to muscle in on the Nomad rackets of drugs, protection and nightclub security on the Gold Coast. Peace was restored—at least temporarily—after mediation by senior members of both clubs.

Unfortunately, neither the Finks nor Bandidos was part of the peace deal. In September 2006 the Australian Crime Commission confirmed that these gangs were involved in a major push into tattoo parlours, motorcycle shops, money lending and security firms across Surfers Paradise, where several nightclubs and bars already had close links with bikie gangs. As the Finks and Bandidos moved aggressively into new territories, the Rebels and Nomads were drawn into the violence. One of the first casualties was their 2005 peace compact.

In February 2007 Bandidos and Rebels clashed near Bribie Island, 25 kilometres north of Brisbane. Shots were fired and men were beaten with baseball bats. A few weeks later there was an arson attack on the Rebels' clubhouse in Brisbane. Tit-for-tat shootings and arson attacks continued, causing Queensland's shadow attorney general, Mark McArdle, to declare that escalating violence was an issue of 'enormous concern'.

Meanwhile the *Sunday Mail* quoted the state's police minister, Judy Spence, as saying that hospitals and charities were giving bikie gangs a 'veneer of respectability' by accepting their donations. The newspaper noted caustically that while the police minister was issuing her statement of concern, her police were being hired and paid to patrol a Bandidos' charity day on the Sunshine Coast (it was the fourth year the Bandidos had run the event). The contradiction was acknowledged by the Bandidos, whose sergeant-at-arms and chief organiser told the *Sunday Mail* that it was a 'double standard' for the police minister to criticise donations and then accept payments from a motorcycle gang. 'We had to pay them [the police] to be here,' he said. 'They were quite happy to take our money [around $3000].' About 100 Bandidos in full colours were among at least 8000 people who attended the event.

While bikie gangs in other states at least paid lip service to the idea of coexistence, in New South Wales rivalry invariably led to violence.

On 23 November 2005 the young Milad Sande—who four years earlier had been involved in the sale of rocket launchers stolen from the Australian army—was found dead in Cromwell Park, Malabar, in Sydney's south-east. He had been shot in the head. Sande had just delivered $2 million worth of pseudoephedrine to the Bandidos' Downtown chapter for what was to have been a joint Bandidos and Nomads amphetamine cook.

Milad's cousin, Danny Sande, was president of the Bandidos' Blacktown chapter. During the 1980s–90s his uncle (also named Milad) had been one of Sydney's biggest heroin dealers. The older Milad was also well connected with bikie gangs. The Sandes were good friends with the Nomads' chief, Sam Ibrahim, and his brother Michael, a Nomads associate. Through Sam Ibrahim the Nomads had a significant criminal presence in Kings Cross.

Milad Sande's murder triggered a violent joint response by the Bandidos and the Nomads. Both had been ripped off in a double-cross and both stood to lose money and 'respect'. Several Bandidos believed to have been involved in the double-cross, including Felix Lyle, the Bandidos' Downtown chapter president, were taken to one of the gang's clubhouses, where they were beaten and tortured in the presence of the Bandidos' Sydney chapter president, Rodney Monk. They were stripped of their colours and expelled from the Bandidos. Monk took over. In February 2006 one of the former Bandidos was again kidnapped and tortured. Three hundred thousand dollars is rumoured to have been paid to the Bandidos and Nomads for his return.

In June 2009, four years after Sande's murder, the government issued a $100,000 reward for information leading to the arrest of those responsible, but the reward has not been claimed and the murder remains unsolved.

Despite the beatings of Lyle and the others, neither club was satisfied. Lyle was secretly a part-owner of the trendy Gas nightclub, near Sydney's Central railway station. As a result of his expulsion he was no longer a Bandido. Lyle was told to employ Nomads as security for his club and to pay what they demanded. Things were getting too hot and too expensive for Lyle. Before long he sold the club.

The new owners looked elsewhere for security and the Nomads did not appreciate the rebuff. On 25 August three men dressed in black and wearing balaclavas fired more than 30 shots at the club, using a shotgun, rifle and pistol. Two hundred terrified patrons scrambled for cover. No one was injured but a message had been delivered to the club owners. Damage to the club was estimated at around $25,000. It was the fifth bikie shooting in a Sydney nightclub in eight months.

About the same time Sam Ibrahim, leader of the Nomads' Parramatta chapter, issued a public challenge through the *Sunday Telegraph* to fight Rebels president Alex Vella to the death. In an article headlined 'Bikie call to arms' Ibrahim was quoted taunting Vella, 'take me on, just me and you ... guns or fists, anywhere, anytime'. According to Ibrahim the challenge was made in a bid to end an escalating turf war and to avoid shedding innocent blood. Vella did not take up the offer.

During December 2006 Sam Ibrahim; the Nomads' national president, Scott Orrock; Orrock's predecessor, Greg Craig; and the president of the Nomads' Sydney West chapter, Paul Griffin, were arrested in Sydney and charged with crimes ranging from attempted murder and assault inflicting grievous bodily harm to firearms and affray. The charges stemmed from the 32-year jail sentence imposed on Richard Walsh. Walsh had been on 'Nomad business' when arrested. The Parramatta chapter accused the Newcastle chapter of not providing the obligatory financial assistance to support Walsh's family.

A meeting was arranged at the Nomads' Newcastle clubhouse at 15 Chin Chen Street, Islington, on Sunday 12 September 2004, to resolve the dispute. On that day more than 20 members of the Parramatta and Sydney West chapters rode in convoy to Newcastle in full colours. As soon as he entered the compound Ibrahim made his intentions clear: there was going to be no discussion. Ibrahim pulled his gun and shot Dale Campton, the sergeant-at-arms of the Newcastle chapter, in both legs, then shot at the legs of Mark Chrystie, the Newcastle club president, but missed. He aimed at Leo Bagnall's chest and pulled the trigger several times, but the gun jammed. As Ibrahim shouted for another gun, Orrock aimed at Bagnall and shot him in the right leg.

After the shooting stopped, Newcastle gang members were herded into their clubhouse. Campton was bashed and stripped of his colours. Several Harley Davidsons were taken as part payment for the money owed to the Walsh family. Ibrahim demanded a further $70,000, supposedly to pay for Walsh's legal costs.

The Sydney visitors split up and left the clubhouse before police arrived. As they made their way back to Sydney, about 15 of the gang were stopped on the freeway near the small village of Mooney Mooney, near the Hawkesbury River, by heavily armed police wearing bulletproof vests. Five were arrested for relatively minor offences.

The demands for payment continued throughout 2005 and into 2006. On 19 April 2006 Griffin telephoned Campton and threatened, 'You've got to come up with the money ... it has been fucking 18 months and you haven't paid a cent.' It was too much for Campton: he made the decision to roll.

On 28 June 2006 Campton met Griffin and asked, '... why did Sam do that to me [shoot me]?'

The response, 'I'm not Sam, ask Critter [Mark Chrystie].'

A month later Campton was still making excuses for not paying the money. In another telephone conversation, Griffin told him to 'sell the fucking house to pay it'.

Police continued to record their meetings and conversations. If it wasn't bad enough for the bikies that one of their sergeants-at-arms had turned informer, his evidence was supported by the Newcastle gang's high-tech security systems—systems that were intended to keep police at bay. Their closed-circuit television and audio monitors had caught much of the affray and the recordings were seized by police. Sam Ibrahim and Scott Orrock were charged; bail was refused.

Despite the electronic evidence available and the rollovers, other Nomads were not keen to testify against their attackers or to explain their own involvement. In October 2008, after almost two years in jail, Ibrahim and two other Nomads, including national president Scott Orrock, were acquitted. A few weeks later Ibrahim was released on bail. As part of his bail conditions he was barred from associating with any Nomads or visiting any Nomads clubhouse.

In 2007, while Ibrahim was in jail, the Nomads' Parramatta chapter which he founded and led disbanded after the firebombing of its Granville clubhouse—part of an escalating bikie war in New South Wales.

On 15 March about 20 armed and hooded bikers, believed to be members of the Comancheros, forced their way into the Mr Goodbar club in Paddington, punching patrons and club employees, smashing glasses and bottles, trashing the club and firing shots into the ceiling. Among the 150 patrons were Fadi Khalifeh, a bodyguard of John Ibrahim, members of the Bra Boys, including Koby Abberton, and models and television stars attending a private function.

Sydney Morning Herald journalists Kate McClymont and David Braithwaite reported that 'Witnesses said Mr Khalifeh had been outside the nightclub when he was dragged indoors by several of the hooded men, then assaulted.'

The same month, the Rebels' new clubhouse at Wickham in Newcastle was the target of an arson attack.

Three weeks later Scott Orrock's Skin Deep tattoo parlour in the inner Sydney suburb of Newtown was shot up during the night. Orrock—who by this time was on bail over the shootings and assaults at the gang's Newcastle clubhouse—told the *Daily Telegraph* that he was 'really fucking angry' and challenged those who'd shot up his shop and burnt the clubhouse to meet him face-to-face.

Less than a week later, in the early hours of the morning, around 30 members of the Nomads and Bandidos outlaw motorcycle gangs confronted each other in Sydney's Darling Harbour. Shots were fired. By the time police arrived, the bikies had gone.

On 17 April the Bandidos' clubhouse in inner-city Petersham was sprayed with gunfire. A fortnight later the Comancheros' clubhouse in neighbouring Marrickville was torched. The next night two men were seriously wounded in a drive-by shooting outside the Nomad-linked nightclub DMC (previously known as the UN) in Oxford Street, Paddington. This was followed two nights later by an attempted fire-bombing of the Bandidos' Petersham clubhouse. Club members refused police permission to enter and preferred to stay inside the burning clubhouse rather than come out. The fire was extinguished and no one was seriously injured.

The violence that was rampant in New South Wales was spilling over to other states. In Victoria the Bandidos' Breakwater clubrooms, near Geelong, were riddled with bullets on

28 February 2007. On 2 April a man with links to the Rebels was shot at Whittington near Geelong. The next few months saw seven tit-for-tat shootings around Geelong and an arson attack on the Rebels' headquarters. Victoria Police claimed the violence was part of a bikie turf war being fought in Australia's east coast states.

The bikies were also consolidating their power in other ways. In September 2006 the *West Australian* newspaper reported an investigation by Victorian police which revealed that 'motorcycle gangs were major players in the drug trade, gun running and tax avoidance, and had attacked businesses that had cooperated with police, invested heavily in the Australian mining industry, intimidated potential rival bidders at property auctions and infiltrated confidential government computer records.'

In Western Australia, both the police and government expressed concern at the involvement of outlaw motorcycle gangs in the amphetamine trade and at their infiltration of legitimate businesses—often using standover tactics and intimidation—to launder profits. In 2004 the Western Australian police commissioner sought the removal of fortifications to the Gypsy Jokers' clubhouse in an industrial area of Maddington in Perth. The clubhouse had a concrete front wall, surveillance cameras, steel doors and modified timber doors. The commissioner claimed that the clubhouse was 'habitually used as a place of resort by members of a class of people a significant number of whom may reasonably be suspected to be involved in organised crime'. The Gypsy Jokers defended the fortification of their clubhouse as 'necessary because the area had high rates of burglary and car theft'. It was a novel but unsuccessful defence. The court supported the commissioner, who listed 59 members of the chapter, all but one of whom had a criminal record, and 130 charges against members or associates.

In November 2006, during a debate in the Western Australian Legislative Assembly on the threat of outlaw motorcycle gangs, the deputy speaker said:

> I received a letter ... from the member for Midland in the following terms —That this House expresses grave concern that the war currently being waged on the streets of Perth between rival outlaw motorcycle gangs threatens public safety and holds law enforcement in contempt ... The House notes that outlaw motorcycle gangs are heavily involved in organised crime, including the manufacture and distribution of hard drugs, extortion and standover tactics.

In a series of police raids carried out in the months preceding the parliamentary debate, 44 search warrants were executed on bikie clubhouses and homes. Fifty unlicensed firearms including pistols, shotguns, rifles and machine guns; 16,000 rounds of ammunition; 10 sticks of power gel, detonators and other assorted weapons, including replica guns, batons, swords and large baseball bats; and drugs including cannabis, ecstasy, amphetamines and LSD were seized.

Bikies had been major weapons suppliers to crime gangs since the mid 1990s. In January 2007 Natalie O'Brien of the *Australian* newspaper reported on leaked secret police intelligence reports from the late 1990s onwards about the theft of Australian Defence Force weapons from the National Storage Distribution Centre at Moorebank, about 30 kilometres south-west of Sydney. The stolen weapons included machine guns and automatic assault rifles. According to the reports, '[S]taff in the armoury' were involved in the theft of military firearms and some staff 'were in collusion with outlaw motorcycle gangs'. The New South Wales Police Executive was warned of the thefts and risks posed on at least four occasions: twice during 1998, once during 2000 and once during 2001. O'Brien reported that internal navy and military investigations during the late 1990s found that the theft of military weapons had begun in the 1980s.

One week after O'Brien's article in the *Australian* the Australian Crime Commission announced the formation of a national task force to 'better guide national investigative and policy action' against bikies as a result of a 'significant expansion in the activities of outlaw motorcycle gangs in 2005–6'. According to the commission, outlaw motorcycle gangs were involved in a wide range of criminal activities including murder, drug manufacturing and trafficking, firearms trafficking, extortion, prostitution, robbery, theft, fraud, money laundering and rebirthing of stolen motor vehicles. The head of the Australian Crime Commission, Alastair Milroy, declared, 'OMCG criminal activity presents a significant threat to Australia and its interests.'

Within weeks, 200 police from Queensland and New South Wales, as well as officers from Queensland's Crime and Misconduct Commission and the Australian Crime Commission, raided about 50 properties in Byron Bay, Tweed Heads, the Gold Coast, Logan, Brisbane, Ipswich and Redcliffe. All the properties were connected with the manufacture and distribution of amphetamines by the Gold Coast, Ipswich and Byron Bay chapters of the Nomads outlaw motorcycle gang. More than 20 people linked to the Nomads were arrested and charged with offences including drug trafficking, producing dangerous drugs and possessing concealable firearms.

The operation had been planned before the Australian Crime Commission revealed the formation of a bikie task force but it was a convenient arrangement: a highly publicised announcement followed by a highly publicised police swoop in two states.

Governments and police forces across Australia were beginning to feel the heat of various reports highlighting the relentless growth of bikie gangs and bikie crime. In its 2005–06 Annual Report the Australian Crime Commission reported that there were 35 outlaw motorcycle gangs across Australia, 18 of which operated in New South Wales, 17 in Victoria, and 11 and eight in Queensland and South Australia respectively. Between two and six gangs were identified in each of the other states and territories.

According to the commission, these gangs were broken up into 212 chapters. More than 26 new chapters had been established in recent years—13 in New South Wales and six in Queensland alone. Gang membership had increased to a total of 3500 full-patch members. (The New South Wales Crime Commission has estimated that prospective members, nominees and associates together constitute about ten times the number of full-patch members.)

This increase is part of an ongoing cycle of growth and decline in bikie numbers. In the late 1980s there were around 21 outlaw motorcycle gangs operating across Australia. The next half decade saw dramatic growth. By 1994 there were 52 outlaw motorcycle gangs, though gang membership numbers were not known. This was followed by an almost decade-long decline in gang numbers before another resurgence began in the late 1990s–early 2000s. That resurgence continues to this day.

Adding to the pressure on law enforcement bodies was the federal Parliamentary Joint Committee (PJC) on the Australian Crime Commission. A short time before the release of the Australian Crime Commission's report, the PJC announced its 'Inquiry into the Future Impact of Serious and Organised Crime on Australian Society'. The issue of outlaw motorcycle gangs would be raised and the commission would be asked what it was doing about the threat.

On 30 April 2007 the committee's deputy chair, Duncan Kerr, speaking in Perth, said:

One of the things that has troubled me about evidence over a decade on this committee ... is that we are constantly hearing that outlaw motorcycle gangs are the driving force for the distribution of amphetamines, and that they are growing in power and influence. They have been the subject of references for the former National Crime Authority. They continue to be a focus of the Australian Crime Commission ... It seems odd that a group that self-identifies its membership in such an overt way would be so difficult to contain. I am puzzled at the failures of, I suppose, a decade of law enforcement to really get a grip on outlaw motorcycle gangs ... On the face of it, it is surprising that a group that stands out in such an identified way is not capable of being addressed in a pretty straightforward manner.

On the subject of bikie crime in Perth, Kerr said:

We know that Western Australia has been a place where outlaw motorcycle gangs have really consolidated and built a strong presence. You do have the legislation that allows you to knock down fortresses. You now have both state and federal coercive powers. They have been applied against outlaw motorcycle gangs, and yet we have this constant repetition of this being a growing rather than a reducing area of concern.

The next day, at a public hearing in Melbourne, Kerr went further:

The AFP and the Australian Crime Commission all assert that their efforts are designed to disrupt the toughest of the tough in terms of the organised crime networks. Yet we constantly hear that we are getting more robust and resilient organised crime groups. We have not had much capacity, for example, in the outlaw motorcycle gang area. A group which self-identifies should be pretty easy to pick on the streets. Even with that group we are told that they are expanding and that they control the distribution of amphetamines. What was an emerging threat, barely on the horizon when I was minister for justice (11 years ago), has become now one of the key areas of discussion in law enforcement. We do not seem to be very capable of actually hitting those that we designate as targets.

A week later—after more than two decades of escalating bikie violence around New South Wales—Police Commissioner Ken Moroney announced a crackdown, with a particular focus on 'recent "tit-for-tat" retribution attacks' involving the Nomads, Comancheros, Bandidos and Rebels. 'Police action will be direct and immediate,' Moroney declared.

The belated promise of action came eight years after Moroney, as deputy commissioner responsible for Crime Agencies and other specialist commands; Jeff Jarratt, deputy commissioner responsible for local area commands and regions; and the commissioner, Peter Ryan, were warned of the threat posed by outlaw motorcycle gangs but refused to support a major long-term offensive against them. The briefing was given by Assistant Commissioner Clive Small, one of the authors of this book, in late 1999. It highlighted the resourcing implications of the forthcoming Olympic Games on the investigation of organised and other serious crime during 2000.

Small's briefing proposed that two primary long-term investigations be undertaken by Crime Agencies. One would be into the bikies, specifically the Rebels, Bandidos, Nomads, Comancheros and Black Uhlans. (Of Small's list all except the Black Uhlans would be listed as targets by Moroney eight years later.) The other would be into a major Lebanese organised crime family which remains largely untouched and continues with business as usual to this day.

While the wording of the 1999 warning and proposed action was different in its detail, the same themes had been strongly put to the police executive seven years earlier. In 1992 police analysts Mark Loves and Jim Shearan, both members of the Tactical Intelligence Section, New South Wales Police State Intelligence Group, prepared a report entitled 'Outlaw Motorcycle Gangs: A portrait of deviance'. The authors warned:

> Outlaw motorcycle clubs are organised to the point where a large quantity of counter intelligence against law enforcement bodies is available. Wives or associates of members

have been known to obtain employment in Government Departments, such as the Road Traffic Authority, Telecom, the Taxation Department, and the Police Department. This enables the bike gang [to gain] access to all areas of confidential information ... Incidents of 'bikers' photographing police and writing down a police officer's name, rank, and station on their own counter intelligence forms are more common than generally thought ... Many bike gangs now maintain computer files of local police, their vehicles and where they live.

Moroney's 2007 crackdown was a response to warnings issued more than a decade earlier. Like the Australian Crime Commission (of whose board Moroney, as New South Wales police commissioner, was a member), he had good political reasons for announcing a 'get tough' campaign against the bikies. Within weeks both Moroney and the Australian Crime Commission were due to be grilled by the PJC on the failure of law enforcement to deal with bikies. As a result of the crackdown Moroney could count on a few bikie arrests to deflect accusations of inaction.

The arrests duly followed. In mid June 2007 masked and heavily armed members of the State Protection Group were involved in a series of raids in Taree which resulted in the arrest of six members of the Rebels on various drug charges. During the previous five weeks the police had visited 250 bikie clubhouses. According to police, the raids were proof of their commitment to the crackdown. They failed to explain how 250 clubhouses had come to be established or how many times during the past ten years or so they had been visited by police.

On 8 June Moroney appeared before the PJC. Bikies were now his first priority: 'Firstly, I address the issue of outlaw motorcycle gangs. The conflict—which in one sense is not necessarily new—that we have seen in New South Wales in more recent times and that we have evidenced in the state of South Australia in recent days indicates that conflict within the outlaw motorcycle gangs themselves is increasing.' Moroney highlighted the growing threat of outlaw motorcycle gangs and the 'convergence between the activities of outlaw motorcycle gangs and, in some instances, Middle Eastern organised crime groups'. A 'coordinated national approach' was required, he said, to address outlaw motorcycle gangs.

Fifteen months later, in its report 'Inquiry into the Future Impact of Serious and Organised Crime on Australian Society', the PJC concluded: 'Within Australia, outlaw motorcycle gangs continue to dominate serious and organised crime, particularly in the area of illegal drug manufacture and distribution.' Again, the report failed to explain how this had been allowed to happen.

On 14 March 2009 about 700 members of bikie gangs including the Hells Angels, Gypsy Jokers, Rebels, Finks and Descendants gathered in the Barossa Valley town of Gawler, 40 kilometres north of Adelaide, before setting off on a ride in protest against recent anti-bikie laws described by the state government as the 'world's toughest'. The *Serious and Organised Crime Control Act*, which came into effect in June 2008, allows the police commissioner to ask the state government to 'declare' illegal a bikie club, making individual members liable to harsh sanctions if they associate or communicate with one another.

The semblance of unity between traditional rival clubs

was dismissed by Premier Mike Rann as a 'stunt'. The ride, dubbed 'The Freedom Run', was an exercise, said Rann, aimed at convincing 'other states not to follow us, it's about intimidation'.

Heralding the success of its newly established anti-bikie police task force, the South Australian government reported that in the 12 months up to November 2008, the task force had made 283 arrests. However, as journalist Larine Statham of the *Independent Weekly* pointed out, 'almost two-thirds were not actually bikie gang members'.

Despite the vaunted police crackdowns, the last few months of 2008 saw an orgy of bikie violence in Sydney. On the night of 5 October 2008 41-year-old Todd Anthony O'Connor was gunned down in a back street in the inner-city suburb of Tempe. O'Connor was alleged to be collecting a debt of nearly $400,000 on behalf of an associate when he was hit with shotgun blasts in the head and neck. As a teenager in the mid 1980s O'Connor had worked as a strip club bouncer in Kings Cross. Later he ran nightclubs and strip clubs. In 1995 he was charged with two counts of supplying drugs and one of possessing an unlicensed firearm; by 2001, after several court appearances and appeals, all three charges had been dropped. O'Connor was again arrested in 1997 for three drug supply charges. In 1998 he pleaded guilty to two of the charges and was given 250 hours' community service. The third charge was dropped.

O'Connor was a close friend of the Ibrahim family and had travelled overseas with John and Fadi Ibrahim. In the early 2000s he became a member of the Parramatta chapter of the Nomads outlaw motorcycle gang headed by Sam Ibrahim and is said to have been a founding member of Notorious when the Parramatta chapter closed. O'Connor is alleged to have taken over the operation of an amphetamine syndicate after Michael Ibrahim was jailed in 2007. It has been suggested that his assassination was connected with the murder of Milad Sande in 2005 and the attempted murder of Fadi Ibrahim in 2009.

In April 2009 27-year-old Hugo Jacobs was charged with murdering O'Connor but had not faced his trial at the time of writing. Police are still seeking a second suspect.

After O'Connor's murder at least 15 drive-by shootings took place across Sydney in 16 days during late November and December. A number of bikies and their associates were injured in the attacks, along with several innocent people. The hostilities continued in 2009 with clubhouses being attacked and drive-by shootings.

In February 13 men, believed to be Comancheros or associates of the gang, walked into a car yard in Liverpool in Sydney's south-west, assaulted three male employees, locking one of them in a car boot, and stole 12 cars from the yard. At the time of writing ten cars had been recovered and one person charged with aggravated robbery, aggravated kidnapping, participating in a criminal group and other offences.

Around the same time police raided homes near Penrith, 50 kilometres west of Sydney's central business district, and arrested a member of the Life and Death outlaw motorcycle gang, seizing a shotgun, ammunition and several cannabis plants.

On 22 March 29-year-old Hells Angel associate Anthony Zervas was bashed to death in a brawl at the Sydney airport domestic terminal between Comancheros and Hells Angels. Violence broke out after the two gangs found themselves on the same plane returning from Melbourne. The fatal bashing,

which occurred in front of hundreds of innocent citizens
—adults and children—and received international media
coverage, became the trigger for intense media, community
and political pressure. The frenzy increased nine days later
when Zervas's 32-year-old brother, Peter, a senior Hells
Angel, was shot four times (but not killed) while driving into
the carpark beneath the Lakemba apartment block where
his mother lived. Anthony Zervas had a long criminal record
that included charges for violence and drug offences. Peter
was sentenced to five years' jail in 2005 for shooting a man
in the leg at a party in Brighton-Le-Sands. He was released
from jail in 2008.

By mid August 11 Comancheros had been charged
with murder over the airport brawl. Three other men,
two with links to the Hells Angels, were charged with
affray. As the police investigation was underway, the New
South Wales government announced that 975 people had
been charged by police strike force Ranmore during a
two-year crackdown on bikie gangs. The *Sydney Morning
Herald* journalist Geesche Jacobsen noted, however, that
most had been charged only for minor offences. Jacobsen
wrote that:

> Overall, 975 people were charged with 2171 offences
> under Operation Ranmore ... However, figures obtained
> under freedom-of-information laws show that in that time
> only nine people were charged specifically with being
> a member of a criminal gang. Nearly 300 people were
> charged with traffic offences, more than 140 with 'judicial'
> offences, such as breaching bail, and 110 with property and
> street offences.

The figures revealed that only 40 of those arrested had been charged by the state's Gang Squad. Most charges were laid by local police.

The disclosure was a major embarrassment to the government. It didn't matter that some of the Gang Squad's 40 arrests were for serious crimes or that they were the hard-earned result of protracted and complex investigation. They were caught up in a whirlwind of government spin—the release implied that all arrests involving bikie gang members were equally serious and equally valuable to the crackdown—the effect of which was to undermine the squad's credibility.

The South Australian government had been similarly caught out a few months earlier. It was careful not to make the same mistake twice. In July 2009 the government announced that during the previous 18 months South Australia's Crime Gangs Task Force had arrested or reported 163 outlaw motorcycle gang members and 328 bikie associates; issued 134 barring orders; seized more than 70,000 street deals of amphetamines, ecstasy, cannabis and other drugs, more than 100 firearms, and almost $800,000 in cash. This time the government clearly identified which arrests involved bikie gang members and which involved associates.

In August 'Ferret', a member of the Finks outlaw motorcycle gang, joined members of the Rebels to address the National Press Club in Canberra. 'Ferret's aim was to argue the case of the newly formed United Motorcycle Council of New South Wales and to criticise new anti-bikie laws. 'I'm not trying to say all bikers are saints, just like not all politicians or police are squeaky clean,' 'Ferret' argued. 'But I would say that there is more organised criminal activity every day in Australia's governments and police services than you would find at your local biker clubhouse.' It was an interesting argument and it augured a new phase in the fight against organised crime. Outlaw motorcycle gangs have learned well from politicians: spin can be more powerful than facts. Some outlaw motorcycle gangs have now hired public relations firms to tidy up their public image. Warning his colleagues, the government and the public not to be fooled by the 'new age' bikies, New South Wales Deputy Police Commissioner Nick Kaldas declared, 'Just because bikies deliver teddy bears to children's hospitals once a year doesn't mean they're not criminals the other 364 days.'

Inevitably, the New South Wales government responded to the public furore over the airport brawl by announcing a raft of stringent new bikie laws two months later. Unlike previous legislative crackdowns, these laws would be modelled on anti-terrorism legislation. In an article headlined 'Rees goes gangbusters with draconian response' *Sydney Morning Herald* journalist Richard Ackland described New South Wales Police Commissioner Andrew Scipione as having 'whipped up the spectre of terrorism'. The head of the Office of the Director of Public Prosecutions, Nicholas Cowdery QC, questioned the aims of the legislation. 'This legislation,' said Cowdery, 'has been described as laws against "bikie gangs" and as "gang laws". However, it is not confined in its terms to "outlaw motorcycle gangs" and its potential reach is much broader. Where will the line be drawn?'

The laws allow the police commissioner to apply to the Supreme Court to proscribe criminal gangs and to jail, for up to five years, 'controlled persons' found associating with each other (there are some exceptions to the 'association' provisions—for example, close family members). The laws also provide for penalties of up to five years' jail for members of a proscribed gang who 'recruit' others. A controlled person loses any state-granted licence to conduct a business. Cowdery argued that there was no need for new laws, but rather for more rigorous policing and enforcement of existing legislation—specifically, the anti-criminal group provisions passed in 2007.

Over the years police have conducted some very successful operations against outlaw motorcycle gangs, locking up principals for long periods, seizing their assets and otherwise disrupting their operations. The problem has been the lack of political will to continue this pressure over time. Instead, governments have tended to seize on short-term successes as final outcomes rather than as important steps in an ongoing battle, placing political opportunism above long-term social and economic wellbeing and national security.

In August 2009 the Parliamentary Joint Committee on the Australian Crime Commission released a report of its inquiry into the legislative arrangements to outlaw serious and organised crime groups. Outlaw motorcycle gangs feature prominently in the review. The report referred to the 'significant expansion in the activities of OMCGs in 2005–06' identified by the Australian Crime Commission's Outlaw Motorcycle Gangs National Intelligence Task Force.

The South Australian government submitted that outlaw motorcycle gangs presented 'the greatest serious and organised crime threat in that state' and pointed to the growing connection between street gangs and bikie gangs. Assistant Commissioner Harrison from the South Australia Police told the committee: 'We are now seeing individual members of street and youth gangs graduating to nominees or prospects of outlaw motorcycle gangs, and we are also seeing some of them made full members of outlaw motorcycle gangs. We know that there is a direct correlation between some outlaw motorcycle gangs and some street gangs.'

The assistant commissioner's comments echoed those of Alastair Milroy, then chief executive of the Australian Crime Commission, to Natalie O'Brien of the *Australian* some months earlier. In June 2008 O'Brien reported that police intelligence showed bikie groups, including the Bandidos, Hells Angels, Rebels and Lone Wolf, were actively recruiting teenagers in New South Wales, the Gold Coast and South Australia to distance themselves from their criminal activities. According to O'Brien, one bikie group was giving these recruits handguns and drugs in exchange for their services. Milroy told O'Brien, 'Several OMCGs [outlaw motorcycle groups] are using street gangs to perform high-risk criminal activities, such as drug distribution, extortion and blackmail ... This offers the OMCGs a level of protection from exposure to law enforcement.' The assistant commissioner also noted the formation of alliances between gangs that would have been unlikely in the past: 'We are finding that there is diversification and interrelationships between outlaw motorcycle gangs and the more traditionally based ethnic serious and organised [crime] groups of the past.'

The South Australian government also identified outlaw motorcycle gangs as a threat to other jurisdictions, but not everyone agreed. A number of submissions argued that while some members of outlaw motorcycle gangs were criminals who committed crime together, the individuals themselves were the problem, not the gangs.

Whilst not denying the role of Australian bikie gangs in organised crime, Kevin Kitson, acting chief executive officer with the Australian Crime Commission, 'was clear' the committee observed, 'that this was not the issue on which the ACC currently believes it should focus its efforts'. Kitson explained that the ACC's strategy was to 'identify serious criminal targets through identification of criminal business structures and money flows'. He went on: 'OMCGs continue to feature in the Australian criminal landscape; of that there is no question. We would make a distinction between the operation of those groups as networked entities and the criminal enterprises of a number of the significant individuals within those groups. There is no doubt that in some instances those individuals operate entirely as individuals.'

In Kitson's view the Australian Crime Commission's involvement in combating this national threat should be a low priority because outlaw motorcycle gangs do not meet the definition of formal 'criminal business structures' that he (and, presumably, the commission executives and the police commissioners who sit on the commission's board) identifies as the commission's priority. Kitson's determination to play down the threat posed by outlaw motorcycle gangs and reduce the priority they should be given by the commission seems to contradict statements made by its own chief executive. Kitson's stance is also at odds with the commission's assessment that outlaw motorcycle gangs have expanded in recent years, and with evidence contained in the PJC's 2007 report 'Inquiry into the Future Impact of Serious and Organised Crime in Australian Society'. It also seems to fly in the face of comments made by Prime Minister Kevin Rudd, who only a few months earlier promised a bikie crackdown, describing bikie violence as 'absolutely unacceptable' and 'repugnant'. According to the *Age*'s Michelle Grattan, Rudd admitted, 'We have a problem on our hands.' Bikie thugs, he said, should receive 'zero tolerance'.

Kitson's (and the Australian Crime Commission's) argument that bikie gangs are really just groups of individuals, some of whom are involved in crime, appears to contradict the major premise of new legislation that targets bikie gangs not as groups of individuals but as 'criminal organisations'.

For the time being, it is the bikies themselves who are calling the tune.

As previous generations have discovered, extreme violence conducted in the public eye is bad news for organised crime. Guns have been put away and traditional rivals have agreed to a truce. But how long will it last?

CHAPTER TEN

Organised crime and terrorism

Terrorism is not new to Australia. More than 140 years ago, on 12 March 1868, 35-year-old Henry James O'Farrell, an Irish Nationalist, shot and wounded the Duke of Edinburgh while he was picnicking at Clontarf on Sydney's north shore during a visit to Australia. O'Farrell was arrested, tried and convicted. One month after the shooting he was hanged at Darlinghurst Gaol. The country's next terrorist attack occurred almost 50 years later, on 1 January 1915, when two men shot dead four people and wounded seven more before being killed by police and soldiers at Broken Hill. The killers, 41-year-old Badsha Mahommed Gool and 61-year-old Mullah Abdullah, were from what is now Pakistan. Both men left notes saying the attack was in response to the hostilities between the Ottoman and British Empires. It was Australia's first experience of Islamic terrorism.

These early attacks aside, it is generally believed that Australia was—with one exception—relatively immune from terrorism until quite recently. (The exception is the 1978 bomb attack outside Sydney's Hilton Hotel that killed a police officer and two civilians and injured seven others. The Australian prime minister and 11 visiting heads of state were staying in the hotel.) The truth, however, is that over the past half century numerous acts of violence have been directed towards the state and its institutions. The 1977 murder of political activist and anti-drugs campaigner Donald Mackay in Griffith and the 1994 bombing of the Adelaide office of the National Crime Authority are two examples of politically motivated violence. They were carried out by a criminal organisation—the 'ndrangheta or Calabrian Mafia—that operates outside the control of the legitimate government and is well known in its Calabrian homeland for its 'war' against the state. In Australia the 'ndrangheta followed a similar pattern, both attacking and perverting the institutions of the state when threatened. Representatives of the state, in the form of Labor politician Al Grassby and others, were used to defend it or deny its existence. At the same time it protected itself by infiltrating and corrupting state institutions including immigration, law enforcement, the legal profession and the judiciary.

Between 1966 and 2009 Australia has been the target of more than 200 terrorist acts or relevant events (see Appendix). This is a conservative estimate. The past decade has seen increasing public and political anxiety about terrorism. In response politicians have drawn an increasingly artificial distinction between terrorism and crime. All acts of terrorism are crimes.

Australia's attitude to terrorism changed dramatically as a result of four acts committed overseas. The first was the coordinated attack on the World Trade Center in New York and the Pentagon in Washington on 11 September 2001. Nineteen hijackers and almost 3000 innocent people died, including 22 Australians. The second occurred on 12 October 2002 on the Indonesian island of Bali, when a suicide bomber detonated a bomb in the popular Paddy's Pub in the tourist district of Kuta. Moments later a more powerful car bomb was detonated by a second suicide bomber outside the Sari Club, opposite Paddy's Pub. The bombings killed 202 people, including 88 Australians. A further 209 people were injured. A third bomb exploded outside the United States consulate in Denpasar but caused only minor damage. The bombings were described by Indonesia's chief of police, General Da'i Bachtiar, as the 'worst act of terror in Indonesia's history'. They had been carried out by members of the Islamist group Jemaah Islamiyah. Three members of the group were tried, found guilty and sentenced to death. On 9 November 2008 they were executed by firing squad. A fourth was sentenced to life in jail.

On 9 September 2004 a one-tonne bomb was packed into a small Daihatsu delivery van and detonated outside the Australian embassy in Jakarta, killing nine people, including the suicide bomber, and wounding more than 150. Several other embassies and nearby buildings were damaged. Jemaah Islamiyah was blamed for the bombing.

The fourth attack occurred thirteen months later on the evening of 1 October 2005 when Jemaah Islamiyah suicide bombers set off bombs in three cafés at Jimbaran Beach, Kuta. Twenty people were killed, including the three suicide bombers, and 129 were wounded. Four of those killed and 19 of the injured were Australians. A month later one of the masterminds of the bombing was killed in a shootout with Indonesian police.

The same year the Australian government published a report entitled 'Transnational Terrorism: The threat to Australia'. The report stated: 'Australia is a terrorist target, both as a Western nation and in its own right. Intelligence confirms we were a target before the 11 September 2001 attacks, and we are still a target. Our interests both at home and abroad are in the terrorists' sights.'

David Wright-Neville, in his paper 'The Politics of Fear: Counter-terrorism and Australian democracy', notes that in the five years since 9/11 'the Australian government has introduced more than 50 separate pieces of Commonwealth legislation dealing entirely or in part with terrorism-related matters'. During the same period the states and territories introduced 'over 40 separate pieces of similar legislation, most of which are designed to harmonise federal and state counter-terrorism laws'.

Despite the number of terrorist acts (around 150) committed in Australia or against Australians between 1966 and 2000, Wright-Neville notes that before 2001 'the last piece of legislation to touch (albeit remotely) on terrorism-related matters was the *Air Navigation Act* passed by the federal parliament in 1991'. Terrorist acts during this period include the attempted hijacking of a Pan American aircraft at Sydney's International Airport in 1979 (the hijacker was shot dead by police when he tried to set off a bomb he was carrying); a series of Family Law Court bombings and killings in the 1980s which claimed three lives (including that of one family court judge); and the assassination, on 17 December 1980, of Turkish Consul General Sarik Ariyak and his bodyguard outside the consul general's home in Sydney's eastern suburbs. The killings of Ariyak and his bodyguard were the work of Armenian terrorists who left the country immediately after the hit. The assassins are believed to have been helped by supporters inside Australia.

In another report titled 'Terrorism in Australia: 1966–1994', then Senior Constable Wayne Hoffman of the New South Wales Police noted that in mid 1985 the Commonwealth police had 'warned Victoria Police that a Turkish terrorist organisation might have been selling weapons—hand grenades, machine guns and pistols—to Vietnamese criminal gangs [operating in Victoria] ... The Turkish group sold to the Vietnamese, who were locked in a continuing war with Chinese criminal bands in Sydney and Melbourne.'

In 1986 a car packed with 50 to 60 sticks of gelignite exploded outside the Victoria Police headquarters complex in Russell Street, Melbourne, killing one police officer and injuring ten police and 11 members of the public. Three Melbourne criminals were eventually jailed for the bombing: two were sentenced to life while the third was jailed for 13 years. The bombing was said to have been a revenge attack on police for earlier convictions.

The same year an attempt was made to bomb the Turkish consulate in Melbourne. The bomber, an Armenian resident in Australia, was killed as he tried to set off the bomb. Later investigations uncovered a network of Australian citizens of Armenian background who had assisted in the planned bombing.

In March 1988 two petrol bombs were thrown at the diplomatic residence of the South African consul in Canberra. A fortnight later a South African diplomat's vehicle was destroyed by fire. Three months afterwards the vehicle of the

United States defence attaché was firebombed in Canberra. The three bombings are believed to be linked.

In 1991 the federal government identified 19 terrorist groups as having active supporters and/or representatives in Australia. They were:

- Syrian National Socialist Party in Syria
- Palestinian Liberation Organisation
- Main People's Congress (Arab People's Congress) in Libya
- Hezbollah in Lebanon
- Lebanese Forces in Lebanon
- Progressive Socialist Party in Lebanon
- Gush Emunim, Israeli right-wing group
- Fedayin-e-Khalq in Iran
- Mujahedeen Khalq Group (People's Holy Warriors)
- Hamas
- Armenian Liberation Army in Armenia
- Islamic fundamentalists in Indonesia and Malaysia
- Moro National Liberation Front in the Philippines
- Khmer Rouge in Cambodia
- African National Congress in South Africa
- Provisional IRA in Ireland
- Australian Neo-Nazi groups such as National Action; National Socialist Defending Australian People; White Australian Resistance (formerly White Aryan Resistance); and Australian National Socialist Movement.

The number of extremist Muslim groups on the list reflects the growing influence of radical Islam on terrorists and would-be terrorists—a trend that in the following years became increasingly apparent both in Australia and elsewhere.

An Australian link to the 1993 World Trade Center bombing in New York was not disclosed for seven years and revealed significant failures by intelligence and investigative authorities, both in the US and Australia. About 12.15 pm on 26 February 1993 a bomb weighing 550 to 750 kilograms, hidden in a van, was detonated on the second level of the World Trade Center's underground carpark. The blast made a crater nearly 46 metres in diameter and five floors deep. Six people were killed and more than a thousand injured. Within weeks two men, Mohammad Salameh and Nidal Ayyad, were arrested by the FBI. A third man, Mahmud Abouhalima, fled the United States the day after the bombing. He was later arrested in Egypt and extradited back to the United States. Ahmad M. Ajaj, who had entered the United States from Pakistan; Ramzi Yousef, who had been on the same flight as Ajaj but was refused entry to the US; and a sixth person known only as 'Yassin' were also identified as being involved in the bombing.

The following year Salameh, Ayyad, Abouhalima and Ajaj were convicted of the bombing and sentenced to life in jail. In 1995 Yousef was arrested in Pakistan and extradited to the United States. He was tried and convicted of another terrorist attack and sentenced to life in jail. Two years later he was convicted of the World Trade Center bombing. Several more alleged conspirators in the bombing were convicted of other terrorist activities.

In 2000 Australian security agencies investigated phone calls made to several Sydney addresses before and immediately after the bombing—but by then it was too late. At least two of the conspirators had made calls lasting from nine to 19 minutes to businesses in Dean Park and Yagoona in

Sydney's western suburbs. At the time of his arrest Salameh was preparing to apply for migration to Australia.

It was also around 2000 that a new trend started to emerge. Australian-based individuals and groups began travelling overseas to undertake training with terrorist groups or to carry out terrorist attacks in other countries.

Among them was Noorpolat Abdulla, a Uighur who migrated with his family to Australia in the early 1980s to escape political oppression in China. In 1986 Abdulla became an Australian citizen. In 2000 he was rounded up with around a hundred others in the former Soviet Republic of Kazakhstan and questioned over the murder of two Kazakh police. Thirteen months later Abdulla was convicted of preparing a terrorist attack and sentenced to 15 years' jail.

Around the same time Belal Khazaal, who had migrated to Australia from Lebanon with his family as a three-year-old child, was reportedly sending recruits overseas to train in Afghanistan. Khazaal first came to the attention of the Australian Security Intelligence Organisation (ASIO) in 1994. Over the next ten years the Qantas cleaner and occasional journalist was interviewed several times by ASIO. In 2004 the ABC's *Four Corners* program cited US Central Intelligence Agency (CIA) reports claiming that Khazaal had trained in a military camp in Afghanistan in 1998 and was a confidant of al-Qaeda's leader, Osama bin Laden, and his deputy, Ayman Al-Zawahiri. The CIA documents named Khazaal as 'reportedly planning an explosives attack against some US embassies ... the current target is in Venezuela ... Khazaal also has plans to attack with explosives US interests in the Philippines.' They also tied Khazaal to a Spanish al-Qaeda operative,

Abu Dahdah, who was alleged to have strong links with one of the masterminds behind the September 11 attacks. Khazaal had asked Dahdah to help move an associate secretly around Europe.

In December 2003 Khazaal and his brother Maher were convicted and sentenced in absentia to five years' jail by a military tribunal in Lebanon for donating money to an Islamic group which had orchestrated a string of bomb attacks in Lebanon. Two years later Khazaal was again convicted in absentia by a military tribunal of terrorism-related charges that included financing and directing the activities of Saleh Jamal (see later in this chapter) and providing him with false travel documents. Khazaal was sentenced to 15 years' jail.

In September 2009 Khazaal was sentenced in Sydney to a minimum 12-year jail term. Ordering him to serve at least nine years behind bars, Justice Megan Latham said his crime was 'not far from the worst category of the offence'. She said the 'terrorism training manual'—which was published on a website endorsed by al-Qaeda—advocated 'widespread and indiscriminate loss of life'. The 110-page book singled out world leaders, including former US president George W. Bush, as targets for assassination and contained detailed instructions on how to shoot down planes, attack vehicles and set boobytraps. An application by the Lebanese government for Khazaal's extradition to Lebanon to serve his outstanding jail sentences will be considered after he has served his time in New South Wales.

In 2001 the Australian government deported Ahmad Abdul Rahman Awdah Al Joufi, a Saudi national and suspected al-Qaeda member, after he arrived in Melbourne on a false passport. The purpose of his visit to Australia was said to be the recruitment of frontline fighters for a jihad or 'holy war' against Russia.

In 2005 Tallaal Adrey, an Australian citizen from Auburn in Sydney's western suburbs, was arrested in Kuwait and convicted of weapons and ammunition charges, including trading ammunition for the purpose of murder, and sentenced to four years' jail. Adrey was among 37 Islamists placed on trial as members of the Peninsula Lions. This group has been linked with the Saudi-based al-Haramain Brigade, a subgroup of the al-Qaeda Organisation of the Arabian Peninsula, which claims to be behind a number of bombings and violent attacks in Saudi Arabia. Adrey was not charged with membership of this organisation.

The rise in overseas activities by Australian-based terrorists and their supporters during the past decade has paralleled an increase in terrorist activity inside Australia. On 22 May 2000 the police strike force charged with the protection of the Sydney Olympic Games arrested a 28-year-old Maori man after he had made numerous threats to Olympic organisers. The man had changed his name by deed poll from Dion Monaghan to that of Adolf Hitler's private secretary, Martin Bormann. Ingredients for making explosives (including hydrochloric acid, chlorine, petrol and fertiliser) and a home-made rocket launcher were found by police in a bunker below his Summer Hill home. The following year Bormann pleaded guilty to two counts of possessing explosive substances, carrying a knife in a public place and unauthorised use of a rocket launcher and sentenced to 15 months' jail. Having already served 16 months in custody, he was eligible for immediate release but was kept in custody pending his deportation to New Zealand on racial vilification grounds.

In New Zealand the same year, police raided houses in

Auckland and found evidence of a conspiracy to blow up the nuclear research reactor at Lucas Heights in Sydney's south. The houses were home to Afghan refugees and the raids were part of an investigation into a people-smuggling racket to bring illegal immigrants from Afghanistan to New Zealand. The living room of one house had been converted into a virtual command centre complete with a conference room and maps highlighting the nuclear reactor and detailing its access and exit routes. Three people were arrested but they were eventually charged and convicted of only minor offences.

The following year Mohammed Afroz Abdul Razak (Afroz) was arrested in India and confessed to being part of an al-Qaeda cell using India as a base from which to launch attacks similar to those of 9/11 against Britain, Australia and India. He had trained as a pilot in both Britain and Australia. In 2005 Afroz was sentenced to seven years' jail for plotting attacks against a friendly nation and forging documents.

In 2003, 50-year-old Jack Roche was convicted and jailed for nine years for conspiring to destroy the Israeli embassy in Canberra and the Israeli consulate in Sydney. Roche was released on parole in May 2007. Born Paul George Holland, Roche had migrated from the UK to Australia in 1978. After converting to Islam around 1992, he met the head of the Jemaah Islamiyah terrorist group in Sydney. In the mid 1990s Roche travelled to Indonesia where he studied Islam before returning to Australia. In early 2000 he flew to Pakistan and travelled to Afghanistan for military training. While in Afghanistan he met al-Qaeda leaders including Osama bin Laden. He returned to Australia the same year.

The year Roche was convicted, 25-year-old French terrorist Willie Brigitte—also known as Mohammed

Abderrahman, Mohammed Ibrahim Abderrahman, Abou Maimouna, Salahouddin, Jamal and 'Abderrahman the West Indian'—arrived in Sydney and married 26-year-old Australian Melanie Brown, a Muslim convert, after meeting her only five times. At the time Brown, a former soldier in the Australian army, denied it was a marriage of convenience intended to enable Brigitte to stay in Australia. 'We married for the pleasure of God. It's very different to anything you would understand because you are not Muslim,' Brown told *Sydney Morning Herald* journalist Ellen Connolly. According to Brown, it had been Mohamed Ndaw's praise of Brigitte that convinced her to marry him. 'Mohamed was Willie's friend,' she told Connolly, 'and obviously he told his wife who repeated it to me.' Ndaw had told Brown that 'Willie Brigitte was the best brother that he knew'. In return Brigitte described Ndaw as his 'closest and most trusted friend'. In 2004 Ndaw was deported to his native Senegal on security grounds.

Ndaw was the brother-in-law of Australian-born 'Abdul' (not his real name) and a close friend of Brown and Brigitte. In 2005 'Abdul' was among a group of at least 16 Muslims who trained at terrorists camps in New South Wales and was one of 22 arrested later that year in Sydney and Melbourne. In 2004 Brigitte was arrested by Australian federal police and deported to France where he was detained for terrorist activities. After his detention, Brown said she was leaving Brigitte as a result of disclosures to her by French authorities.

The following year the deputy director-general of ASIO told a Security in Government Conference in Canberra that Brigitte's deportation had prevented a terrorist attack in Australia. ASIO and the federal police had reportedly acted on information from French authorities that Brigitte had links to al-Qaeda and was planning a terrorist attack, possibly on the Lucas Heights research reactor and military installations.

In March 2007 a French court found Brigitte guilty of planning terrorist attacks in Australia and sentenced him to nine years' jail. The court also found that after converting to Islam in 1998 Brigitte had become involved with a group allied to al-Qaeda. French anti-terrorist investigators had known of Brigitte since at least the late 1990s. They had tracked his movements in 1999 when he studied at a religious school in Pakistan and later when he underwent military training with weapons and explosives.

In its 2004–05 Annual Report ASIO drew attention to the threat from 'home-grown' terrorists. In August 2005 the *Age*'s political editor, Michelle Grattan, reported former ASIO officer Michael Roach as saying that Australia had about a dozen terrorist cells, with up to 60 individuals in Sydney and Melbourne. According to Grattan, Australian Federal Police Commissioner Mick Keelty had confirmed this assessment.

Two years later *Sun-Herald* journalist Alex Mitchell revealed that 12 of the 37 high-risk inmates in the Supermax facility inside Goulburn jail had converted to fundamentalist Islam. The men were known as the 'Supermax Jihadists'. Their conversions were masterminded by Bassam Hamzy, a violent criminal jailed for 21 years for the murder of an 18-year-old man and the wounding of another outside a Paddington nightclub in 1998. Mitchell reported that 'Prison officers have confiscated pictures of Osama bin Laden from the walls of Hamzy's cell. Prisoners have been captured on surveillance tapes kneeling in front of Hamzy and kissing his hands.'

While in jail the converts had received regular payments of about $100 which appeared to be from family members, but inquiries by Corrective Services officers revealed the payments had been organised by Hamzy through his outside contacts and sympathisers.

Two of the converts, one a convicted murderer and the other a rapist, married Muslim women in marriage ceremonies using a three-way telephone hook-up involving the prisoner, his bride and an imam. In one of these cases, the prisoner began an illicit relationship with a female prison psychologist whom he converted to Islam. She was forced to resign when the relationship was discovered. In the other case, Hamzy had arranged contact between the prisoner and his Muslim bride. According to Corrective Services Commissioner Ron Woodham, a third convert spoke openly about martyrdom and boasted of being 'prepared to die for the cause'.

The disclosures from Goulburn jail should not have been a surprise. In November 2005 *US News & World Report* correspondent David Kaplan observed that the prime training ground for Europe's jihadist criminals 'may well be prison':

[A]s much as half of France's prison population is now believed to be Muslim. In Spanish jails, where Islamic radicals have recruited for a decade, the number has reached some 10 per cent. Ahmidan, leader of the Madrid bombing cell, is thought to have been radicalized while serving time in Spain and Morocco. Prison was also the recruiting center for many of the 40-plus suspects nabbed by Spanish authorities last year for plotting a sequel to the Madrid bombings, an attack with a half ton of explosives on Spain's national criminal court. Nearly half the group had rap sheets with charges ranging from drug trafficking to forgery and fraud.

Kaplan also reported that '[n]early half of the 41 groups on the [US] government's list of terrorist organisations are tied to narcotics trafficking, according to DEA [Drug Enforcement Administration] statistics'.

In 2003 Dr Michael Waller, an expert on terrorist groups, gave evidence before the US Senate's Subcommittee on Terrorism, Technology and Homeland Security. Speaking on 'Terrorist Recruitment and Infiltration in the United States: Prisons and Military as an Operational Base', Waller pointed out that 'The prison recruitment question is occurring world-wide.' It was, he argued, part of a larger campaign to build terrorist support networks. 'Estimates place the number of Muslim prison recruits at between 15–20% of the [US] prison population ... Currently, there are approximately 350,000 Muslims in Federal, state and local prisons—with 30,000–40,000 being added to that number each year ... These inmates mostly came into prison as non-Muslims.' Waller noted that 'For many disaffected young people, their first contact with Islam comes in jail. Over the past 30 years, [radical] Islam has become a powerful force in America's correctional system ... al-Qaeda and other [terrorist] organi-zations have found men who have already been convicted of violent crimes and have little or no loyalty to the United States ... and many inmates are anxious to hear how they can attack the institutions of America.'

Waller quoted the observation of Theodore Dalrymple, a psychiatrist with experience of British prisons, that Islam had assumed an influence in British jails disproportionate to the number of Muslim inmates—4000 among a jail population of 67,500. Five years later, in November 2008, the *Daily Mail* reported that one-third of the 458 'most dangerous men in the country' held in Whitemoor Prison near March in Cambridgeshire were Muslim and that they included al-Qaeda terrorists. The same year the chief inspector of prisons for England and Wales, Anne Owers, reported that some terrorist detainees committed to a radical interpretation of Islam were pressuring other prisoners to convert.

In New South Wales the ambiguous distinction between crime and terrorism was further blurred by the emergence of Middle Eastern crime gangs in the aftermath of the Wood Royal Commission into the New South Wales Police Service. Saleh Jamal, a member of gangs led by Danny Karam and Michael Kanaan, was arrested and charged with the 1998 shooting attack on the Lakemba Police Station in south-west Sydney. As a member of the Karam and Kanaan gangs, Jamal is suspected of having been involved in several other shootings and murders during the early 2000s. In jail, Jamal came under the influence of hardened criminals who had already converted. These prisoners had assumed the role of Islamic teachers as a means of building a gang within the jail system. Jamal spent two years in jail before being granted bail in 2001. With his brothers, Mohammed Omar (commonly known as Omar) and Ahmed, Jamal joined the Haldon Street prayer hall at Lakemba in Sydney's south-west, some of whose members were associated with Brigitte, Khazaal and other Islamic radicals.

In March 2004, while still on bail, Saleh Jamal fled Australia on a false passport provided by Khazaal. Two months later he was arrested in Lebanon for terrorism offences. The charges related to the detonation of bombs in McDonald's restaurants in Syria. In February 2005 Jamal was convicted of possessing weapons and explosives, using a forged Australian passport, forming a terrorist group and planning acts that endangered state security and sentenced to five years' jail with hard labour. In April 2006 the Lebanese Court of Appeal overturned Jamal's conviction on terrorism charges and he was extradited to Sydney. A year later Jamal was sentenced to nine years' jail over the 1998 kneecapping of Elias Elias at Greenacre in Sydney's south-west. Time spent in jail in both Sydney and in Lebanon was taken into account by the court. The court also took into account claims by Jamal that he had been tortured while in jail in Lebanon.

Jamal claimed that in 2005 Australian federal police had offered him a reduced jail sentence in Australia if he returned and pleaded guilty to planning an attack on Sydney Harbour and turned informant on men he had allegedly recruited to jihad.

Saleh Jamal's brothers, Ahmed and Omar, were also in jail, one in Iraq and the other in Australia. Ahmed was captured in northern Iraq in August 2004 and since then has been held in jail in the Kurdish city of Suliamaniyah because of his alleged links to terrorism. Omar was arrested in Sydney the following year, with eight others, on charges of conspiring to manufacture explosives in preparation for a terrorist attack, firearms and related crimes.

At the same time, 13 people were arrested in Melbourne and charged with being members of a terrorist organisation, planning terrorist attacks and other crimes. In the raids police seized chemicals used in the manufacture of bombs, lab equipment and weapons, and found a variety of documents including instructions on bomb-making, sabotage, counter-surveillance and targeting embassies and other buildings.

The Melbourne cell had been under physical and electronic surveillance by law enforcement and security agencies for at least 16 months. Its connection with the Sydney cell was discovered as the investigation progressed. In the lead-up to the arrests, the Melbourne cell was heard to complain that the Sydney cell was ahead of them in planning an attack, despite the fact that their planning had begun later.

A member of the Sydney cell, 26-year-old Mazen Touma of Bankstown, was a close associate of the Darwiche crime gang. In 2001 Touma had set up a 'friend' who had robbed one of Darwiche's drug runners for a payback kneecapping at Punchbowl. Mazen Touma's cousin, Mohammed, was another member of the gang. Mazen had told a friend that he planned to die in a jihad which he described as 'an obligation for every Muslim'. Allah, he said, would give him a paradise for his martyrdom. In another conversation Touma and 28-year-old Indonesian 'Bilal' (not his real name) spoke about how they would have to be healthy 'to shoot some motherfuckers'.

In November 2003 Mohammed Touma had been arrested and charged with weapons and related offences and possession of property believed stolen. Five months later he was granted bail with reporting conditions and a security of $20,000. Touma was forced to surrender his passport but waited only a short time before fleeing Australia on a false passport and is now believed to be living in the Middle East. He is wanted for the murder of Ahmed Fahda at Punchbowl on 30 October 2003 and other crimes. Six years after Fahda's murder Abdul Darwiche was shot and killed in a Punchbowl street by Ahmed's younger brother, Mohammed 'Blackie' Fahda.

'Hussein' (not his real name) was another of those arrested in the Sydney swoops. Two years earlier he had bought five rocket launchers through Eddie Darwiche. The launchers, which have still not been recovered, were among the ten stolen from an Australian Defence Force base in Sydney's west. 'Hussein' had been involved in planning terrorist activities since at least 2000. In that year a terrorist training camp was discovered in the New South Wales southern tablelands on a property owned by three of 'Hussein's brothers and a fourth person. Explosions and automatic gunfire had been heard coming from the property. 'Hussein' and his brothers told police that the property was used by Sydney's hardline Islamic Youth Movement, but only for 'hunting trips'.

In December 2004 'Hussein', Mazen Touma and Bangladeshi 'Azooz' (not his real name) were apprehended by police within the 1.6-kilometre exclusion zone around Sydney's Lucas Heights nuclear reactor. A padlock on a gate leading to the reactor's reservoir had been cut. According to police, 'all three persons gave different versions of the day's events'. None of the men was charged.

The following year two New South Wales properties were used as training camps in preparation for jihad. In March 'Azooz', 'Abdul', Khaled Cheikho and others went to a 9000-hectare property called Curranyalpa, 140 kilometres south-west of Bourke. The recreational 'hunting party' had booked the property under the name 'Adam Georges', an alias of Khaled's nephew Moustafa Cheikho. Police found ammunition shell cases, one badly burnt and melted battery, sparkplugs and a quantity of unidentifiable melted material at the camp site.

A month later another 'hunting party' went to a 17,000-hectare property called Mulga Creek Station, 70 kilometres south-east of Bourke. They booked the property using the name 'Andrew Scott'. This 'hunting party' included 'Azooz', Mazen Touma, 'Hussein', and Khaled and Moustafa Cheikho. In court police claimed 'These camping and hunting trips are part of the jihad [holy war] training being undertaken by this group ... [The trips] are consistent with the usual modus operandi of terrorists prior to attacks.'

In November 2006, 35-year-old Marek Samulski (commonly known as Abdul Malik), a Sydney man of Polish extraction who had moved with his family to Lebanon two years earlier, and 19 other men were detained in a swoop by Yemeni secret police. Among the 19 were Australians Mohammed and Abdullah Ayub, sons of the former head of Jemaah Islamiyah's Australian terror cell, Abdul Rahim Ayub, and two senior al-Qaeda leaders. According to journalists Cameron Stewart and Martin Chulov of the *Australian*, Yemeni authorities said the raid had 'dismantled an al-Qaeda cell and disrupted a gun-running ring to neighbouring Somalia'. The elder sister of the Ayub brothers, Rahma, is the wife of Khaled Cheikho, who was arrested and charged in Sydney with terrorist offences in 2005.

The leader of the Sydney and Melbourne terrorist cells was 45-year-old 'Rajab' (not his real name), a radical Islamist. 'Rajab' was born around 1960 in Algeria and arrived in Australia in 1989 on a visitor's visa. He became a prohibited person and for more than six years fought attempts by Australian authorities to deport him. In 1992 he married a Lebanese woman who was an Australian citizen and with whom he has six children. Two years later he became an Australian citizen, though he also retained his Algerian citizenship.

By this time 'Rajab' was associating with extremist Muslim elements in Melbourne. He gradually extended his influence into New South Wales, creating a second band of followers. From around 2000 'Rajab' made frequent trips to Algeria, Lebanon and Brunei. In 2005 ASIO revoked his passport. With 'Rajab's encouragement, several of his followers travelled overseas for terrorist training.

In 2005 'Rajab' publicly complained that there were two laws: Australian law and Islamic law. 'My religion doesn't tolerate other religion ... The only one law which needs to spread, it can be here or anywhere else, has to be Islam,' and declared 'Jihad is a part of my religion.'

In secretly recorded law enforcement intercepts, members of 'Rajab's group, who cannot be named for legal reasons, were heard encouraging one another to plan a large-scale terrorist attack: 'You shouldn't kill just one, two or three ... Do a big thing.'

'Like Madrid,' one person replies.

On another occasion there was discussion about the then Prime Minister John Howard and how he had taken the lives of Muslim 'brothers'. 'If he kills our kids, we kill [inaudible] little kids,' another says.

Other intercepts recorded various members of the group expressing their approval of terrorist acts overseas such as the 2004 bombing of the Australian Embassy in Jakarta, discussing matyrdom, the killing of innocent women and children and suicide missions.

As they prepared for jihad the Melbourne cell filmed the Australian Stock Exchange and the city's main Flinders Street Station and collected maps of Casselden Place, the Melbourne headquarters of the Departments of Foreign Affairs and Trade and Immigration.

The source of funds for their jihad was credit card and identity fraud, the theft and rebirthing of motor vehicles and motorbikes, and stolen SIM cards. The men also discussed 'bashing and robbing' people to get money.

Among those arrested in Sydney was 'Azooz' who was charged with making false statements to ASIO to cover his links with Willie Brigitte—the lies included denying 23 telephone contacts with Brigitte (Brigitte had rung 'Azooz's butcher shop on more than 40 occasions) and setting up three safe houses for him in Sydney's south-western suburbs, two in Lakemba and one in Wiley Park. In 2005 the *Australian*'s Nick Leys reported '["Azooz"] has also been linked to Asman Hashim, a Malaysian survival and weapons skills boot camp trainer for Jemaah Islamiyah, who was in Australia from mid-2001 to 2003.' During this period Hashim stayed at a flat in Dee Why, a beachside suburb on Sydney's north shore. Previously the flat had been used as a safe house for Jemaah Islamiyah members. According to Leys, 'Hashim was believed to be part of JI's forward party to Australia, sent to recruit and to train ... [He] organised survival camps in the Blue Mountains based on camps he had run in the Philippines.' When arrested in Malaysia in 2004 by Special Branch officers, Hashim claimed that '["Azooz"] had been a regular at the camps [in the Blue Mountains] and was a key player.'

Twelve of the 13 alleged Melbourne conspirators eventually faced trial. It started in the Victorian Supreme Court in February 2008 and lasted seven months. During the trial it was disclosed that various possible targets were discussed, including the 2005 AFL Grand Final at the MCG, Melbourne's Crown Casino during Grand Prix week and the final of the pre-season AFL competition in 2006, but no specific target had been selected.

Seven of the 12 were found guilty by the jury and given long jail sentences. The jury acquitted four of those charged and could not reach verdicts on charges against another, 31-year-old Shane Kent, known by the name Yasin.

In mid 2001 Kent is alleged to have trained at a terrorist camp in Pakistan before proceeding to al-Qaeda's al-Faruq training camp for foreign jihadis in Afghanistan. He is said to have met bin Laden and committed himself to violent jihad. On 28 July 2009, as Kent's retrial was about to begin in the Victorian Supreme Court, he pleaded guilty to being a member of a terrorist organisation between July 2004 and November 2005 and making a document connected with the preparation of a terrorist act. On 2 September 2009 Kent was sentenced to five years' jail. With time already served, Kent will be eligible for parole in mid 2010.

A thirteenth conspirator, Izzydeen Atik, pleaded guilty and gave evidence for the prosecution at the trial. He was jailed for five and a half years. In 2002 Atik had been convicted of credit card fraud and given a suspended sentence. While receiving social security benefits he was living in a luxury townhouse and employed a butler.

Jury selection for the Sydney trial began in February 2008. A pool of 5000 potential jurors was narrowed down to 15 people. Jury selection was followed by eight months of legal argument, by the end of which four of the nine Sydney accused—29-year-old Mirsad Mulahalilovic, 24-year-old 'Abdul', 25-year-old Mazen Touma and 38-year-old 'Bilal' —had pleaded guilty to lesser charges and been sentenced to jail terms ranging from four years and eight months to 18 years.

The trial, which was held in a purpose-built high security court in Parramatta in Sydney's west, finally began in November 2008. Over the next ten months the jury heard evidence from 300 witnesses and was presented with court statements from another 2100 people as well as 3000 exhibits and electronic evidence equivalent to almost 900 million pages. The prosecution argued that the group strongly adhered to the Islamic faith and were motivated by the pursuit of violent jihad. They believed, the prosecution argued, that jihad—holy war—was founded in the teachings of Islam.

In mid September 2009 the jury retired to consider the evidence. On 16 October they returned their verdict, finding the five accused—40-year-old 'Azooz'; 36-year-old Khaled Cheikho, 32-year-old Moustafa Cheikho, 44-year-old 'Hussein' and 24-year-old Mohammed Omar Jamal—guilty of conspiring to commit acts in preparation for a terrorist act or acts. The jury had not been told about the four accused who had pleaded guilty before the trial began. At the time of writing, the five found guilty at trial had not been sentenced.

Several of those jailed had only converted to Islam in the 18 months before they were arrested in 2005.

The events described in this chapter, together with the chronology of terrorist acts at the end of the book (see Appendix) tell us much about the evolution of terrorism in Australia during the past four and a half decades. Nearly two-thirds of the more than 150 incidents that took place in Australia between 1966 and the destruction of the Twin Towers on 11 September 2001 targeted the diplomats, property or businesses of foreign countries, primarily Israel (18), Yugoslavia (14), Serbia (8), China (7), the United States and India (6 each), South Africa (4), Turkey and Croatia (3 each).

Around a third of the incidents targeted Australian government officials and interests on Australian soil. There were only three attacks on Australian interests and people overseas—the most significant being 9/11 itself—and three incidents of people and groups based in Australia training for attacks overseas.

However, the 40 or so incidents since 9/11 show a very different picture. The proportion of terrorist acts directed at non-Australian targets inside Australia declined dramatically, with just two against US interests and one each against Sri Lanka and Lebanon. There were three attacks on mosques (but none before 2001). Eight incidents involved Australian targets. Australians and/or Australian interests were targeted in four overseas incidents and there were 11 incidents of Australian-based individuals and groups travelling overseas to carry out terrorist activities in other countries. Since 2001 both actual and planned incidents have been designed to cause more deaths and injuries and greater damage to property than in the decades before 2001. Targets have also been more indiscriminate, with the victims often innocent civilian citizens.

The global nature of modern terrorism has put new demands on domestic law enforcement agencies, which have sometimes struggled to distinguish between intelligence and evidence. On 2 July 2007 the Australian Federal Police (AFP) arrested Mohamed Haneef, an Indian doctor, at Brisbane international airport as he prepared to board a plane to India on a one-way ticket. The AFP suspected Haneef of being involved in two failed London car bomb attacks and an attack on Glasgow airport in which a flaming jeep was driven into the doors of the arrivals terminal. Haneef was held without charge under Australia's anti-terrorism laws.

A fortnight later he was charged with recklessly providing support to a terrorist organisation. There was enormous media interest in Haneef's arrest, detention and charging. Sensational leaks—some entirely false—fuelled speculation about the ongoing investigation and the alleged guilt of Dr Haneef, even after the terrorism charge against Haneef was dropped on 27 July.

Eight months later the federal government established the Clarke Inquiry into the Case of Dr Mohamed Haneef. Some time after the Clarke Inquiry began the AFP announced that Haneef was no longer a person of interest. Clarke was scathing about the decision. 'I do not find that surprising,' he said. 'I could find no evidence that he was associated with or had foreknowledge of the terrorist events.' Clarke found that Haneef was wrongly charged and that it took too long to clear him.

In its own defence the AFP submitted to the inquiry that 'terrorism investigations are often complex and demanding, involving large volumes of information that must be collected, processed and analysed in a limited time frame'. Such investigations can also involve multiple jurisdictions, both in Australia and abroad. Clarke himself agreed: '[W]hat started as a small investigation blew out, involving nearly 50 people from Perth to North Queensland and occupying the attention of many officers, from the AFP, the Queensland Police Service, other members of the Australian Intelligence Community (in particular, ASIO and the Defence Signals Directorate) and the Australian Customs Service.'

Clarke found that the investigation was conducted in an environment that lacked operational protocols and investigational structures and was hamstrung by an inadequate case management system. He commented, 'There does not appear to have been any systematic process for recording and updating the information received in the course of the investigation and for keeping track of significant avenues of inquiry.'

Clarke also registered his surprise that 'not one of the people involved in the police investigation and the charging whom the Inquiry interviewed stood back at any time prior to the decision to charge and reflected on what Dr Haneef was known to have done'. Among other things, Clarke recommended that 'appropriate operational protocols and major incident room structure' for counter-terrorism investigations and 'a national case management system for major police investigations' be developed and adopted 'as a matter of urgency'.

Despite the seriousness of the findings, Clarke was far from satisfied with his own inquiry. In September 2009 he told the Commonwealth Ombudsman's Conference in Canberra that his inquiry into the botched investigation 'had no power' at all and was unable to compel agencies to produce evidence or to demand the appearance of former ministers. Such powers, he said, would have enabled the inquiry to reach a firm finding on whether there had been a criminal 'conspiracy' in which the former immigration minister Kevin Andrews came under political pressure to take action against Haneef. (The minister revoked Haneef's passport.)

Clarke's report on the fiasco that was the Haneef case offers important insights into the wider failings that have hampered Australia's fight against organised crime. The principles that apply to the investigation of terrorism are the same as those that apply to all crimes. Indeed, in its 2007–08 Annual Report the AFP claims 'to treat terrorism as a criminal offence'.

Whatever the crime—from shop stealing and house-breaking to murder, drug trafficking and terrorism—the investigative principles are the same: ethical conduct, a strategic focus and operational discipline. The variables are scale and complexity. The Haneef case was large and complex but there have been many investigations, by both state and federal police, that have been larger and more complex. The systems and processes, and the forensic, organisational and strategic principles that delivered successful results in those investigations, are the very ones identified by the Clarke Inquiry as lacking from the AFP's investigation of Haneef.

One of the most significant changes to the business of terrorism has been its source of funding. In the past 20 years state-sponsored funding for international terrorist groups has greatly diminished. In its place, many groups have turned to crime. In 2005 Robert Charles, described by reporter David Kaplan as 'the State Department's former point man on narcotics', was quoted as saying that 'Transnational crime is converging with the terrorist world.' His view was echoed by Antonio Maria Costa, the head of the United Nations Office on Drugs and Crime. 'The world is seeing the birth of a new hybrid of organized crime terrorist organizations,' said Costa. 'We are breaking new ground.'

Kaplan's article in *US News & World Report* cited several examples of this convergence. One was the 2004 train bombings in Madrid that killed 191 people and wounded another 1800. The group behind the bombings was funded almost entirely from hashish and ecstasy trafficking. Their drug network extended from Morocco through Spain to Belgium and the Netherlands. Drug trafficking also funded the attempted bombings of US and British ships in Gibraltar in 2002, and the 2003 attacks in Casablanca that killed 45 people.

The 2002 Bali bombings carried out by Jemaah Islamiyah were funded, in part, by jewellery store robberies. In 2004 an al-Qaeda affiliate, the Moroccan Islamic Combatant Group, robbed six ATMs of more than a million dollars to fund its terrorist activities. In his article Kaplan referred to reports from France and Italy about jihadists selling heroin on the streets and handing 80 per cent of the take to their cell leader.

The same trend—of terrorists resorting to crime and criminals gravitating to terrorism—is apparent in Australia. Examples include Saleh Jamal, a member of Danny Karam and Michael Kanaan's crime gangs; Belal Khazaal, who provided Jamal with a false passport to flee Australia; Tallaal Adrey, who was involved in weapons trading; Mazen Touma, who was closely associated with the Darwiche gang; and the Islamic extremists rounded up by Operation Pendennis in Melbourne and Sydney who funded their would-be terrorist activities from crimes such as credit card fraud and the theft and rebirthing of motor vehicles.

History shows that terrorists don't need a lot of money. In November 2008 Robert Windrem and Garrett Haake analysed the cost of several international terrorist attacks for the *NBC World News*. The cost estimates were drawn from reports and statements obtained from the United Nations, the US Central Intelligence Agency, the US Department of Justice and the 9/11 Commission. Windrem and Haake noted that the simplest first-generation suicide bombs constructed by the Palestinian Islamist group Hamas cost no more than $200. The World Trade Center bombing in 1993 was estimated to have cost US$31,000; the attack on the USS *Cole* in 2000, which killed 17 people, cost between US$5000 and US$10,000; the 2002 Bali bombings between US$75,000 and US$80,000; the Madrid train bombings in 2004 cost US$10,000 and the attacks on London's public transport system in 2005 (three bombs exploded at underground railway stations and a fourth exploded on a bus) which killed 56 people and injured around 700 cost US$14,000.

A former official of the US Treasury's Office of Foreign Assets Control told Windrem and Haake: 'Terrorism is unfortunately not a rich man's sport.'

None of the planned attacks in Australia required a lot of money. When police swooped on the Melbourne cell in 2005 they found only $18,000 in the *sandooq* (the pooled profits from their criminal activities). As one officer involved in the investigation of several terrorist operations has observed, 'They [terrorist cells] run on the smell of an oily rag.'

Orthodox crime—from local crime to transnational organised crime—offers other rewards to terrorists by inflicting social, economic and physical damage on the host country. But these benefits come with a cost. Involvement in crime increases the risk of detection, arrest and prosecution. Terrorist attacks may be prevented by chance arrests for non-terrorist crimes. The investigation of non-terrorist crimes may compromise or uncover more serious terrorist activities or reveal the existence of previously unknown terrorist cells and individuals, enabling law enforcement to take pre-emptive action.

Arguably it is their increasing involvement in orthodox crime that could prove to be the terrorists' Achilles heel. The model for this style of indirect law enforcement is the FBI's pursuit of the Chicago gangster Al Capone. Despite his notoriety for everything from bootlegging to murder,

Capone proved impossible to convict on these or racketeering charges. The FBI, however, succeeded in having him jailed for contempt of court before the US Treasury Department finally put him away for eleven years for tax evasion.

A Capone-style strategy can be used to tackle terrorism as well as organised crime. In both, prosecutors can have difficulty proving the principal crimes beyond a reasonable doubt. Convicting and jailing the perpetrators on lesser charges serves several purposes. It disrupts their activities and often leads to the discovery of evidence for other crimes, including the principal crimes.

The strategy is not without its critics, who want to see criminals punished for their principal crimes rather than for lesser crimes with lesser penalties. The family and friends of someone who has been killed in a terrorist bombing are unlikely to feel that justice has been done if they see the offender jailed for passport fraud or possession of explosives. But in the global war against terrorism and organised crime the Capone strategy has an important role to play—provided rival law enforcement agencies can be made to cooperate rather than compete.

The relationship between Australian law enforcement agencies is especially fraught. In the case of organised crime, jurisdiction belongs primarily to the states rather than the commonwealth. There is little incentive for the Australian Federal Police to devote valuable resources to areas that are low on their internal list of organisational priorities. The same questions that undermine commonwealth–state co-operation also bedevil interstate investigations: Whose turf? How much is it going to cost? Who gets the credit? Who pays? Who gets the blame if something goes wrong?

On 20 August 2009 Jonathon Pearlman wrote in the *Sydney Morning Herald* that 'Australia's domestic spy agency, ASIO, could be expanded into an FBI-style agency that targets a range of threats such as organised crime and border security.' Pearlman quoted Dr David McKnight, an associate professor of journalism at the University of New South Wales who has written extensively about ASIO, as saying that this would mark a 'profound' change for ASIO. 'There has been a long, historic tension between the ASIO and the Commonwealth and [later the] federal police. This could exacerbate that tension.' Dr McKnight pointed out, however, that 'the two agencies have had to work together since 2001, so plans to broaden ASIO's role could reflect a better working relationship'.

The *Sydney Morning Herald* reported that possible changes to the role of ASIO 'have the backing of senior officials in the prime minister's and attorney-general's departments'. Getting commonwealth agencies to cooperate rather than compete is vital—but it is only half the battle. The states and territories have a long tradition of rivalry and blame-shifting. The ability to overcome that tradition will be the real measure of Australia's seriousness in the fight against organised crime and terrorism.

Afterword

Organised crime has had a profound impact on Australia's social, political and economic wellbeing. Between $4 billion and $12 billion in drug money alone is sent offshore every year. The shootings, bombings and arson attacks carried out since the mid 1980s by outlaw motorcycle gangs have claimed at least 100 lives. A dozen murders and more than 100 shootings were committed in the wave of Middle Eastern violence and other crime that swept across south and south-west Sydney from the late 1990s to 2004.

The impact of terrorism has been different to that of organised crime and is reflected in the 90 pieces of federal, state and territory legislation enacted since 2001. Critics argue that this legislation has reduced human rights and given too much power to governments, through law enforcement and security organisations, to intrude into people's lives. The new laws have also been dismissed as political 'quick fixes' rather than genuine solutions.

Supporters, on the other hand, insist that such laws are necessary to protect the freedoms that come with living in a democratic society. (At the time of writing, Federal Attorney General Robert McClelland produced a discussion paper outlining a broad range of reforms. Some of the suggested reforms would strengthen existing legislation and create new law enforcement powers while others would have the opposite effect, increasing accountability and rolling back excessive powers.)

Whichever view one holds, the fact is that the threat of terrorism is real and growing. The Australian Federal Police 2007–08 Annual Report reveals that during the year it investigated 40 new terrorist cases, finalised 35 cases, and still had 76 cases on hand at the end of the reporting year. Very few criminal prosecutions or other legal actions appear to have resulted from these investigations.

Organised crime and terrorism will never be eradicated, but they can be contained. The challenge we face is twofold. One is to avoid sacrificing our traditional values of personal freedom and democratic accountability in return for short-term gains. The other is to develop and implement law enforcement strategies that are as sophisticated and effective as the criminals they are designed to catch.

By and large, the criminal justice system has served us well, but it must be continually reviewed and, where appropriate, adjusted to deal with new threats. These adjustments must never be at the expense of public confidence in its contribution to the freedoms and benefits we expect from a democracy. Fairness, and the perception of fairness, is fundamental to that confidence.

Too often, the political response to organised crime and terrorism has been the same: the spontaneous announcement of new legislation aimed not at the roots of the problem but at the visible manifestation of it: the outlawing of bikie gangs, for instance, as a substitute for the painstaking investigation and dismantling of the bikies' role in the trafficking of illegal drugs and other serious crime. We have referred to the argument of Nicholas Cowdery QC, the director of the New South Wales Office of Public Prosecutions, and others, that what is needed is not new legislation but the rigorous policing and enforcement of the legislation that exists. Cowdery's observation is equally valid whether applied to organised crime or terrorism, and we support his view.

As we have shown, both in this and our earlier book, *Smack Express,* state and federal law enforcement authorities have had significant victories in the fight against organised crime gangs, locking up principals for long periods, seizing their assets and otherwise disrupting their operations. But the focus on individual arrests, seizures and confiscations means that no matter how important a single bust might appear to be, the damage inflicted will only be temporary. The gangs simply retreat and regroup, often emerging stronger than they were before. The underlying structures of organised crime remain intact. Long-term disruption of organised crime depends on constant police pressure, particularly once gangs have been weakened. This pressure is expensive in terms of both money and resources. It takes political courage to sustain it—the sort of courage that is rarely rewarded at the ballot box.

Like the business of crime, the business of terrorism is changing with the times. The terrorists are learning new methods, using new weapons and finding new sources of funding. The least we can demand is that law enforcement agencies, and the governments they answer to, show themselves to be equally adaptable, equally resourceful and equally determined.

APPENDIX

Politically motivated violence in Australia (1966–2009)

The term 'politically motivated violence' is taken from the *Australian Security Intelligence Organisation Act 1979*. It refers to acts or threats of violence or unlawful harm intended to achieve a political objective, and acts that are likely to lead to violence and are intended to overthrow Australia's system of government. The popular term is 'terrorism'. The following is a comprehensive list of terrorist incidents and documented terrorist threats in Australia, and against Australians overseas, since 1966. Some of those accused or investigated were acquitted or were never charged, and their inclusion in this list does not imply that they were guilty of any offence.

The chronology has been compiled from a variety of sources including: a report by New South Wales Senior Constable Wayne Hoffman, 'Terrorism in Australia: 1966–1994'; Parliament of Australia, 'Terrorism in the Nineties: Issues and Problems (1970–92)'; Global Terrorism Database, Study of Terrorism and Responses to Terrorism (START), A Center of Excellence of the US Department of Homeland Security based at the University of Maryland; annual reports of the Australian Security Intelligence Organisation, the Australian Federal Police and various state and territory law enforcement agencies; speeches and media reports.

1966

1.	**21/06/66.** The Leader of the Federal Opposition, Arthur Calwell, shot at point blank range through the closed window of his car at Mosman, Sydney, by 19-year-old Peter Kocan. Calwell had just addressed an anti-Vietnam conscription meeting at the town hall. His face was cut by flying glass. Kocan was confined to a mental institution.

2.	**17/11/66.** Parcel bomb mailed to pro-Yugoslav supporter exploded prematurely in the mail room of the Melbourne General Post Office.

1968

3.	**08/08/68.** Petrol bombs detonated in an attempt to destroy the offices of the US Consulate-General in Melbourne.

1970

4.	**01/01/70.** Police foiled a planned bomb attack on a Serbian Orthodox Church in Canberra.

5.   **21/10/70.** Bomb attack on the Yugoslav Consulate-General in Melbourne.

1971

6.   **17/01/71.** Bomb attack on the Soviet Embassy in Canberra.

7.   **04/04/71.** Bomb attack on a Serbian Orthodox Church in Melbourne.

8.   **12/09/71.** Attempted arson attack on a Serbian Orthodox Church in Melbourne.

9.   **23/11/71.** Bomb attack on a Yugoslav travel agency in Sydney.

10.   **19/12/71.** Bomb attack on a theatre in Sydney.

1972

11.   **11/01/72.** Bomb attack on a Serbian Orthodox Church in Canberra.

12.   **14/02/72.** Armed assault on the Yugoslav Consulate in Perth.

13.   **16/02/72.** Bomb attacks on two Yugoslav tourist agencies in Sydney.

14.   **20/04/72.** Bomb attack on the Brisbane office of the Communist Party of Australia. It was the anniversary of Hitler's birth and the Australian National Socialist Party is believed to have been responsible for the attack.

15.   **26/04/72.** Bomb attack on the Melbourne residence of a pro-Yugoslav political figure.

16.   **17/09/72.** Bomb exploded inside the Yugoslav General Trade and Tourist Agency in Sydney, injuring 16 people.

17–21. **09/72.** Five Black September Organisation letter bombs addressed to Israeli diplomats in Sydney and Canberra intercepted in post offices in Australia.

22–23. **03/10/72.** Two letter bombs addressed to Israeli officials in Sydney intercepted by the postal service.

24. **06/10/72.** Schoolchildren and their teacher kidnapped and held for ransom in Victoria. (This became known as the Faraday hostages/extortion case.)

25. **02/11/72.** Letter bomb sent to a prominent member of the Jewish community in Australia.

26. **08/12/72.** Bomb attack on Serbian Orthodox Church in Brisbane.

1973

27. **24/01/73.** Letter bomb addressed to a Jewish businessman in New South Wales intercepted at the post office.

28. **09/04/73.** Arson attack on the office of a Croatian newspaper editor in Melbourne.

1974

29. **24/12/74.** Firebomb attack on Pan American ticket office in Sydney.

1975

30. **25/05/75.** Bomb attack on the Sunny Adriatic Trade and Tourist Centre (Yugoslav) in Melbourne.

31–32. **19/11/75.** Letter bombs addressed to the Queensland premier exploded when opened, injuring staff. A similar device sent to the prime minister was detected and defused.

1977

33–34. **15/02/77.** Edwin John Eastwood kidnapped schoolchildren and teacher at Wooreen in Victoria. Eastwood demanded a ransom of US$7 million, guns, drugs and the release of 17 inmates from Pentridge Prison. Eastwood was shot through the right knee and captured. Three months earlier Eastwood had escaped from Geelong Prison where he was serving a 15-year sentence for a similar offence in 1972. After pleading guilty to 15 counts of kidnapping and 10 related charges, Eastwood was sentenced to 21 years' jail, to be served cumulatively with the 11 years remaining on the previous sentence.

35. **15/07/77.** Griffith anti-drugs campaigner and political activist Donald Mackay murdered in Griffith by the `ndrangheta (also known as the Honoured Society or Calabrian Mafia).

36. **29/08/77.** Arson attack on the Indian High Commission in Canberra.

37. **31/08/77.** Arson attack on the Australian Atomic Energy Commission in Sydney.

38. **15/09/77.** Indian Defence Attaché and his wife kidnapped in Canberra. The Defence Attaché was stabbed in the chest.

39. **19/10/77.** Air India employee stabbed in Melbourne.

40. **04/12/77.** Bomb attack on Yugoslav Airlines office in Melbourne.

41–43. **24/12/77.** Gelignite bomb attack on the statue of Yugoslav General Draza Mihailovic in Canberra— it was the third attempt to destroy the statue by bombing in seven years. The others occurred in January 1970 and January 1972.

1978

44. **13/02/78.** Bomb exploded outside the Hilton Hotel in Sydney, killing one police officer and two civilians and injuring seven others. The Australian prime minister and 11 visiting heads of state were staying in the building at the time.

45. **25/03/78.** Bomb found and defused in the Indian High Commissioner's residence in Canberra.

46. **18/05/78.** Bomb exploded outside New South Wales Police headquarters in Sydney, causing extensive damage.

47. **27/05/78.** Bomb attack on the residence of the Indian Ambassador in Sydney.

48. **02/09/78.** Police arrested Croatians involved in military training at Eden on the New South Wales south coast. They were preparing for an armed incursion into Yugoslavia. Previous armed incursions into Yugoslavia by Australian Croats occurred in 1963 and 1972.

49. **13/11/78.** Six people hospitalised after Iraqi officials presented poisoned sweets to participants at the Assyrian Universal Alliance (AUA) Congress in Fairfield in Sydney's west.

1979

50. **04/1/79.** Bomb attack on the home of an Australian government intelligence analyst in Canberra.

51. **08/02/79.** Security forces and police discovered conspiracy to bomb Yugoslav targets and water pipelines in Sydney.

52. **04/04/79.** Attempt to hijack a Pan American plane at Sydney airport. The hijacker, who was armed with a bomb, was shot and killed by police.

53.   **24/04/79.** Letter bomb sent to Boans department store in Perth exploded, injuring nine people.

1980

54.   **23/06/80.** Family Law Court Judge David Opas shot dead at his home in Sydney. Attacks on judges of the court continued for six years.

55.   **06/11/80.** One person injured during an armed assault at the Sydney home of Nicholas Papallo, honorary vice-consul for Italy.

56.   **20/11/80.** Bomb attack on the Iwasaki Tourist Resort at Yeppoon in Queensland, causing serious damage.

57.   **17/12/80.** Turkish Consul General Sarik Ariyak and his bodyguard assassinated outside the consul general's home in Sydney. Justice Commandos of the Armenian Genocide claimed responsibility. Levon Demirian, a member of the Armenian Revolutionary Federation, was suspected of involvement in the assassinations.

58.   **17/12/80.** Bomb attack on Woolworths store in Warilla, south of Wollongong.

59.   **19/12/80.** Bomb attack destroyed Woolworths store at Maitland near Newcastle.

60.   **24/12/80.** Two people injured in a bomb attack on a Woolworths store in the Sydney central business district.

1982

61.   **05/82.** Bomb attack damaged Woolworths store at Liverpool.

62.   **23/12/82.** Bomb attack on Israeli Consulate in Sydney.

63.   **23/12/82.** Two bombs exploded in the carpark of the Hakoah Club in Sydney. A third bomb failed to detonate.

1983

64.   **12/11/83.** Gelignite and ammonium nitrate bomb found and defused at the Lucas Heights nuclear reactor in Sydney.

1984

65.   **06/03/84.** One person injured in a bomb attack on the home of Family Law Court Judge Richard Gee in Sydney.

66.   **15/04/84.** Bomb attack on the Family Law Court building at Parramatta in Sydney's west.

67.   **04/07/84.** Family Law Court Judge Ray Watson injured and his wife, Pearl, killed in a bomb attack on their apartment at Greenwich on Sydney's lower north shore.

1985

68.   **1985.** Commonwealth Police intelligence alleged that Vietnamese criminals in Melbourne were buying weapons from Turkish terrorists. The weapons were said to include hand grenades, machine guns and pistols, to be used by Vietnamese gangs in an ongoing feud with Chinese criminal groups in Sydney and Melbourne.

69.   **05/85.** Bomb attack on the Coroner's Court in Melbourne.

70.   **15/06/85.** Bomb attack on the vehicle of Bronwyn Ridgeway, assistant secretary of the New South Wales Nurses' Association.

71. **05/07/85.** Bomb attack on the Union Carbide factory in Rosebery in south-eastern Sydney. A group calling itself the Pacific Peacemakers claimed responsibility.

72. **13/07/85.** Two shots fired at the Vietnamese Embassy in Canberra.

73. **21/07/85.** One person killed and 48 injured in a bomb attack on the Jehovah's Witness Kingdom Hall at Casula in Sydney's south-west. The attack was believed to have been connected with Family Law Court bombings.

74. **19/09/85.** Car bomb exploded at Canterbury Race-course in Sydney, injuring one person.

1986

75. **27/03/86.** Car bomb attack on police headquarters in Russell Street, Melbourne. One police officer was killed, and ten police and eleven civilians were injured. Three Melbourne criminals were eventually jailed for the bombing.

76. **23/11/86.** Bomb exploded in the carpark under the offices of the Turkish Consulate General in South Yarra, Melbourne. The bomber, Hagop Levonian, a member of the Armenian Revolutionary Federation, was killed when the device exploded prematurely. Levonian's co-conspirator, Levon Demirian, was charged with the murder of Levonian and conspiring with Levonian to carry out the bombing. He was convicted of both charges in 1987 and sentenced to 25 years' jail. The murder conviction was quashed on appeal and he served ten years for conspiracy. At the time of his arrest in Sydney, Demirian had been preparing to leave Australia for Beirut. Demirian was

a suspect in the 1980 assassination of Turkish Consul General Sarik Ariyak.

1987

77.   **19/01/87.** Bomb exploded in the sorting room of the Roma Street Mail Exchange in Brisbane, injuring six. An anti-Turkish group calling itself the Greek-Bulgarian-Armenian Front was believed to be responsible for the attack.

78.   **10/87.** Nearly 600 kilograms of explosives stolen from mining sites in several states by a drug syndicate, including Lebanese criminals, with the aim of bombing police stations and vehicles in Sydney and Melbourne. Police arrested the ringleaders before the explosives could be used.

1988

79.   **22/03/88.** Two petrol bombs thrown at the residence of an employee of the South African Embassy in Canberra. The attack was linked to Australia's anti-apartheid stance.

80.   **10/04/88.** Firebomb attack on the car and Canberra home of Jan Hough, third secretary at the South African Embassy. Part of his house was also destroyed. Documents linked the March and April attacks.

81.   **02/07/88.** Firebomb attack on the Yugoslav Club in Adelaide.

82.   **18/07/88.** Firebomb attack on the car of United States Defence Attaché Colonel Dean Stickwell in Canberra. Police suspected links with attacks on the South African Consulate and staff on 22 March and 10 April.

83. **01/09/88.** China City restaurant in Como, Western Australia, torched by the Neo-Nazi Australian Nationalist Movement.

84. **01/09/88.** Mandarin Chinese restaurant in Como, Western Australia, torched by the Australian Nationalist Movement.

85. **12/10/88.** Two police ambushed and killed in Walsh Street, Melbourne. Both killers were later killed in police raids.

86. **16/11/88.** 'Necklacing' of an effigy outside the home of an anti-apartheid activist in Sydney.

87. **22/11/88.** Golden House Chinese restaurant in Bellevue, Western Australia, torched by the Australian Nationalist Movement.

88. **27/11/88.** Croatian youth shot while demonstrating outside the Yugoslav Consulate General in Sydney.

1989

89. **16/01/89.** Attempt by the Australian Nationalist Movement to torch the Ko Sing Chinese restaurant at Ferndale in Western Australia.

90. **19/01/89.** Ling Nan Chinese restaurant in Perth, Western Australia, torched by the Australian Nationalist Movement.

91. **27/01/89.** Sydney home of Eddie Funde, Australian representative of the African National Congress, shot up. Two members of National Action were charged and jailed for two years. Three years later Dr James Saleam, former leader of National Action and later leader of the Australia First Party (NSW), was sentenced to three and a half years' jail for being an accessory before the fact to the attack.

92.   **21/05/89.** Arson attack on Abbey's Bookshop in Sydney—believed to be the result of the bookshop selling Salman Rushdie's novel *The Satanic Verses*.

93.   **25/05/89.** Bomb attack on Ko Sing Chinese restaurant at Ferndale in Western Australia. The attack—the second in five months—was believed to have been carried out by the Australian Nationalist Movement.

94.   **01/09/89.** David Locke, a member of the right-wing Australian Nationalist Movement, killed in Perth by two other members of the group who suspected him of being an ASIO or police informer.

95.   **27/10/89.** Incendiary device thrown at the home of a US Embassy employee in Sydney.

1990

96.   **21/04/90.** David Noble, a member of the right-wing group National Action, murdered with an axe in Sydney by other members of the group after a party in the Melbourne suburb of Pascoe Vale South to celebrate Hitler's birthday. Dane Sweetman was subsequently sentenced to 20 years' jail.

1991

97.   **23/01/91.** Firebomb attack on Rooty Hill Islamic Centre in Sydney's west.

98.   **25/01/91.** Firebomb attack on a Jewish kindergarten in Melbourne.

99.   **25/01/91.** Lebanese-Australian man arrested in Sydney for planning to hijack an aircraft to Iraq.

100. **06/02/91.** Lebanese-Australian man apprehended in possession of a rifle near the Iraqi Embassy and the Prime Minister's Lodge in Canberra.

101.   **20/02/91.** Firebomb attack on the American Australian Association building in Sydney.

102.   **26/02/91.** Firebomb attack on the Sephardi Synagogue in Sydney.

103.   **05/03/91.** Firebomb attack on the Bankstown and District War Memorial Synagogue in Sydney's south-west.

104.   **05/03/91.** Firebomb attack on the Air Force Navy Club in Sydney.

105.   **12/03/91.** Attempt to firebomb the North Shore Synagogue and Masada College in Sydney.

106.   **28/03/91.** Firebomb attack on the southern Sydney Illawarra Synagogue.

107.   **03/04/91.** Attempt to petrol bomb a Serbian church in Melbourne.

108.   **18/04/91.** Chairman of the Coptic Human Rights Commission, Dr Makeen Morcos, assassinated in Sydney after giving a radio talk criticising Islamists and the Egyptian government for harassing and murdering Coptic Christians. The assailants were thought to have been agents of the Egyptian government or members of an Australian-based cell of an Islamist group.

109.   **20/04/91.** National Action member Wayne Smith murdered in Sydney because of suspicions that he was an ASIO or police informant. Another National Action member was subsequently convicted of the murder.

110.   The federal government identified 19 terrorist groups as having active supporters and/or representatives in Australia. They were
    • African National Congress in South Africa
    • Armenian Liberation Army in Armenia

- Australian Neo-Nazi groups such as National Action; National Socialists Defending Australian People; White Australian Resistance (formerly White Aryan Resistance); and the Australian National Socialist Movement
- Fedayin-e-Khalq in Iran
- Gush Emunim, Israeli right-wing group
- Hamas
- Hezbollah in Lebanon
- Islamic fundamentalists in Indonesia and Malaysia
- Khmer Rouge in Cambodia
- Lebanese Forces in Lebanon
- Main People's Congress (Arab People's Congress) in Libya
- Moro National Liberation Front in the Philippines
- Mujahedeen Khalq Group (People's Holy Warriors)
- Palestinian Liberation Organisation
- Progressive Socialist Party in Lebanon
- Provisional IRA in Ireland
- Syrian National Socialist Party in Syria.

111. **03/09/91.** Bomb attack on Perth headquarters of the Western Australian government's Lotteries office.
112. **12/09/91.** Shotgun fired at a window of the Indonesian Consulate in Darwin.
113. **15/09/91.** Molotov cocktails thrown at the venue of a Serbian function in Melbourne.
114. **15/09/91.** Firebomb attack on the Melbourne home of a politically active Croatian family.
115. **23/09/91.** Six Molotov cocktails thrown at a Serbian community centre in Melbourne.

1992

116. **11/01/92.** Arson attack on the United States Consulate in Brisbane.

117. **06/04/92.** Several staff injured during an attack on the Iranian Embassy in Canberra by members of a Mujahedeen group.

118. **05/06/92.** Reverend Doug Good of Western Australia stabbed to death in the rectory next to the Fremantle Church of Christ by an Iranian Muslim while preparing to officiate at a marriage between a Christian man and an Iranian woman who had converted from Islam to Christianity. Good's killer was sentenced to six years' jail for the 'unintentional killing'.

119. **12/11/92.** Property damaged during an attack on the Indonesian Consulate in Darwin by East Timorese Activists.

1993

120. **26/02/93.** Six people killed and more than 1000 injured in a bomb attack on World Trade Center in New York. Mohammad Salameh and Nidal Ayyad were arrested in the US shortly after the bombing. Mahmud Abouhalima was arrested in Egypt and extradited back to the United States. Ahmad M Ajaj, who entered the United States from Pakistan; Ramzi Yousef, who was on the same flight as Ajaj but was refused entry to the US; and a sixth person known only as 'Yassin' were also identified as being involved in the bombing. Salameh, Abouhalima and Ajaj were convicted of the bombing and sentenced to life in jail. In 1995 Yousef was arrested in Pakistan and extradited

to the United States, where he was tried and convicted of another terrorist attack and sentenced to life in jail. Two years later he was convicted of the World Trade Center bombing. Several others believed to be involved in the bombing were convicted of terrorist offences. Seven years later police confirmed telephone contacts with supporters in New South Wales both before and immediately after the bombing.

121. **03/93.** Firebomb attack on Foo Win Chinese restaurant in Perth. The attack was believed to have been carried out by the Australian Nationalist Movement.

122. **28/06/93.** About 25 Kurds barricaded themselves inside the UN building in Sydney demanding support from Australian government against Turkish oppression of Kurds.

123. **01/08/93.** Firebomb attack on Illawarra Synagogue in southern Sydney—the second attack in just over three years.

1994

124. **28/01/94.** Firebomb attack on the Mexican Consulate in Sydney, believed to have been carried out by members of the Zapatista National Liberation Army.

125. **02/03/94.** One officer killed and several injured in a bomb attack on National Crime Authority offices in Adelaide. The bombing was believed to have been carried out by a member of the `ndrangheta—the Calabrian Mafia.

126. **14/03/94.** Bomb attack on the offices of a Greek-Australian organisation in Melbourne.

127. **18/03/94.** Firebomb attack on a Greek Orthodox Church in Sydney.

128. **25/03/94.** Attack by pro-Kurdish group on the German Consulate in Melbourne.
129. **05/09/94.** Labor MP for Cabramatta, John Newman, murdered on the orders of his political rival Phuong Canh Ngo.

1995

130. **Mid 1995.** Singapore-based terrorism expert Rohan Gunaratna reported the Liberation Tigers of Tamil Elam (LTTE) as buying aircraft, arms and explosives from Australia. As late as 2006 LTTE bought remote control devices to detonate bombs in Sri Lanka. Recovered devices had Australian markings.
131. **17/06/95.** Firebomb attack on the French Consulate in Perth—believed to have been carried out by the Pacific Popular Front.
132. **22/06/95.** Bomb attack on a Serbian restaurant in Sydney.

1996

133. **1996.** Egyptian exile Mohamed Hassanien deported over his alleged association with Jemaah Islamiyah. Hassanien had entered Australia from Denmark on a false passport, allegedly with local assistance. The deportation followed a tip-off that he could be planning terrorist attacks against Jewish targets in Australia.
134. **06/96.** Ahmad al-Hamwi, better known as Abu Omar, was given asylum in Australia and took up residency in Sydney's south-west. He told the Refugee Review Tribunal that he had no involvement in terrorism. Reports later emerged that police

in the Philippines believed that only a year earlier Omar had been a director of the International Relations and Information Centre (IRIC), an Islamic charity based in Manila that was linked to the foiled 1995 Bojinka plot—sometimes described as a precursor to 9/11—and to the 1993 World Trade Center bomber, Ramzi Yousef. Omar was a relative by marriage to Osama bin Laden. In 2006 Australian security and immigration authorities investigated the circumstances under which Omar was allowed into Australia and his alleged connections with Islamic militant groups. Al-Hamwi has not been accused of any offence in Australia. It was reported at the time that he had declined to comment on the allegations about his past.

135.   **03/08/96.** Pipe bomb attack on Australian government offices in Coffs Harbour on New South Wales north coast.

136.   **23/10/96.** Bomb exploded at Circular Quay railway station, Sydney.

137.   **27/10/96.** Bomb exploded at Central railway station, Sydney.

138.   **31/10/96.** Bomb exploded at St James railway station, Sydney.

139.   **29/12/96.** Bomb detected and defused at Wynyard railway station, Sydney. The four attacks were believed to have been carried out by the same person or persons.

1997

140.   **21/08/97.** Bomb attack on the home of an Australian government official in Canberra.

141.   **1997–2000.** Turkish immigrant Mehmet Akin Kayirici sent letters to various consulates threatening to shoot down planes carrying US, French, English and Israeli athletes coming to the Sydney Olympics. He also threatened to attack the Opening Ceremony unless $100 million ransom was paid and Israel released imprisoned colleagues. Kayirici claimed to be part of a 15-strong terrorist cell operating in Australia. Arrested in March 2000, he was charged with sending threatening letters and threatening to destroy an aircraft. In 2001 he was jailed for six years.

1998

142.   **22/09/98.** Three Molotov cocktails thrown at offices of the Jabiluka uranium mine in Darwin.

143.   **01/11/98.** Lakemba Police Station in Sydney's south-west attacked in a drive-by shooting. (See March 2004 re Saleh Jamal.)

2000

144.   **2000.** Phone intercept recorded Lebanese Muslim Zecky 'Zac' Mallah discussing the idea of being a suicide bomber with a well-known radical Sydney sheik associated with the extremist Islamic Youth Movement. Mallah was arrested in September 2003. (See September 2003 for further information regarding Mallah.)

145.   **2000.** Jack Roche planned bomb attacks on the Israeli Embassy in Canberra and the Israeli Consulate in Sydney. In June 2003 Roche was sentenced to nine years' jail in Western Australia.

146. **03/00.** New Zealand police raided houses in Auckland and found evidence of a conspiracy to blow up the nuclear research reactor at Lucas Heights. The residents were Afghan refugees. Some were believed to have had military training and fought in Afghanistan, Iraq, Iran, Bosnia, Chechnya, Somalia and Sri Lanka. The group was also involved in people smuggling, money laundering and other criminal activities. Only minor charges were laid.

147. **22/05/00.** After numerous threats against Olympic organisers police searched a property in the Blue Mountains and homes in two Sydney suburbs, seizing chemicals, a computer and records. They arrested a New Zealand man for possession of explosives. The man, Dion Monaghan, had changed his name to that of Nazi henchman Martin Bormann. The following year Bormann pleaded guilty to possessing explosives, carrying a knife in a public place and unauthorised use of a home-made rocket launcher and was sentenced to 15 months' jail. He was released immediately due to time already served and deported to New Zealand on the grounds of racial vilification.

148. **Mid 2000.** Security agencies received information that Lebanese-born Sydney airport baggage handler Belal Khazaal had sent recruits to train in Afghanistan. Khazaal was believed to have helped train terrorist recruits, some linked to al-Qaeda, on a property near Braidwood in New South Wales. Evidence of military weapons and explosives was found on the property. After several years back in Lebanon, Khazaal returned to settle in Lakemba and became a prominent member of the Islamic Youth Movement.

He was alleged to be a member of al-Qaeda and to have undergone military training in Afghanistan in early 1998. In 2003 Khazaal was convicted in absentia by a military tribunal for bombing attacks in Lebanon and sentenced to jail. (See March 2003 and June 2004 for further information re Khazaal.)

149. **Mid 2000.** Five people deported from Australia for having links to extremist groups in the Middle East, Europe and Asia.

150. **09/00.** Australian citizen Noorpolat Abdulla arrested after two local police were shot dead in the Soviet Republic of Kazakhstan. Abdulla was convicted of preparing a terrorist attack and sentenced to 15 years' jail.

151. **Before 2001.** Al-Qaeda and Jemaah Islamiyah actively canvassed attacks in Australia according to the Deputy Director-General of ASIO.

2001

152. **06/01.** Australian Army Captain Shane Della-Vedova, an ammunitions technical officer and ordnance specialist, stole ten rocket launchers. One was sold to a Lebanese drug trafficker associated with gangs including the Bandidos outlaw motor cycle gang. Most, if not all, eventually fell into the hands of Adnan Darwiche and his gang, several of whose members became involved in terrorism. Some rocket launchers were on-sold to 'Hussein' (not his real name), who was arrested in 2005 during Operation Pendennis. In 2007 Della-Vedova was sentenced to ten years' jail for the theft and sale of the rocket launchers. Only one has been recovered.

153.   **07/01.** Steven Rogers, a security guard at a Melbourne abortion clinic, shot and killed by anti-abortionist Peter James Knight.

154.   **08/01.** Khalid Sheikh Mohammed, al-Qaeda's chief operational planner, applied for and was issued with an Australian visa in a false name. The visa was not used and was later cancelled. Authorities believe Khalid was planning to come to Australia for 'operational' purposes.

155.   **11/09/01.** Nineteen al-Qaeda hijackers crashed two planes into the World Trade Center in New York, and a third into the Pentagon in Washington. A fourth hijacked plane crashed in a field in Somerset County, Pennsylvania. Nearly 3000 people died in the attacks, including 22 Australians. Eight years later, and almost seven years after his capture in Pakistan, US authorities announced that Khalid Sheikh Mohammed, the alleged mastermind of the attacks, and four other conspirators, would be tried in a civil court in New York just a few blocks from Ground Zero.

156.   **14/09/01.** Two Molotov cocktails thrown at a mosque in Brisbane's southside suburb of Holland Park.

157.   **23/09/01.** Firebomb attack on a mosque in the Brisbane suburb of Kuraby. In December 2002 24-year-old Terrence George Hanlon was jailed for six years for the attack.

158.   **30/09/01.** Foiled attack on a mosque in Brisbane's south-west suburb of Darra.

159.   **05/10/01.** Egyptian-born Australian Mamdouh Habib arrested in Pakistan and detained at Guantanamo

Bay by US authorities after undertaking an al-Qaeda training course in a camp near Kabul. Habib admitted links with conspirators involved in the 1993 bombing of the World Trade Center in New York. Habib later recanted some of the admissions allegedly made at the time of his arrest, saying they had been made under duress. All charges were eventually dropped and Habib returned to Australia in 2005.

160.   **15/10/01.** Letter contaminated with an undisclosed chemical sent to the US Consulate in Melbourne.

161.   **03/11/01.** Osama bin Laden publicly declared Australia to be a legitimate target for terrorist attacks.

162.   **11/01.** The Australian government deported Ahmad Abdul Rahman Awdah Al Joufi, a Saudi national and suspected al-Qaeda member, from Melbourne, after he arrived on a false passport, reportedly to recruit fighters for a jihad against Russia. Joufi was described as a recruiter and fundraiser for Chechen Islamic fighters and an Osama bin Laden loyalist for at least ten years. He fought as a volunteer in Chechnya during the mid 1990s and reached the rank of unit commander.

163.   **12/01.** Security forces disrupted a Jemaah Islamiyah bombing campaign against western interests in Singapore, including the Australian High Commission. Over several months 36 people—32 of them identified as being members of Jemaah Islamiyah—were arrested in relation to the plot.

164.   **12/01.** Twenty-six-year-old Mohammed Afroz Abdul Razak arrested in India. He confessed to being part of an al-Qaeda cell using India as a base

to launch attacks in Britain, Australia and India. The Australian target was said to be Melbourne's Rialto Towers. Afroz trained as a pilot in both Britain and Australia. In 2005 he was sentenced to seven years' jail for plotting attacks against a friendly nation and forging documents.

165.   **12/01.** After converting to Islam, Australian-born David Hicks was captured in Afghanistan. He was held in Guantanamo Bay until 2007 when he pleaded guilty to 'providing material support for terrorism'. Hicks was returned to Australia to serve the remaining nine months of a suspended seven-year sentence.

2002

166.   **12/10/02.** Bomb attack on tourist nightclubs in Bali killed 202 people, including 88 Australians, and injured another 209.

2003

167.   **01/03.** Australian Jack 'Jihad Jack' Thomas, 30, arrested in Pakistan. Thomas admitted training at the al-Faruq camp in Afghanistan. Bin Laden visited the camp three times during that period. He also admitted to receiving about $5000 from al-Qaeda sources. According to BBC News Thomas admitted that an al-Qaeda operative told him Bin Laden wanted a 'white boy' to carry out terrorist attacks in Australia. In 2006 Thomas was found guilty of receiving funds from a terrorist organisation and possessing a falsified passport. Both convictions were quashed on appeal. At the retrial Thomas was acquitted of receiving funds from

al-Qaeda but convicted of possessing a falsified passport and sentenced to nine months' jail. He was immediately released due to time already served. He has been acquitted of all terrorism charges.

168. **2003.** ASIO and the Australian Federal Police foiled a plan by Willie Brigitte, working with Lashkar-e-Taiba, an Islamic group fighting against Indian control of Kashmir, to carry out a terrorist attack against Lucas Heights nuclear research reactor. He was deported and held by French authorities. Convicted in 2007 of planning terrorism attacks in Australia, he was sentenced to nine years' jail. Brigitte was a close associate of Faheem Lodhi, a Pakistani–Australian later convicted of terrorist offences.

169. **2003.** 'Imad' (not his real name) of Greenacre in Sydney's south-west, who supplied weapons to the Darwiche gang and other Lebanese gangs, travelled to Lebanon where he traded weapons with Hezbollah and supplied them with false Australian passports which were later used to visit Australia. 'Imad' was detained in Lebanon for possessing false passports, then returned to Australia, where he continued to supply weapons to criminal gangs.

170. **09/03.** Police raided Zeky (Zac) Mallah's Condell Park home, near Bankstown in Sydney's south-west. They found a gun, ammunition and a note to ASIO saying he wanted to 'take the life of every ASIO officer I can get my hands on'. Mallah was convicted on firearms offences and fined $1400. Later he was charged with planning a suicide attack on the Sydney offices of the Department of Foreign Affairs and Trade or ASIO. In 2005 he was acquitted

of both terrorism charges but pleaded guilty to threatening to kill commonwealth officers and sentenced to two years' jail.

171.   **12/03.** Belal and his brother Maher Khazaal were convicted in absentia by a military tribunal in Lebanon of helping fund a series of bomb attacks by an Islamic group and sentenced to five years' jail. In 2000 Belal was involved in sending recruits to Lebanon and training recruits in New South Wales.

2004

172–74. **01/02/04.** Three Chinese restaurants in Perth's southern suburbs, the Spearwood, the Foo Win and the Lakelands, were firebombed and daubed with swastikas. One of the restaurants, the Foo Win, was also attacked in 1993 and in July 2004.

175.   **02/04.** Perth petrol station owned by an Iraqi daubed with swastikas in a racist attack.

176.   **03/04.** Saleh Jamal was a key figure in gangs led by Danny Karam and Michael Kanaan. He had come under the influence of radical Islamic teachers during an earlier 12-month sentence for supplying cannabis. While on bail for the 1998 shooting attack on the Lakemba Police Station, Jamal fled Australia on a false passport provided by Belal Khazaal. Two months later he was arrested for terrorism offences in Lebanon. He was convicted of possessing weapons and explosives, using a forged Australian passport, forming a terrorist group and planning acts that endanger state security and sentenced to five years' jail. In 2006 the Lebanese Court of Appeal overturned Jamal's conviction. He

was extradited to Sydney and sentenced to nine years' jail for shooting with intent to cause grievous bodily harm and discharging a firearm in a public place. In November 2009 Jamal was convicted of the drive-by shooting of the Lakemba Police Station.

177. **15/04/04.** Sydney medical student Izhar ul-Haque charged with 'training with a terrorist organisation'. The training allegedly occurred during a visit to Pakistan and involved the Lashkar-e-Taiba. In November 2007 the New South Wales Supreme Court ruled that 'misconduct' by the AFP and ASIO officers made their interviews with ul-Haque inadmissible. All charges were dropped.

178. **22/04/04.** Sydney architect Faheem Lodhi arrested and charged with terrorism-related offences linked to the ul-Haque investigation. Lodhi was convicted on 19 June 2006 of acts done in preparation for a terrorist act, including a plot to blow up a national electricity grid, and sentenced to 20 years' jail. He had made regular trips to Pakistan and around 2002 became involved in Lashkar-e-Taiba in Pakistan. Lodhi was a close associate of Willie Brigitte.

179. **02/06/04.** Former Qantas cleaner Belal Khazaal was charged with collecting or making documents likely to facilitate terrorist acts (he had produced a 110-page jihad book in Arabic called 'Provision in the Rules of Jihad—Short Wise Rules and Organisational Structures that Concern every Fighter and Mujahid Fighting against the Infidels') and inciting others to engage in a terrorist act. Khazaal was reportedly planning to bomb US embassies in Venezuela and elsewhere as well as US interests in the Philippines. On

11 September 2008 Khazaal was found guilty in the New South Wales Supreme Court on the first charge. He was sentenced to a maximum of 12 years' jail. The jury failed to agree on the second charge.

180.   **17/07/04.** A Perth synagogue was attacked and daubed with swastikas and racist graffiti.

181–83.**19/07/04.** The Foo Win and two other Chinese restaurants in Perth's southern suburbs were plastered with swastikas and racist slogans by members of the Australian Nationalist Movement. The Foo Win had been firebombed five months earlier. It had also been attacked in 1993.

184.   **09/09/04.** One-tonne bomb exploded outside the Australian Embassy in Kuningan District, South Jakarta, killing nine people including the suicide bomber and several embassy employees. More than 150 people were wounded. Two plotters were jailed and a third was executed. Jemaah Islamiyah was believed to be responsible.

185.   **09/04.** Ahmad Jamal, younger brother of Saleh, arrested in the Kurdish city of Mosul in Iraq. Interviewed by security forces, Jamal said he travelled to Iraq to kill Americans. (He later claimed the admissions were made under duress.) He was deported to Australia in March 2007.

2005

186.   **14/02/05.** Australian citizen Tallaal Adrey from Auburn in Sydney's west arrested in Kuwait with 36 members of the Peninsula Lions Islamist group, which is believed to have links with al-Qaeda in Iraq. Adrey was convicted of weapons possession, weapons trading,

ammunition possession, and ammunition trading for the purpose of murder and sentenced to four years' jail. Adrey was not charged with membership of the Peninsula Lions Islamist group or al-Qaeda.

187. **24/02/05.** Military tribunal in Lebanon convicted Belal Khazaal in absentia of terrorism-related charges, including financing and directing the activities of Saleh Jamal and providing him with false travel documents, and sentenced him to 15 years' jail.

188. **01/10/05.** Three suicide bombers exploded bombs in Kuta, Bali, killing the bombers and 17 others, including four Australians, and injuring 129, including 19 Australians.

2006

189. Late 2005–early 2006. Thirteen people in Melbourne and nine in Sydney were arrested and charged with various terrorist offences as part of an 18-month federal–state operation named Pendennis. Algerian-born Muslim cleric 'Rajab' was the spiritual leader of the cells. Those arrested in Sydney included 21-year-old Mohammed Omar Jamal, younger brother of Saleh; 40-year-old 'Hussein' who, a few years earlier, had bought five rocket launchers through Eddie Darwiche and whose cousin Ahmed Elomar was arrested in Lebanon in 2007; 25-year-old Mazen Touma; and 36-year-old 'Azooz', an associate of Willie Birgitte, who, with 'Hussein', had been stopped by police near the Lucas Heights research reactor. In 2008 seven of those charged in Melbourne were convicted and given long jail sentences. An eighth person had pleaded guilty to a lesser charge and was jailed before the trial

began. The following year a ninth person, Shane Kent, pleaded guilty to being a member of a terrorist organisation and was sentenced to jail. In October 2009 five of the nine people charged in Sydney were convicted by a jury. The remaining four had earlier pleaded guilty to various charges and had been jailed.

190.	**24/3/06.** Hassan Kalache and his partner, Jill Courtney, a Muslim convert, charged in Sydney with conspiracy to murder and conspiracy to cause explosives to be placed in or near a public place. In February 2008 both were acquitted of the charges. Kalache was already serving 22 years for murdering a drug rival in 2002.

191.	**09/05/06.** Brisbane schoolteacher John Howard Amundsen charged with making explosive devices in preparation for a terrorist attack: 53 kilograms of explosives were found in his home. The terrorism charge was dropped in February 2007 and replaced with lesser charge of possessing incendiary devices. Amundsen was sentenced to six years' jail.

192.	**17/10/06.** Polish-born Australian Marek Samulski (commonly known as Abdul Malik), and two other Australians, Abdullah and Mohammed Ayub, were among 20 people arrested in Yemen for allegedly smuggling arms into Somalia for terrorist purposes. The Ayub brothers—sons of Abdul Rahim Ayub, former head of Jemaah Islamiyah's Australian cell— were detained for two weeks and released. Their elder sister was married to Khaled Cheikho, who was arrested during Operation Pendennis.

193.	**10/06.** Australian citizen Warya Kanie, 39, detained in Iraq by coalition forces for allegedly engaging in anti-coalition activities in Baghdad. Kanie entered Australia around 2004 as part of the humanitarian refugee program, before travelling to Iraq. He was released after nine months without charge.

2007

194. **01/05/07.** Two men were arrested and charged in Melbourne with being members of a terrorist group, financing terrorism and providing material support for terrorism. Further detail is not included, for legal reasons.

195. **24/06/07.** Lebanese Australian Bassem al-Sayyed, his wife and five other militants killed in a ten-hour fire-fight with Lebanese soldiers in Tripoli's Abu Samra district, part of a month-long battle between the army and Fatah al-Islam militants at a Palestinian refugee camp. Al-Sayyed had moved from Sydney to northern Lebanon a year earlier. Four other Sydney men were arrested. Ibrahim Sabouh and Omar al-Hadba were charged with terrorism offences: carrying weapons, undermining the state's authority and participating in the killing of civilians and military personnel. Allegedly half a tonne of weapons and explosives were found in al-Hadba's workshop in Tripoli. Sabouh was charged with offences in connection with Fatah al-Islam. At the time of writing al-Hadba and Sabouh are facing trials in Lebanon. Australian boxing champion Ahmed Elomar was also arrested, but released without charge.

196. **02/07/07.** Mohamed Haneef arrested in connection with two failed car bomb attacks in London and an attack on Glasgow airport four days earlier. Haneef

was held without charge under Australia's anti-terrorism laws. A fortnight later he was charged with recklessly providing support to a terrorist organisation. The terrorism charge against Haneef was dropped on 27 July. The Clarke Inquiry into the handling of the Haneef matter found mistakes by the AFP, the Office of the Commonwealth Director of Public Prosecutions and the Minister for Immigration and Citizenship, the Hon. Kevin Andrews MP. Haneef was cleared of involvement in any terrorist activities.

2008

197. **14/01/08.** Terrorists attacked the Serena Hotel in Kabul, Afghanistan, the temporary home of the Australian Embassy. During a gun battle two suicide bombers detonated bombs, killing seven—including the two bombers—and injuring five. The Taliban claimed responsibility for the attacks.

198. **14/7/2008.** The AFP arrested 34-year-old Thulasitharan Santhirarajah, the director of a Melbourne business college, on behalf of the FBI for alleged terrorism offences by the Tamil Tigers in the United States. At the time of writing the deportation proceedings against Santhirarajah were ongoing.

2009

199. **2009.** Under the terms of the *Security Legislation Amendment (Terrorism) Act 2002*, the Australian government officially designated certain organisations as terrorist groups. There are 17 organisations on the list. They are:

- Abu Sayyaf Group
- al-Qaeda
- al-Qaeda in Iraq (AQI) (formerly listed as Al-Zarqawi and TQJBR)
- al-Qaeda in the Lands of the Islamic Maghreb (AQIM)
- Ansar al-Islam (formerly known as Ansar al-Sunna)
- Asbat al-Ansar (AAA)
- Hamas's Izz al-Din al-Qassam Brigades
- Hizballah (Hezbollah) External Security Organisation
- Islamic Army of Aden (IAA)
- Islamic Movement of Uzbekistan
- Jaish-e-Mohammed (JeM)
- Jamiat ul-Ansar (formerly known as Harakat Ul-Mujahideen)
- Jemaah Islamiyah
- Kurdistan Workers Party (PKK)
- Lashkar-e Jhangvi (LeJ)
- Lashkar-e-Taiba
- Palestinian Islamic Jihad.

200. **17/07/09.** The JW Marriott and Ritz-Carlton Hotels in Jakarta, Indonesia, were bombed. Seven people, including three Australians and two suicide bombers, were killed. Sixteen others were injured. The bombings had been organised by Noordin M Top, then Indonesia's most wanted Islamist militant. Top had previously been a member of Jemaah Islamiyah but left to set up a more violent splinter group, Tansim Qaudat al-Jihad. In early September Top was killed in a police raid. A video

was found that showed the suicide bombers and recorded the voice of the man believed to have recruited them, Saifuddin Jaelini, declaring, 'Destroy America, destroy Australia, destroy Indonesia.' Police believe Jaelini may take over the terrorist group now that Top is dead.

201.   **04/08/09.** Australian Federal Police, Victoria Police and New South Wales Police carried out raids in Victoria. Twenty-seven-year-old Saney Edow Aweyz, 22-year-old Yacqub Khayre and 25-year-old Abdirahman Ahmad (all Australian citizens born in Somalia), and 25-year-old Nayef El Sayed (Australian citizen born in Lebanon) were arrested and charged with conspiring to carry out an armed suicide attack on the Australian army base at Holsworthy in Sydney's outer south-western suburbs. Police also charged 33-year-old Wissam Mahmoud Fattal, a Sydney man of Lebanese descent who was already in custody in Melbourne over a serious assault. Ahmad was also charged with aiding and abetting a hostile act by a sixth person, Walid Osman Mohamed, in Somalia. Mohamed is believed to be still in Somalia. The five are alleged to have links with the al Shabab group, which has carried out suicide bombings and armed attacks in Somalia. At the time of writing the five had not faced their trial.

202.   **21/08/09.** The federal government added Somali-based al Shabab to its list of terrorist organisations.

Bibliography

Much of the information used in writing this book was obtained first-hand in the course of police investigations, from court records and from personal interviews conducted by the authors. Some sources have been cited in the text; others, for obvious reasons, must remain anonymous. The authors are grateful to all the people they have spoken to, named or unnamed; without their courageous cooperation this book could not have been written.

Books and major articles

Bob Bottom, *Bugged! Legal police telephone taps expose the Mr Bigs of Australia's drug trade*, Sun Books, Melbourne, 1989

——*Shadow of Shame: How the mafia got away with the murder of Donald Mackay*, Sun Books, Melbourne, 1988

Lisa Cahill and Peter Marshall, 'The Worldwide Fight against Transnational Organised Crime: Australia', Technical and Background Paper no. 9, Australian Institute of Criminology, January 2004

Jennifer Cooke and Sandra Harvey, *Done Like a Dinner: Great restaurant crimes*, Park Street Press and Media 21 Publishing, Sydney, 2007

Ross Coulthart and Duncan McNab, *Dead Man Running: An insider's story on one of the world's most feared outlaw motorcycle gangs ... the Bandidos*, Allen & Unwin, Sydney, 2008

Pierre-Arnaud Chouvy, 'Drugs and the Financing of Terrorism', in *Terrorism Monitor*, vol. 2, issue 20, 21 October 2004

Nicholas Cowdery, Director of Public Prosecutions, NSW, 'Effectiveness of the Criminal Law', paper delivered to Legal Studies State Conference, Rosehill, 2008

The Eminent Jurists Panel on Terrorism, Counter-terrorism and Human Rights, 'Assessing Damage, Urging Action', Report, International Commission of Jurists, 2009

Jonathan Fine, 'Contrasting Secular and Religious Terrorism', in *Middle Eastern Quarterly*, vol. 15, no. 1, Winter 2008, pp. 59–69

Daveed Gartenstein-Ross and Kyle Dabruzzi, 'The Convergence of Crime and Terror: Law enforcement opportunities and perils', *Policing Terrorism*, Report for the Manhattan Institute for Policy Research, no. 1, June 2007

Wayne Hoffman, 'Terrorism in Australia: 1966–1994', Report (unpublished), February 1994

International Institute for Counter Terrorism and the Israeli Anti-Drug Authority, 'Position Paper: the Connection between Terrorism, Narcotics and International Crime', June 2008

David E. Kaplan, 'Paying for Terror: How jihadist groups use crime to pay for attacks worldwide', *US News & World Report*, 27 November 2005

Mark Loves and Jim Shearan, 'Outlaw Motorcycle Gangs: A portrait of deviance', Report (unpublished), Tactical Intelligence Section, State Intelligence Group, New South Wales Police, 1992

Athol Moffitt, *A Quarter to Midnight: The Australian crisis—Organised crime and the decline of the institutions of state*, Angus & Robertson, North Ryde, 1985

Sean Padraic, as told by Trevor Haken, *Sympathy for the Devil: Confessions of a corrupt police officer*, ABC Books, Sydney, 2005

Lindsay Simpson and Sandra Harvey, *Brothers in Arms: The inside story of two bikie gangs*, Allen & Unwin, Sydney, 1989

Clive Small and Tom Gilling, *Smack Express: How organised crime got hooked on drugs*, Allen & Unwin, 2009

Arthur Veno, *The Brotherhoods: Inside the outlaw motorcycle clubs*, Allen & Unwin, 2003

Michael Waller, 'Terrorist Recruitment and Infiltration in the United States: Prisons and military as an operational base', Evidence to the US Senate's Subcommittee on Terrorism, Technology and Homeland Security, 14 October 2003

David Wright-Neville, 'The Politics of Fear: Counter-terrorism and Australian democracy', Elcano Royal Institute of International and Strategic Studies, Working Papers, issue 27, 19 October 2006

Australian Government publications and official reports

Australian Crime Commission, Australian Crime Commission Annual Report 2003–04, December 2004

——'The future impact of serious and organised crime on Australian society', Submission to the Parliamentary Joint Committee on the Australian Crime Commission, 2007

——'Horizons: Call for comment—Futures scanning 2009', January 2008

——'Organised Crime in Australia', Report, 2008

——'Organised Crime in Australia', Report, 2009

Australian Government, 'Transnational Terrorism: The threat to Australia', 2004

Australian Security Intelligence Organisation Report to Parliament 2004–05

——Report to Parliament 2005–06

——Report to Parliament 2006–07

——Report to Parliament 2007–08

Commonwealth–New South Wales Joint Drug Task Force on Drug Trafficking, 'Investigation of Harry Wainwright, Nugan Hand Limited and its associated companies and the affairs of Murray Stewart Riley and his associates as recommended by the Further Report of the Royal Commission into Drug Trafficking, May 1980', Report, vol. 1, January 1982; vol. 2, June 1982; vol. 3, October 1982; and vol. 4, March 1983

Commonwealth of Australia, Standing Committee on Legal and Constitutional Affairs, Estimates, *Hansard*, 23 February 2009

BIBLIOGRAPHY

John Cusack, American Consulate General, 'Report to the Honourable John V. Dillon, Under Secretary, State of Victoria, Treasury Building', Melbourne, 11 August 1964

Deputy Director-General, Australian Security Intelligence Organisation, Address to Security in Government Conference, Canberra, 10 May 2005

First Assistant Director-General, Security Division, Australian Security Intelligence Organisation, 'Extending National Security Intelligence', Address to Safeguarding Australia Conference, July 2005

Independent Commission Against Corruption, 'Report on the Investigation into Allegations Made by Louis Bayeh about the Member for Londonderry, Paul Gibson MP', December 1998

——'Report on the Investigation into the Department of Corrective Services: First Report: The Conduct of Prison Officer Toso Lila (Josh) Sua and Matters Related Thereto', 1998

——'Report on Investigation into the Relationship Between Police and Criminals: First Report', 1994

——'Report on Investigation into the Relationship Between Police and Criminals: Second Report 1994

——'Report on the Investigation into Matters Relating to Police and Confidential Information', 1994

——'Report on Investigation Relating to the Raid on Frank Hakim's Office', December 1989

The Hon. Mr Justice Athol Moffitt, Royal Commissioner, 'Allegations of Organised Crime in Clubs', NSW Government Printer, 1974

National Crime Authority, 'Organised Crime in Australia: NCA Commentary 2001', 2001

——'Operation Cerberus: Italo-Australian Organised Crime Bulletin', November 1995

Parliamentary Joint Committee on the Australian Crime Commission, 'Inquiry into the Future Impact of Serious and Organised Crime on Australian Society', September 2007

——'Inquiry into the Legislative Arrangements to Outlaw Serious and Organised Crime Groups', August 2009

Parliamentary Joint Committee on the National Crime Authority, 'Asian Organised Crime in Australia', Discussion Paper, February 1995

——'National Crime Authority—An Initial Evaluation', Report, 1988

Police Integrity Commission, 'Report on the Involvement of Officers of the New South Wales Police Service in Relation to Unauthorised Release of Information and the Protection of Illegal Activities', 2001

Christopher Sneddon and John Visser, 'Financial and Organised Crime in Italy', AUSTRAC Papers 2, Australian Government, 1994

The Hon. Mr Justice Donald Gerard Stewart, 'Royal Commission of Inquiry into the Activities of the Nugan Hand Group', Report, Australian Government Publishing Service, Canberra, 1985

US Federal Research Division, Library of Congress, 'Asian Organised Crime and Terrorist Activity in Canada, 1999–2002', 2003

——'Nations Hospitable to Organised Crime and Terrorism', 2003

——'A Global Overview of Narcotics-Funded Terrorist and other Extremist Groups', 2002

Senator the Hon. Amanda Vanstone, Minister for Justice and Customs, Australia, Address to Tenth United Nations Congress on the Prevention of Crime and the Treatment of Offenders, Vienna, 10–17 April 2000

The Hon. Justice J.R.T. Wood, 'Royal Commission into the New South Wales Police Service', Reports, vols I–III, 1 May 1997

——'Royal Commission into the New South Wales Police Service', Transcripts, 1995–1997

The Hon. Mr Justice Phillip Morgan Woodward, Royal Commissioner, 'Report of the Royal Commission into Drug Trafficking', Report, vols 1–3, October 1979

Newspapers and periodicals

Age
Australian
Canberra Times
Daily Mail
Daily Telegraph
Herald Sun
National Times
NBC World News
Sun-Herald
Sunday Mail
Sunday Telegraph
Sydney Morning Herald

Index

INDEX

INDEX

INDEX

INDEX

INDEX